'WHAT IS GOD?'

An investigation of the Perfections of God's Nature

ROBERT L. REYMOND

To the distinguished faculty of
Knox Theological Seminary
with whom it is sheer joy to serve Christ

Dr. E. Calvin Beisner
Dr. Warren A. Gage
Dr. D. James Kennedy
Dr. Samuel P. Lamerson
Dr. Lawrence C. Roff
Dr. Collins D. Weeber
Dr. R. Fowler White

who requested that I deliver this series of addresses
on the attributes of God
to the seminary family in the Knox Seminary chapel

'WHAT IS GOD?'

An investigation of the Perfections of God's Nature

ROBERT L. REYMOND

ΠENTOR

© Robert L. Reymond 2007

ISBN 1-84550-228-0
ISBN 978-1-84550-228-7

10 9 8 7 6 5 4 3 2 1

Published in 2007
in the
Mentor Imprint
by
Christian Focus Publications Ltd.,
Geanies House, Fearn, Ross-shire,
IV20 1TW, Great Britain

www.christianfocus.com

Cover design by Alister MacInnes

Printed and bound by Bell & Bain, Glasgow

Contents

Get you up to a high mountain, O Zion,
herald of good tidings;
lift up your voice with strength, O Jerusalem,
herald of good tidings,
lift it up, fear not;
say to the cities of Judah,
'BEHOLD YOUR GOD!'
– Isaiah 40:9

PREFACE

This book contains the eleven addresses on the attributes of God[1] that the faculty of Knox Theological Seminary invited me to deliver to the Knox Seminary student body during the Fall semester of 2003. Using the answer provided by the fourth question of the *Westminster Shorter Catechism*, 'What is God?'[2] as my frame of

---

[1] I prefer the word 'perfections' over the word 'attributes' since their referents in God are intrinsic to him and not 'items' that are 'assigned to' (*ad* – 'to'; *tribuô* – 'assign') him. However, because the latter is the more common term I will use it in these addresses as long as the term is understood as I define it in the first lecture as 'ascriptions to God that his *self*-revelation in Holy Scripture declares are intrinsically true of him'.

[2] 'God is a Spirit, infinite, eternal, and unchangeable in his being, wisdom, power, holiness, justice, goodness, and truth.' The *Shorter Catechism* ascribes ten attributes to God here. Are there more? Yes, certainly, for we shall see that these ten subsume other attributes of like kind under them. John of Damascus in his classic summary, *Exposition of the Orthodox Faith*, 1, 8, lists eighteen. Frankly, we do not and cannot know the number of God's attributes. Being infinite as he is, God must possess countless attributes about which we know nothing beyond the fact that they will all be consistent with the ones about which we do know. Granted the following are poetic expressions but Frederick W. Faber sang of the 'God of a *thousand* attributes' while E. Lange (1650–1727), translated by John Wesley, and Charles Wesley, both probably closer to the truth, exclaimed respectively:

> O God, thy being who can sound?
> Thee to perfection who can know?

reference I delivered these addresses on consecutive Thursday mornings in the scheduled seminary chapel services (which explains their odd number), and they appear here virtually as I delivered them with little substantive and only minor editorial work having been done on them after they were delivered. I want to express my gratitude to the Knox faculty for their kind invitation to deliver these addresses. I also want to thank both the faculty and the student body (who, I was painfully aware as I delivered them, listened intently to them) for their expressions of appreciation for them.

Naturally, no single address in this series, in isolation from the others, completely and entirely depicts the God of the Bible. But I believe these eleven, taken together, provide an accurate and composite picture of the one living and true God both as he is in himself and as he has revealed himself to us. In these addresses I also applied each divine attribute to the original audience[3] to demonstrate the practical value of preaching on God's attributes but I have hardly exhausted what can be done in regard to their application. And while I recognize that something is always lost when public addresses appear in print I trust that the God who is described in these addresses will bless their publication and by them encourage many pastors, in the words of Isaiah, to 'lift up [their] voices with strength, fear not, and say to [their people], "*Behold your God!*"' For as the Septuagint, the early church's Bible, suggests in Isaiah 40:9 by twice employing the term 'herald of good tidings'[4] to describe

---

O height immense! No words are found
Thy *countless* attributes to show.

and

Sovereign Father, heavenly King,
Thee we now presume to sing;
Glad thine attributes confess,
Glorious all and *numberless*!

[3]In a few instances I adapted ideas for application from Charles Haddon Spurgeon and Arthur W. Pink.

the one who proclaims 'Behold your God!', pastors may be assured that when they preach on the character of God they are proclaiming a necessary aspect of the 'good news' of the gospel itself. While the original audience of these addresses was primarily seminary faculty and seminarians, some of whom sat with open Hebrew Bibles and/or Greek New Testaments before them, I make no apology for urging that pastors need to inform their congregations of the very same truths about God that I brought to the attention of the Knox faculty and students because nothing is more needful for God's people in this day of theological illiteracy than to know what their God is actually like. And I am confident that their congregations will be able to comprehend this material if their pastors will make the effort to digest it and expound it to them. I can guarantee that their congregations will hear surprising and wonderful things about their God in every sermon that their pastors preach about him!

Even though publishing one's prayers comes dangerously close to praying at street corners to be seen by men, I decided after some reflection to allow the prayers I prayed at the beginning and end of each address to remain with them – yes, I write out my public prayers, believing that the Holy Spirit can lead me in my composition of them in my study just as certainly as he can lead me in my composition of them from the pulpit – because I hope they will stimulate and encourage pastors to think about and to frame their own public prayers to fit their sermon subjects in a God-honoring way without the repetitive words 'And God' and 'just' before virtually every phrase that one hears so much today in public prayers. Christian pastors should not be afraid of writing their public prayers. After all, most of the biblical psalms are just that – written public prayers.

---

[4]*ho euangelizomenos* is from the same verb root from which we derive our words 'evangelize' and 'evangel' ('gospel').

The inserted words from the original languages in transliterated form in some Bible verses cited in these addresses have been provided in this printed version of them for the benefit of the busy preacher. Footnotes have been included, not only because it is simply common courtesy to give credit to sources quoted, but also because I assume that most preachers who will read these addresses will either need or want the information they contain in order to do further research on their own. I made no reference to these footnotes, of course, as I delivered these addresses.

Pastors should feel free to use these addresses in any way that will aid them as they preach on God's attributes. I only request, if they find anything in them that they decide they can use, that they *not* feel they must credit me for the use of the material. The truth that I have attempted to proclaim belongs not to me but to the church of Jesus Christ. Therefore, they may use this material freely without obtaining permission from me. I would suggest, if pastors choose to follow my example and read lengthy lists of biblical texts, that in order to save time they should do as I did and simply read the texts without their references, informing their congregations beforehand that they can and will provide chapters and verses to any who desire to have them. I would also suggest, since some of these addresses such as the eleventh on the Trinity obviously are too long to be delivered on one occasion, that they plan ahead and be prepared either to eliminate some material (which is the choice I made) or to preach more than one sermon on a given attribute (which time constraints would not allow me to do).

One last word of explanation: The perceptive reader may have noted from his perusal of the table of contents that I did not deliver an address as such on proving the existence of God. I did not do this for three reasons: first, my assignment was to speak on God's attributes, and it seemed to me that the nature of my assignment as it was explained to me presupposed God's existence just as the Bible presupposes it; second, 'bare existence' *per se* is not an attribute that distinguishes in any way the God said to exist from other things since anything that has meaning exists. Simply to prove that an entity exists is of no value since, as I have said, anything that has any faint meaning at all exists. But it makes a great deal of difference whether this entity is 'a dream, a mirage, the square root of minus one, or the infinite personal triune God of Holy Scripture' (Gordon H. Clark). So the question that needs to be addressed is not, 'Does God exist?' Of course God exists! The far more important question is '*What* is God?' It is this question that I attempt to answer by this series, not by drawing on *my* musings about God, but by setting forth as faithfully as I can what God has revealed about himself in Holy Scripture.

My third reason is this: *no one needs to have God's existence proven to him.* Every human being already has a God-created innate knowledge of God (Rom. 1:21) – John Calvin called this knowledge man's *sensus deitatis, sensus divinitatis,* and *semen religiosus*[5] – by virtue of the light of nature within him and general revelation outside of him, and he knows in his heart, because of the requirements of the law that God has written on his heart (Rom. 2:15), that someday God will judge him for his transgressions of that law (Rom. 1:32). Really, then, no actual atheist exists anywhere among mankind; only theists exist, a very small percentage of whom *claim* to be atheists.[6] These 'practicing atheists' believe with the greatest leap of the imagination – against both the *sine qua non* ('without which nothing') of all scientific inquiry that 'out of nothing, nothing comes'

---

[5]'Sense [or perception] of deity' (*Institutes,* 1.3.1), 'sense [or perception] of divinity' (1.3.3), and 'seed of religion' (1.3.1; 1.4.1; 1.4.4).

[6]This means incidentally that it is not atheists who go to hell; only theists go to hell.

11

and its corollary that if something now exists then something (and the biblical God is certainly something!) has always existed – that the entire material universe of which they themselves are a part accidentally 'decayed' (Alan Guth's term) into being *out of nothing* according to established laws of physics and that this universe is therefore the product of an *impersonal* beginning plus time plus chance and is thus the *sole* and *final* reality. Sir James Jeans believed he could assert without fear of refutation that 'into [the] universe [the human race] has stumbled, if not exactly by mistake, at least as the result of what may properly be described as an accident';[7] Sir Arthur Eddington declared in his *New Pathways in Science* that the human race is 'one of the gruesome results of [Nature's] occasional failure [to take] antiseptic precautions';[8] the National Association of Biology Teachers here in the United States has explicitly declared that all life is the outcome of 'an unsupervised, impersonal, unpredictable, and natural process', that is to say, all life originated by chance; (atheist Quentin Smith asserts: '... the most reasonable belief is that we came from nothing, by nothing, and for nothing);[9] and Oxford biologist Richard Dawkins states that Darwin's theory of natural selection 'makes it possible to be an intellectually fulfilled atheist'.[10] But does it? In my opinion, these assertions are laughable, for Darwinian scientists have to believe, at bottom, that

♦ Nothing produced everything
♦ Random chance produced this finely tuned universe

---

[7]James Jeans, *The Mysterious Universe* (New York: Macmillan, 1930), 4.

[8]Arthur E. Eddington, *New Pathways in Science* (New York: Macmillan, 1935), 310.

[9]William Lane Craig and Quentin Smith, *Theism, Atheism, and Big Bang Cosmology* (Oxford: Clarendon, 1993), 135.

[10]Richard Dawkins, *The Blind Watchmaker* (New York: Norton, 1986), 6.

+ Non-life produced life
+ Chaos produced information
+ Mindless matter produced the conscious mind
+ Non-reason produced reason, and
+ Non-Purpose produced humans who are obsessed with purpose.[11]

Furthermore, does Darwinianism make an unbiased atheist? These Darwinian scientists presume at the outset of their research a *naturalistic* view of reality that is profoundly atheistic.[12] They presuppose as a *matter of first principle* that purposeless *material* processes do all the work of biological creation because, according to their philosophy, *nothing else is available*. They have *pre-defined* their task as biologists to be the discovery of the most plausible – or the least implausible – *naturalistic* or *materialistic* explanation of how biological evolution occurs. This approach, of course, rules out an intelligent Creator, requiring adherence at the outset to the Darwinian worldview that assumes that the material universe is all that exists. This is hardly doing 'unbiased science' as it should be done. Rather, this is a prejudicial naturalistic philosophy of science that is biased to the core and dictates the materialistic

---

[11]A variation of Lee Strobel, *The Case for a Creator* (Grand Rapids: Zondervan, 2004), 277.

[12]This presumption is the 'Achilles' heel' of the entire evolutionary enterprise. Evolutionary scientists, acknowledging as they must that they are working with a *naturalistic* philosophy of science, make a fatal admission here. Their acknowledgement patently reveals that the theory of Darwinian evolution does not present to the public value-free data. Philip E. Johnson, in 'Shouting "Heresy" in the Temple of Darwin,' *Christianity Today* (Oct 24, 1994), 26, rightly observes: 'Biologists have authority to tell us facts that they know from the study of biology, but they have no intellectual or moral authority to order us to adopt a particular philosophy that they prefer.' And once these biologists admit that behind their 'biological facts' lies their naturalistic philosophy of science, nonbiologists should understand that they may decide whether they want to believe what the biological evolutionists are saying about origins.

outcome of all scientific pronouncements before the facts are even known and considered.[13]

The findings of molecular biology, for example, not to mention the recent findings of cosmology, physics, astronomy, and biology, fly in the face of the evolutionary assumption. Darwin wrote in his *The Origin of Species*:

> If it could be demonstrated that any complex organ existed which could not possibly have been formed by numerous, successive, slight modifications, my theory would completely break down.[14]

Michael J. Behe, in *Darwin's Black Box: The Biochemical Challenge to Evolution* (New York: Free Press, 1996), advances the sustained argument that the countless molecular systems in the simplest living cell are *irreducibly complex* – chemical 'machines' made up of finely calibrated interdependent parts – which means they cannot have originated by a gradual step-by-step process. All these parts had to be there in the cell from the start – each doing its specific thing – or life never would have begun. In sum, our stunningly complex living cell systems must have originated already complete in order to function at all, thus suggesting that an intelligent designer is the cell's originator. The force of this argument has not been lost on octogenarian Antony Flew – for decades the icon and champion of atheism for unbelievers – who recently declared that the intelligent design argument convinced him that he had to abandon his avowed atheism (he is now a deist)![15] It should also be noted that chance cannot be

---

[13]For more on this, see Gene Edward Veith, 'Science's new heresy trial,' *World* (February 19, 2005), 26.

[14]Charles Darwin, *The Origin of Species* (Sixth edition; New York: University Press, 1998), 154.

[15]Antony Flew and Gary R. Habermas, 'My Pilgrimage from Atheism to Theism: An Exclusive Interview with Former British Atheist Professor Antony Flew,' in *Philosophia Christi* (Winter 2005), the journal of the Evangelical Philosophical Society, edited by Craig J. Hazen.

a cause of anything because chance is not a material thing. It is not being, not energy, not mass, not power, not intelligence. It is only a mathematical concept we employ to calculate possibilities, and in the present instance the mathematical odds that this universe with its complexity created itself is one over infinity or zero. To prefer, then, the notion that 'nothing'[16] created the universe over the opening words of Genesis, 'In the beginning God created the universe,' represents the nadir of theoretical thought and leaps over reason into the sea of absurdity. For it is nothing short of absurdity to personalize nature as, for example, Peter Atkins, a secular physicist, does when he says: 'Once molecules have learned to compete and to create other molecules in their own image, elephants and things resembling elephants will in due course be found roaming through the countryside.'[17]

Nevertheless, these 'practicing atheists' insist that the burden of proof lies with acknowledged theists to prove God's existence to them. But wait: 'This is *my* Father's world'; I am not the trespasser here. In reality, it is they who should justify their atheism in this theistic world. The burden of proof is actually theirs to prove that this physical world is the sole and final reality and that *no* supernatural *spiritual* being anywhere exists. Though they strive mightily to do so, this they cannot do since one cannot prove a universal negative. Thus their 'atheism' is *their* unproven 'grand assumption' – an assumption by the way with which they cannot live consistently,[18] for it often takes, as the English poet Robert Browning says in his poem, *Bishop Blougram's Apology* (lines

---

[16]I am informed that these theoretical physicists, to hedge their bets here, now propose around fourteen different kinds of 'nothing', which would be laughable if it were not so tragic.

[17]Cited by Colin E. Gunton, *The Triune Creator. A Historical and Systematic Study* (Grand Rapids: Eerdmans, 1998), 38.

[18]Francis Schaeffer, as much as any man of his time, made this point again and again in his trilogy, *The God Who Is There, He Is There and He Is Not Silent*, and *Escape from Reason*.

182-87), little more than 'a sunset touch, a fancy from a flower-bell, someone's death, a chorus-ending from Euripides, – and that's enough for fifty hopes and fears ... to rap and knock and enter in [their] soul,' and thus to disquiet their avowed atheism. And before Browning John Calvin correctly insisted that their knowledge of God is ineradicable so that 'willy-nilly they from time to time feel an inkling of what they desire not to believe'.[19] I hope this brief exposition of atheism will suffice as a substitute for an address as such on the existence of God.[20]

I will affirm here, however, that I believe that the triune God of the Bible is the one living and true God because he has revealed himself to all mankind, first, *generally* by his works of creation – which creation reflects *cosmos* (order) rather than *chaos* (disorder) (Rom. 1:18-23) – and providence (Acts 17:25b-28); second, *propositionally* by the divinely inspired Scriptures of the Old and New Testaments (2 Tim. 3:15-17; 2 Pet. 1:20-21); third, *personally* in his incarnate divine Son, the Lord Jesus Christ, who died, rose bodily from death on the third day after he was crucified, and showed himself alive by 'many convincing proofs' (*pollois tekmēriois*) (Acts 1:3); and fourth, *savingly* – in the case of us who are his elect – by his Word and animating Spirit. And I intend in these several addresses to expound upon the nature of *this* God who has revealed himself to us in Holy Scripture. So if you have come this far with me I invite you to continue to read and to 'behold your God' as the incomprehensible supreme Spirit who is

infinite in his being,
  eternal in his being,
    unchangeable in his being,

---

[19]John Calvin, *Institutes of the Christian Religion*, 1.3.2.

[20]I deal with this issue of God's existence much more fully in my *A New Systematic Theology of the Christian Faith* (Second edition; Nashville, Tennessee: Thomas Nelson, 1998), 129-52.

infinite, eternal, and unchangeable in his wisdom,
infinite, eternal, and unchangeable in his power,
infinite, eternal, and unchangeable in his holiness,
infinite, eternal, and unchangeable in his justice,
infinite, eternal, and unchangeable in his goodness,
infinite, eternal, and unchangeable in his truth, and
triune – God's 'special mark' of distinction.

FIRST ADDRESS

'THE INCOMPREHENSIBLE SUPREME SPIRIT'

'You who bring good tidings to Zion, go up on a high mountain. You who bring good tidings to Jerusalem, lift up your voice with a shout, lift it up, do not be afraid; say to the towns of Judah, **'Behold your God!'** (Isa. 40:9)

Esteemed members of the faculty, beloved seminarians, and friends of Knox Theological Seminary. Before I begin this morning's address I must tell you how honored I am to have been asked by the seminary faculty to bring this series of addresses on the attributes of God that I understand as 'ascriptions to God that God's self-revelation in Holy Scripture declares are true of him'. I want to express my appreciation publicly to them now for their kind invitation. And I want to ask you all to pray for me and to trust God with me that by this series of addresses he will bless his Word about himself above all that we could ask or think (Eph. 3:20) and that as his Word goes forth it will 'not return to him empty without accomplishing what he desires' (Isa. 55:11). To him then will go all the glory, and that is as it should be. Let us so pray now.

Prayer:
Almighty God, our Heavenly Father: I thank you for your precious, infallible Word-revelation to us of your divine nature and perfections. Grant us ears truly to hear

19

that revelation both this morning and the remaining Thursday mornings of this semester. Remove the scales from our eyes that we may behold wondrous things out of your Law, and open our hearts to believe and to love your truth. Enable me as one who professes to be a scribe in the Kingdom of God to bring forth treasures, both new and old, from your Word, for the enduring blessing of these your people and for the infinitely worthy cause of Jesus Christ. And may these students be so captivated this semester in all their courses by the beauty and glory of the God who has revealed himself in Jesus Christ that they will feel that theirs will be a life of woe if they do not proclaim him and the whole counsel of God as he has revealed himself in Holy Scripture. I pray these things, for the glory of Jesus, and in his name, Amen.

* * *

Introduction to the series

As I begin this series of addresses on the attributes of the God of Holy Scripture that I am entitling **'What is God?'**. Let me first take a few minutes and give you what, in my opinion, is the primary reason such a topic is absolutely essential for you pastors and seminarians. You are giving your lives in preparation for the gospel ministry. I take for granted that this is the reason you are here in seminary. And you are asking your wives (and husbands) and families to make sacrifices in order that you may be here and acquire the necessary education to conduct your future ministries in a manner that will be acceptable to God and bring everlasting glory to him. You have, I imagine, the confident expectation that upon graduation you will become successful ministers and teachers of the gospel. That's fine and is as it should be. But the Bible has a lot to say about the ingredients that go into making a man a minister approved by God. Leaving aside at this time the regenerating, justifying, adopting, sanctifying, and glorifying work that only God himself can do in bringing you to faith in Christ and nurturing you in your spiritual growth – works, incidentally, that he does for all believers, not just for ministers of the gospel – there are additional measures that you as men preparing for the ministry must take in order to have a fruitful ministry that will know the blessing of God. And one of these measures, if not the primary one, is *the acquisition of a true, deep, and systematic knowledge of the God of Holy Scripture.* Jeremiah 9:23-24 declares:

> This is what the LORD says: 'Let not the wise man boast of his wisdom, or the strong man boast of his might, or the rich man boast of his riches, but let him who boasts boast about this: that he understands and knows me that I am the LORD who does kindness [*hesedh*], justice [*mishpât*], and righteousness [*tsedhâqâh*] in the earth, for in these I delight.'

Daniel 11:32 asserts that 'the people who *know their God* will be strong and will do exploits'. Paul declares that one major aspect of the Christian's walk is 'growing in the *knowledge* of God' (Col. 1:10), while Peter affirms that God gives us 'everything we need for life and godliness *through our knowledge of him*' (2 Pet. 1:3). One thing is certain: no one – neither you nor your parishioners – can trust, serve, or worship an unknown God. If you would trust, serve, and worship him, and do great exploits for him, you must acquire a broad comprehensive knowledge of him.

In his article, 'The Indispensableness of Systematic Theology to the Preacher,' Benjamin B. Warfield, professor of didactic and polemic theology in Princeton Seminary, relates that Professor Flint of Edinburgh, in closing his opening lecture to his class, now many years ago, took the occasion to warn his theological students of what he perceived to be an imminent danger. There was a growing tendency, Professor Flint said, to deem it of primary importance that they should enter upon the ministry, accomplished preachers, and of only secondary importance that they should be scholars, thinkers, theologians. 'It is not so,' he is reported as saying, 'that great or even good preachers are formed. They form themselves before they form their style of preaching. Substance with them precedes appearance, instead of appearance being a substitute for substance. They learn to know the truth before they think of presenting it.... They acquire a solid base for the manifestation of their love of souls through a loving, comprehensive, absorbing study of the truth which saves souls.' In these winged words [Warfield continues] is outlined the case for the indispensableness of Systematic Theology for the preacher. It is summed up in the proposition that it is through the truth that souls are saved, that it is accordingly the primary business of the preacher to present this truth to men, and that it is consequently his fundamental duty to become himself possessed of this truth....[1]

You see, my brothers and sisters, both Scripture and all human experience aswell demonstrate that a person's behavior in the long run corresponds with his beliefs and, humanly speaking, is determined by them. Paul realized this, as evidenced by the fact that in all of his letters his summons to Christians to a high and holy walk are preceded by and grounded in the proclamation of sound doctrine that logically inspires and compels that walk. This points up the necessity for every man who would become an 'expert builder' in the church to impart sound doctrine to those whose souls are under his care. But then, how equally necessary it is, in order to do this, that the one who would indoctrinate others with a given body of truth should acquire a mastery of

[1]Benjamin B. Warfield, 'The Indispensableness of Systematic Theology to the Preacher,' in *Selected Shorter Writings of Benjamin B. Warfield*, edited by John E. Meeter (Nutley, New Jersey: Presbyterian and Reformed, 1973), II, 280.

that same body of truth himself. For it will ever be true, Warfield reminds us, that

> a mutilated gospel [and the airwaves and a plethora of so-called Christian books are filled today with such] produces mutilated lives, and mutilated lives are positive evils. Whatever the preacher may do, [his] hearers will not do without a system of belief; and in their attempt to frame one for the government of their lives out of the fragments of truth which [the indifferent] preacher will grant them, is it any wonder if they should go fatally astray? ...it is not given to one who stands in the pulpit to decide whether or no he shall teach, whether or no he shall communicate to others a *system* of belief which will form lives and determine destinies. It is in his power only to determine what he shall teach, what system of doctrine he shall press upon the acceptance of men; by what body of tenets he will seek to mold their lives and to inform their devotions.... And this is but another way of saying that the *systematic* study of divine truth ... is the most indispensable preparation for the pulpit. Only as the several truths to be presented are known in their relations can they be proclaimed in their right proportions and so taught as to produce their right effects on the soul's life and growth.[2]

As you pastors preach from your pulpits and as you men and women teach from your classroom lecterns as the months and years go by, you are not just to give your people pieces of the puzzle that make up the 'big picture' on the 'puzzle box' of Holy Scripture. You know what I mean: you have all known preachers who preach a sermon one Sunday on Zacchaeus, a sermon the following Sunday on the Genesis flood, a third sermon the following Sunday on circumcision, and so on, whatever catches their fancy. And never do

---

[2]Warfield, 'The Indispensableness of Systematic Theology to the Preacher' in *Selected Shorter Writings*, II, 287-8.

they make any effort to show how these biblical 'puzzle pieces' contribute to the 'big picture' of Scripture. But you are called by God to give your people over time the 'big picture' itself. You are not to preach haphazardly, with no rhyme or reason, week in and week out, on the biblical topics that you happen to like or just tickle your fancy. You should preach with a plan and have it as your goal to make the people of your congregations, each and every one of them, *systematic* theologians, and the surest way to do that is by preaching sermon series on great biblical and doctrinal themes and by *lectio continua* expository preaching of the whole counsel of God through whole books of Scripture and relating what you say expositionally to the Bible's 'big picture'.

Occasionally I reminded the congregations I pastored that historically Presbyterian congregations, unwilling to suffer theologically foolish preaching lightly, have rarely called ignorant pastors to their pulpits. And that is right and proper! But then I pointed out to them that a theologically literate ministry will never tolerate an ignorant laity either. I expected them through my pulpit ministry to grow in their knowledge of their God so that they could in turn correctly minister to others. And in this present context this is just to say that the foundation of all true knowledge of God must be a clear mental apprehension of God's perfections as revealed in Holy Scripture. I would even contend that more than any other topic in these times pastors need to introduce their congregations to the one living and true God of Holy Scripture because nothing is more needful for God's people in this day of rampant theological illiteracy than to know what their God is actually like. For *all* of our problems and the respective solutions to them are ultimately *theological.* Therefore, a true knowledge of God is indispensable to our souls' eternal health and to a sound philosophy of life here and now. So I am praying that we will all grow spiritually this semester as we think about the God who is there, who has spoken to us his Word from another world, and who, after all, is truly the 'Ultimate Who's Who'.

So, pastors and pastors-to-be, covenant with God to learn all you can about him from his inscripturated revelation through this series of addresses this semester and then resolve to preach and to teach what you learn for the improvement of the health and the equipping of his children for those good works that God himself has foreordained that they should do. And while it will ever be the case that it is God alone who gives the increase, bathe your entire labor for him in your fervent prayer to him that you may be used both to plant his Word and to water it in the souls of needy people. When you do that, your sermons will become 'arrows shot from the tense bow-string of conviction and [they] will hit the mark every time' (Francis Landey Patton).

* * *

Turn with me now to this morning's text – John 4:23-25:

> ...the hour is coming [Jesus declared] and now is when the true worshipers [which implies that there are 'false worshipers'] will worship the Father in spirit and truth. For the Father is seeking such ones to worship him. God is spirit, and those who worship him must worship him in spirit and truth. (my own private translation)

Introduction
Before I get into the body of this address I must issue one caveat. You will soon notice that, unlike the Schoolmen of the late Middle Ages who give the impression at times that they know so much about God that they even know 'what he had for breakfast last Sunday morning', I make no such claim. Rather, I will simply attempt to make clear what I think the Bible teaches about God on each selected topic. I will attempt to go as far as the Bible

goes and where it stops, there I will stop. In my opinion this is the safest way to approach the several subjects of this series. So with this understanding between us, let us begin with the following basic assertion: The Christian faith is a monotheistic faith; its monotheism is expressly declared and everywhere assumed by the Old and the New Testaments:

Deuteronomy 4:35, 39: '...the LORD is God; *there is no one else besides him* ['*ên 'ôdh mil^ebhaddô*]'; '...the LORD is God in heaven above and on the earth beneath. *There is no other* ['*ên 'ôdh*].'[3]

Deuteronomy 32:39: 'See now that I myself am He! *There is no god besides me.* I put to death and I bring to life, I have wounded and I will heal, and no one can deliver out of my hand.'

Isaiah 45:5: 'I am the LORD, and *there is no other* ['*ên 'ôdh*]; *apart from me* [*zûlāthî*] there is no God.'

Jeremiah 10:10: '...the LORD is the true God; he is the living God, the everlasting king.'

Mark 12:32: '[There] is one [God], and *there is no other beside him* [*ouk estin allos plēn autou*].'

Romans 3:30: '*There is one God* [*heis ho theos*]....'

1 Corinthians 8:4: 'We know that an idol is nothing at all in the world and that *there is no God except one* [*oudeis theos ei mē heis*].'

1 Timothy 2:5: '...*there is one God* [*Heis ... theos*], and one mediator between God and men, the man Christ Jesus.'

---

[3]I have omitted from this list Deuteronomy 6:4 and its citations in the New Testament because there is some question whether the *Shema* was intended as a monotheistic confession or whether it is a cry of covenant allegiance, that is to say: 'Yahweh is our God, Yahweh alone!' In light of the immediately following call in Deuteronomy 6:5 to love Yahweh exclusively it seems best contextually to take it as the latter.

James 2:19: 'You believe that *there is one God* [*heis estin ho theos*]. Good! Even the demons believe that – and shudder.

This God, according to Holy Scripture, needs nothing outside himself in order to be fully God. He is *self-existent* (sometimes referred to as his aseity because he eternally exists *a se*, 'from himself') which means that God eternally exists necessarily, *self-contained, self-sustaining, self-sufficient,* and *self-revealing,* whose self-revelation is *self-attesting, self-authenticating,* and *self-validating.* Before he created the universe (Gen. 1:1), when he, the triune God, existed all alone, his understanding, his energies, and his love found their proper object within the persons of the Godhead to his own perfect satisfaction and happiness. Holy Scripture teaches us that this one living and true God did not create the universe out of an ontological need to complement himself (Job 41:11; Isa. 40:12-31; Acts 17:25) for he was ontologically exactly the same after his creative activity as before (Ps. 90:2). He 'was under no constraint [from outside himself], no obligation [from outside himself], no necessity [save to himself] to create. That he chose to do so was purely a sovereign act on his part, caused by nothing outside himself.'[4] That is to say, he created this universe solely because he willed to do so (Rev. 4:11) and for the purpose of glorifying himself by the redemptive activity that he would work out on the stage of this small planet (Isa. 43:6-7). In these addresses I will intend by the word 'God' this one living and true God of the Bible. It is the existence of this God alone that I confess. With reference to the claimed existence of any other god as the true god, I am not simply an agnostic; I am a convinced atheist. I deny that any other gods exist save as idolatrous creations in the minds of sinful men who have 'exchanged the truth of God for a lie, and [who]

---

[4]Arthur W. Pink, *The Attributes of God* (Grand Rapids: Baker, 1975), 9-10.

worship and serve the creature rather than the Creator – who is forever praised. Amen' (Rom. 1:25).

The doctrine

Now the *Westminster Shorter Catechism* begins its instruction about this one living and true God in its response to its question, 'What is God,' by declaring: 'God is a Spirit.' So this is where I will begin this series on the attributes of God. This four-word English statement is based upon the three-word statement of Jesus in the Greek text of John 4:24: *pneuma ho theos*, literally, 'spirit [is] the God.' And what we need to do first is to determine the meaning of Jesus' anarthrous use of *pneuma*.

Jesus makes this statement, you will recall, in the context of his discussion with the woman at the well in Samaria. She turned the discussion to the question of the *location* where people should worship God, whether in Samaria or in Jerusalem (John 4:20). Jesus responded by telling her that the worship of God does not require that one be present in either place (John 4:21). This is because true worship has to do, not with a geographic location, but with the nature of the Being of God and the worshiper's inner spiritual condition. So I concur with Leon Morris's wise suggestion that we should omit the indefinite article in our English translation.[5] Apparently, it was not Jesus' intent to teach here that God is *a* spirit in the sense that he is one spirit among many, though that is true enough; rather, he intended to underscore the truth that God's Being is of the *nature* of spirit and is therefore in no way restricted to *spatial* locations. And while it is true that in this particular context Jesus has specifically the Father in mind, that is to say, God the Father is spirit, this statement is equally true of God the Son and God the Holy Spirit, which is just to

---

[5]Leon Morris, *The Gospel of John* (Grand Rapids: Eerdmans, 1971), 271.

say, *all three persons of the Godhead are essentially one undivided spirit.*

But what does it mean to say that God is spirit? Some theologians attempt to isolate out of the sum total of God's Being some one 'primary' (what they call) *metaphysical* essence that stands under and unites together all his 'secondary' *nonmetaphysical* attributes, and they commonly select 'spirit' as that essence. But the Bible does not seem to endorse the notion that we can isolate out of all that the Bible says about God some single metaphysical essence upon which all the others depend for their unity. The Bible says that God is light (1 John 1:5), that God is love (1 John 4:8, 10), that God is a consuming fire (Heb. 12:29). Is God more fundamentally 'spirit' than he is 'light' or 'love' or a 'consuming fire'? I would say no. Morton H. Smith, professor of systematic theology at Greenville (SC) Presbyterian Theological Seminary, seems to concur, observing that

> the same kind of predication is used of [all four statements]. Though these are the only four attributes that are placed in such a proposition in the Bible, they are sufficient for us to conclude that similar statements could be made regarding any of his attributes. 'Every attribute is identical with his being. He is what he has. Whatever God is He is completely and simultaneously.'[6]

Consequently, I would urge that we should not view God's nature as spirit as primary and metaphysical with his other attributes being secondary and ethical (Robert Lewis Dabney will have a bit more to say on this matter in a little while). So we are back to my earlier question, what does Jesus' statement, 'God is spirit,' mean?

---

[6]Morton H. Smith, 'God, The Attributes of,' in *The Encyclopedia of Christianity*, edited by Philip E. Hughes (Marshallton, Delaware: National Foundation of Christian Education, 1972), 4:367.

I would suggest that the word 'spirit' is simply theological shorthand for two other attributes of God.[7] First, to say that the triune God is spirit is to say that God is *personal*. You see, according to the scriptural usage of the word, there is no such thing as *impersonal* spirit. To be spirit is to *be* personal, and the Bible's anthropomorphisms are metaphors designed, in light of God's spiritual essence, to drive home this truth that God is indeed personal. And what does it mean to be personal? To be *personal* is to be, unlike the impersonal stone or inert clay, *self-conscious, self-determining, living, and active*. And the triune God of the Bible is all these things and more – self-conscious, self-determining, living, active, intelligent, and affectionate. He is anything but inert impersonalness: he is the living and active Creator and Architect of the universe, the beneficent Provider of his creature's needs, the Lawgiver and just Judge of mankind, the Advocate of the poor and the oppressed, an empathetic Counselor, the suffering Servant, and the triumphant Deliverer of his people. He is a Man of War (Exod. 15:3), a Dragon Slayer (Rev. 20:1-10), a Bridegroom (Isa. 61:10), a Husband (Isa. 54:5), a King (Isa. 33:22), a Builder and Maker (Heb. 11:10), a Shepherd (Ps. 23:1), a Physician (Exod. 15:26), and much, much more. And as personal spirit God relates to us in an 'I–you' way, *not* in an 'I–it' way. We are not 'things' to him, *and he is not to be a 'thing' to us.*

But right here I must issue a caution: God's 'personalness' should not be taken to mean that God is *one* person; for while it is true that God generally prefers

---

[7] I offer here a brief word about one meaning that it does not have: When Roger Beckwith in 'The Calvinist Doctrine of the Trinity,' *Churchman* 115/4 [2001], 312, argues that the very name of 'Spirit' for the third Person of the Godhead implies his being 'breathed out' from the Father I must demur because the entire Godhead is 'spirit' and is not 'breathed out' from anyone or anything. The word implies nothing in and of itself about the Spirit's relationship with the Father or about any other relationship for that matter.

as a literary convention to speak in his revelation to his people as an 'I' – see for example his 'I am' of Exodus 3:14 – only rarely speaking as a plural subject employing the first person plural 'we' or 'us', yet in the depth of his being, he does speak *within* himself and sometimes to us as a plural subject, one of the many evidences in Scripture that the biblical God is actually *tri-personal.* For example, in Genesis 1:26 God says: 'Let us make man in our image, after our likeness.' In Genesis 3:22 God says: 'The man and the woman have become like one of us, knowing good and evil.' In Genesis 11:7 God says: 'Let us go down and give men different languages.' In Isaiah 6:8 God says: 'Whom shall I send, and who will go for us?' And in John 14:23 Jesus says: 'If anyone loves me, he will obey my teaching. My Father will love him, and *we will come* (*eleusometha*) to him and *we will make* (*poiēsometha*) our home with him.' Therefore, in view of the fact that there are three persons in the Godhead, it is better to say that our God is *personal* than to say that he is *a* person. The God of Scripture is not *a* person; he is *tri-personal.* In the depth of the divine Being of the Godhead exist eternally three persons who stand in an I–you–he essential and personal relation of love with each other. And for any pastor to say from the pulpit that God is *a* person is actually to graze the rim of, if not to cross over into, the modalistic heresy.

I offer no apology for mentioning here, in our discussion of the attributes of God, the truth of the triune character of the Christian God, for in a very real sense, although we do not normally use the term to describe it, God's triunity is another of his distinctive attributes or marks. I will be mentioning his triunity right along as we move through our addresses about God's attributes; indeed, I will reserve my last address for that particular topic. For I take seriously John Calvin's insight that

God ... designates himself [in addition to his spiritual essence] by another special mark to distinguish himself *more precisely* from idols. For he so proclaims himself the *sole* God as to offer himself [at the same time] to be contemplated in three persons. Unless we grasp these [now heed Calvin's next words carefully here], only the bare and empty name of God flits about in our brain *to the exclusion of the true God.*[8]

Note Calvin's last words: 'to the exclusion of the true God.' I hope you got Calvin's point. Calvin had apprehended that the tripersonality of God is not an idea that is to be *added* to one's already complete idea of God but is a truth that enters into the *very idea* of the one living and true God without which he cannot be conceived in the truth of his Being. In other words, since the only God who is there, is, in point of fact, a Trinity, if we think and talk about God and his attributes as if he were simply an undifferentiated divine Monad we are, as a matter of fact, thinking of a God that has no existence. We are thinking of – how does Calvin put it? – 'the bare and empty name of God' that is *not the true God* at all. What this father of the Magisterial Reformation of the sixteenth century is saying is this: If we do not give due regard to God's triunity as we reflect upon him, we have created for ourselves and are talking about an idol. Gregory of Nazianzus (c. 329–c.389) captures my point here well when he states: 'I cannot think on the one without quickly being encircled by the splendor of the three; nor can I discern the three without being straightway carried back to the one.'[9] This is the main reason that Judaism and Islam, while both are monotheistic faiths, are nonetheless both *idolatrous* faiths. Neither of their gods is the true God; their gods are idols because, among other reasons, they are not triune. So we must never think or talk about the God of Christianity unless at the same time we recognize that we are thinking and talking

---

[8] John Calvin, *Institutes*, 1.13.2, emphasis supplied.
[9] Gregory of Nazianzus, 'On Holy Baptism,' oration xl. 41; *Patrologia Graeca*, edited by J. P. Migne (Paris, 1857–66), 36, 418.

about the *triune* God. To talk first about 'God' *per se*, giving no thought to his triunity, according to Calvin, is to talk about an idol. And in our present text Jesus illustrates for us that for which Calvin is contending, for though he says with no apparent specification, 'God is spirit,' the context of his remark makes it clear that he is thinking triunely and intends God the Father, the first person of the holy triune Godhead. We would urge first then that God as spirit is personal or *tri-personal*.

The second thing that God as spirit means is that he is *noncorporeal*, a statement of negation rather than of affirmation, I admit. But this way of talking about God – designated by the church fathers as the *via negationis*, the 'way of negation,' that identifies what God *is* by declaring what he is *not* by means of negating attributes of the finite order as true of him – a way, incidentally, that Louis Berkhof does not think is 'the proper method of dogmatic theology' because 'it takes its starting point in man'[10] but a way the apostle Paul himself endorsed, when describing God, by his use of several privative *alpha* words:[11]

♦ 'immortal' (*aphthartou*) in Romans 1:23 (see also 'immortal' [*aphthartō*] in 1 Timothy 1:17;

♦ 'unsearchable' (*anexeraunētai*) in Romans 11:33;

♦ 'incomprehensible,' lit, 'not to be tracked out' (*anexichniastoi*) in Romans 11:33 (the same word, *anexichniaston*, in Ephesians 3:8 describes the riches of Christ);

---

[10]Louis Berkhof, *Systematic Theology* (New combined edition; Grand Rapids: Eerdmans, 1996), 53, says this because he is very properly concerned that God's self-revelation in his Word should always be the only source of our knowledge of God. But when we see God's Word itself employing the *via negationis* when talking about God we should not declare the method *per se* to be beyond the bounds of scriptural dogmatics.

[11]The Greek alpha (α) is often employed as a prefix to negate the idea of a word or to express the absence of a quality. This use of the Greek alpha is known as the privative alpha.

- indescribable' (*anekdiēgētō*), describing here God's gift to mankind of Jesus Christ, in 2 Corinthians 9:15;
- 'invisible' (*aoratō*) in 1 Timothy 1:17 (see also 'the invisible one' [*ton aoraton*] in Hebrews 11:27);
- 'unapproachable' (*aprositon*) in 1 Timothy 6:16; and
- 'unchangeable' (*to ametatheton* and *ametathetōn*) in Hebrews 6:17-18, describing God's eternal purpose.

And before Paul David had declared that God

- 'neither slumbers nor sleeps. [*lō' yānûm wᵉlō' yîshān*],' that is, he is relentless or ceaseless in his guardian protection of his own, in Psalm 121:4, and
- that God's greatness or majesty (*gᵉdhullāh*) is 'unfathomable' (*'ên hêqer*), that is, is beyond our comprehension, in Psalm 145:3; and that his understanding is
- 'immeasurable' (*'ên mispār*) in Psalm 147:5.

And God himself employs expressions of negation as self-descriptions, declaring for example that he

- 'does not grow tired [*lō' yî'aph*],' that is, he is indefatigable, in Isaiah 40:28; that he
- 'does not grow weary [*lō' yîgā'*],' that is, he is untiring, also in Isaiah 40:28; that
- his understanding is 'unsearchable ['*ên hêqer lithᵉbhûnāthô*],' that is, his understanding cannot be fully comprehended, in Isaiah 40:28; and that
- he 'does not change [*lō' shānîthî*],' that is, he is immutable, in Malachi 3:6.

Hence, God's noncorporeality means that he is without body, body parts, or bodily passions such as hunger for food or the desire to satisfy a sexual drive. He is pure and unqualifiedly noncorporeal Being. We know this is the meaning of 'spirit' from Luke 24:36-43 where, in response to the disciples' assessment that the risen Lord was a 'spirit,' Jesus said: 'Look at my hands and my feet. It is I myself! Touch me and see; for *a spirit does not have flesh and blood* [which is a statement of negation], as you see I have' (24:39).

So when we say that God is spirit we should mean not only that he is *tri-personal* but also that *no property of created matter* may properly be ascribed to his Being. And this means in turn that

♦ he has no extension in space, neither as a vast *solid*, nor as a measureless ocean of *liquid*, nor as an immense volume of *gas* expanded beyond limit; extension, in all these forms, is a property wholly irrelevant to and inappropriately attributed to God as divine spirit;

♦ he has no material size or dimensions, even infinite ones, that is to say, we should not think of God as being 'infinitely large' materially for it is not a *part* of God but all of God who is in every place in the universe (Ps. 139:7-10); nor should we think of him as in any sense 'small' materially for no place in the universe can surround him or contain him (1 Kgs. 8:27), indeed, the heaven of heavens cannot contain him;

♦ he has no material weight (but as we shall see in our third address, *he does have weight*, but of a vastly different kind from any that we know here!), no material mass, no material bulk, no material parts, no material form, no material taste, and no material smell;

♦ he is not like atomic or cosmic energy or vapor or steam or air, all of which are created things;

35

♦ he is not even like *our* spirits, for our spirits are created spirits that can and do exist in only one finite place at a time, namely, within us.[12]

We must simply say that God is 'spirit' and that, whatever else this may mean, it means at the very least that his Being as tri-personal noncorporeal spirit is unlike *any being* about which we know in this material creation. His Being as tri-personal noncorporeal spirit is *uncreated* Being; ours is *created* being. We cannot picture his non-material Being; we cannot imagine his non-material essence (and he forbids us to try), particularly when he informs us as we shall see in later addresses that he is omnipresent, never had a beginning, is infinite, eternal, and immutable in all his attributes, and that he is triune. In short, his tri-personal noncorporeal nature as spirit is simply *incomprehensible* to us.[13] And I find it both intriguing and highly instructive that in Ezekiel 1 the nearer the prophet approached God the more his descriptive words of God reflect God's incomprehensibility:

---

[12]When I say this I do not intend to suggest that our spirits have extension in space.

[13]The word 'incomprehensible' literally means 'impossible to understand', 'unintelligible', or 'unknowable'. By using this word here I do not intend any of these meanings with reference to our knowledge of God in an absolute sense since God is, of course, understandable, intelligible, and knowable, that is to say, apprehensible, to some degree by us because he has revealed something of himself in and by biblical revelation. I hardly need to point out that only God knows God in an absolutely comprehensive way: 'No one knows the Son [comprehensibly] except the Father, and no one knows the Father [comprehensibly] except the Son' (Matt. 11:27); '...no one knows the thoughts of God [comprehensibly] except the Spirit of God' (1 Cor. 2:11). Therefore, though not comprehensible to us in an absolute way, he can be apprehended, that is, partially known, by us. In this specific context I intend to say that we are incapable of fully comprehending the nature of God's noncorporeality beyond the fact of its 'thatness'. But I do not intend that human beings are ignorant of all truths about God's attributes though they are ignorant of many truths about him, even of some truths that he

...there came a voice [writes Ezekiel] from above the expanse over the [living creatures'] heads as they stood with lowered wings. Above the expanse over their heads was *what looked like* a sapphire stone that had the *appearance* of a throne, and high above the *appearance* of the throne was an *appearance like that* of a man. I saw that *what appeared to be* his waist *looked liked* glowing metal, *like the appearance* of fire, and that from there down was *like the appearance of* fire; and brilliant light surrounded him. *Like the appearance* of a rainbow in the clouds on a rainy day, so was the *appearance* around him. This was *the appearance of the likeness* [*mar'eh d*e*muth*] of the glory of the LORD (Ezek. 1:25-28).

Note that while Ezekiel's record itself is comprehensible to us, what Ezekiel saw he describes by employing a number of similes: something 'looked like' a sapphire stone that had the 'appearance' of a throne; then the light about that likeness had the 'appearance' like that of a rainbow, and the one who appeared high above it was 'like a man,' which man-like figure Ezekiel then informs us was 'the appearance of the likeness' of the glory of the Lord. Note that this figure he described was not the Lord as such, not the 'glory of the Lord,' not the 'likeness' of the glory of the Lord, but 'the appearance of the likeness' of the glory of the Lord. And beholding that he fell upon his face. And we too are lost here in adoring wonder! Quite properly then, Blaise Pascal (1623–62), French mathematician and philosopher, said: 'Man must not see nothing at all [when he contemplates the Being of God], nor must he see enough to think that he possesses God, but he must see enough to know that he has lost [that is, cannot fully comprehend] him.' And as Robert Lewis Dabney (1820–98), the Southern Presbyterian theologian, declares:

---

has revealed about himself (this is the reason we continue to study his written Word to us) as well as the unrevealed truths that are mentioned in Deuteronomy 29:29.

God, in revealing himself..., only reveals [the fact of] His being and properties or attributes – His substance remains as invisible as ever. Look back to that whole knowledge of God which we have acquired..., and you will see that it is nothing but a knowledge of attributes. *Of the substance to which these properties are referred, we have only learned that it is.* What it is, remains impenetrable to us. We have named it simple spirit. But is this, after all, more than a name, and the affirmation of an unknown fact to our understandings? For, when we proceed to examine our own conception of spirit, we find that it is *a negation of material attributes only.* Our very attempts to conceive of it ... in its substance are still obstructed by an inability to get out of the materialistic circle of notions.[14]

We can only say that as noncorporeal Being he is *invisible* (another negation) to physical sight. He 'lives in light so brilliant that no human can approach him. No one has ever seen him, nor ever will' (1 Tim. 1:17; 6:16; see Ezekiel's statement: 'brilliant light surrounded him'), and that as noncorporeal Being, that is, as one who in his Being is without material parts, he is also *indivisible* (yet another negation) – what some theologians refer to as his 'simplicity,' using this term in the sense of 'not composed of parts.'

It is true, of course, that the Bible speaks of God as having a face (Exod. 33:20), eyes (Prov. 15:3), an ear (Isa. 37:17), an arm (Exod. 6:6), a right hand (Exod. 3:20), feet (Nahum 1:3) and so on. But in light of the Bible's teaching concerning his noncorporeal nature we must construe such language not literally but metaphorically, the purpose of these anthropomorphisms being to assist people better to understand that God is truly personal.

---

[14]Robert Lewis Dabney, *Lectures in Systematic Theology* (Reprint; Grand Rapids: Zondervan, 1972), 178, emphasis supplied.

Application

Well, so much for the theology inherent within Jesus' statement. Let's relate all this to us in a practical way. First, it is this fact of God's Being as 'spirit' that underlies the Second Commandment that prohibits evéry attempt to fashion an image of God. God says in Exodus 20:4-5:

> Do not make graven [that is, carved, sculpted] images [of me] *of any kind*, or any [painted] likeness [of me] of anything that is in heaven above [that is, the heavenly bodies, clouds, lightning, and birds], or that is in the earth beneath [that is, man, animals, trees, stones, etc.], or that is in the water under the earth [that is, fish, coral reefs, etc.]. You must never worship or bow down to them, for I, the LORD your God, am a jealous God who will not share your affection with any other god.

That is to say, any such image or likeness is not God; it is 'another god'. And Moses reminded the second generation of the nation of Israel that came out of Egypt: 'You saw no form of any kind the day the LORD spoke to you at Horeb out of the fire. Therefore *watch yourselves very carefully*, so that you do not become corrupt and make for yourself an idol, an image of any shape' (Deut. 4:15-16). To think of God's Being in terms of *anything* in the created universe is to misrepresent him, to limit him, to think of him as less or other than he really is. This is the reason God's jealousy is given as the reason for the prohibition against making images of him: he is jealous to protect his glory; he will not share it with anyone or anything else. He eagerly seeks worshipers who think of him as he is – as tri-personal, noncorporeal spirit – and who worship him as such, for to worship anything else is idolatry, and he is angered when his glory is diminished by men falsely misrepresenting him by a likeness to anything in this created universe.

The Roman Catholic Church lives daily with a prime example of a violation of the Second Commandment in its highly acclaimed Sistine Chapel in the Vatican and delights to display it, for there in the chapel ceiling Michelangelo has painted God the Father as a bearded, white-haired elderly man reaching out with his outstretched hand and finger to touch Adam in order to give him life. The ceiling of the Sistine Chapel may display great art, but it also exhibits great disobedience to the Law of God.[15] The result of this and every other similar effort is to fashion an image that is a distortion of God and is thus blasphemous and idolatrous. Pope Gregory I (540–604) had declared that such images are the 'books of the uneducated', but John Calvin rightly asserted: '...bodily images are unworthy of God's majesty because they diminish the fear of him in men and increase error' (*Institutes*, 1.11.6; 1.11-12). They are not necessary, Calvin continued, if the church would do its job of preaching and teaching: '...those in authority in the church turned over to idols the office of teaching for no other reason than that they themselves were mute. Paul testifies that by the true preaching of the gospel "Christ is depicted before our eyes as crucified."' 'From this one fact [the uneducated] could have learned more than from a thousand crosses of wood or stone' (*Institutes*, 1.11.7; see also here 1.11.13).

God, and specifically God the Father, ladies and gentlemen, is not a white-haired elderly man. God the Father is spirit, and they who worship him must worship him *in spirit and truth, that is to say, in spiritual worship that is according to truth.*[16] The Christian must ever be solicitous never even to *think* of God as having

---

[15]The ceiling of the Sistine Chapel, I should note, is not the only such act of disobedience on Rome's part. As Bishop J. C. Ryle writes in his *Warnings to the Churches* (Reprint; Edinburgh: Banner of Truth, 1992), 158, emphasis original: 'Romanism in perfection is a gigantic system of Church-worship, Sacrament-worship, Mary-worship, saint-worship, image-worship, relic-worship, and priest-worship, – ...it is, in one word, a huge organized idolatry.'

any material characteristics. So if you ask me what God looks like, I will not just say: 'I'm not sure' or 'I don't know.' I will say he has no 'looks' in the sense you intend by your question, and I will insist that you give up every attempt to conceive of his Being beyond what is implied in the word 'spirit', namely, his tri-personal noncorporeality.

But I can and will say this to you, and I rejoice with inexpressible joy when I say it – and this is the second application that I want to make – that he who hungers and thirsts by divine grace to know God and what he is like can know him through saving faith in Jesus Christ, for he who by faith knows God's incarnate Son *knows* the Father (John 14:7), and he who has *seen* Christ with the eyes of faith *has seen* the Father (John 14:9), for Christ became and is the *visible* image of the *invisible* God. He is

♦ the Word who existed as God's Son with God the Father before God made anything at all,

♦ the one who is supreme over all, who sits today at the Father's 'right hand', that is, who occupies the place of highest honor in the heaven,

♦ the one through whom God the Father created everything in heaven and earth (John 1:2-3; Col. 1:16; Heb. 1:2),

♦ the one who made the things we can see and the things that we cannot see (Col. 1:16),

♦ the one who holds all creation together (Col. 1:15-17), which means that the so-called

---

[16]In the Greek phrase 'in spirit and truth' of John 4:24 the anarthrous nouns 'spirit' and 'truth' are governed by the single occurrence of the preposition 'in' before 'spirit'. This suggests, just as the only other occurrence of this construction in the Johannine material is in 1 John 3:18 ('in deed and truth') where John intends that love involves deeds that are according to truth, that the entire phrase should be understood as a hendiadys ('one complex idea expressed through two words'), that is, 'in spiritual worship that is according to truth.'

laws of atomic physics are actually the sustaining, adhering work of the Son of God,

♦ the one in whom it pleased God that in him all the fullness of deity should dwell bodily, that is, incarnationally (Col. 1:19; 2:9), and the one who would reconcile this fallen world to God, making peace by means of the blood of his cross (Col. 1:20), and

♦ the one in whom are hid all the treasures of wisdom and knowledge (Col. 2:3).

♦ All which means that the only God who is – the God who revealed himself redemptively in history – is therefore 'Christlike [see John 14:9], and in him there is no un-Christlikeness at all.'[17]

♦ All which means in turn that the triune God has invested the entire salvific enterprise in the person and messianic work of his Son Jesus Christ who is the beginning, the center, and the end of all his will, ways, and works.

As we bring this address to a close, I must ask, in light of God's *incomprehensible* Being as uncreated 'spirit,' whose tripersonal noncorporeal existence is inconceiveable to us, can you now understand *better*

♦ *why it is* that we are to resist every attempt to fashion an image of God's Being with our hands or with our minds;

♦ *why it is* that the world, beginning with itself, cannot and will never find God through the ratiocinations of *its* wisdom (1 Cor. 1:21);

♦ *why it is*, if mankind was ever to know anything truly about him, that God had to reveal himself redemptively and incarnationally in Christ and propositionally in his Word, the Holy Scriptures

---

[17]Michael Ramsay, *God, Christ, and the World* (London: SCM, 1969), 98.

(1 Cor. 2:10-15), which inscripturated Word must never be separated from the incarnate Word;

♦ *why it is*, since no one has ever seen or ever will be able to see God, that his 'one and only [Son, himself] God, who is in the bosom of the Father [*monogenēs theos ho ōn eis ton kolpon tou patros*],' had to 'exegete' (*exēgēsato*) or make the Father known (John 1:18);

♦ *why it is*, since no one knows the Father comprehensively except the Son and he to whom the Son wills to reveal him (Matt. 11:27), that you and I must come to the Son as the Revealer of the Father (Matt. 11:28), and in that knowledge receive eternal life (John 17:3);

♦ *why it is* that Christ alone – who as the Word was with God in the beginning and who is himself God (John 1:1), who became incarnate and lived here on earth among us (John 1:1, 14) – *why it is*, I say, that *he* is the only way to the Father (John 14:6);

♦ *why it is* that *his* name alone is the only name under heaven whereby a person can be saved (Acts 4:12);

♦ *why it is* that *he* alone is the only Mediator between God and man (1 Tim. 2:5);

♦ *why it is* that only the person who has the Son, the only Exegete of God the Father, has life, and why the person who does not have the Son does not have life (1 John 5:12); and

♦ *why it is* that true worshipers must worship God in spirit and truth, that is to say, as he truly is – with spirits that have been regenerated by the Holy Spirit and in accordance with the truth that came through Jesus Christ (John 1:17) who *is* himself the truth (John 14:6) and who came to bear witness to the truth (John 18:37)? You see, only regenerated men can offer true worship through Jesus Christ to the Father.

I am finished, but before I conclude I feel I must say this: as I have been addressing you, if the Spirit of God has convicted you that you are not one of those true worshipers whom the Father seeks to worship him, if the Spirit has quickened in you the realization that you have imagined that you know God when in reality you have sought your knowledge of the glory of God in things other than in the face of Jesus Christ, I implore you, as Christ's ambassador, to submit immediately to his gracious invitation to seek his forgiveness for your idolatry. Place your trust in the only Savior of men who is the only 'Exegete' capable of making the Father known to us. May God help all of us to examine ourselves now to know whether we are in the true Faith.

Let us pray:
Our loving God, this morning we have been reflecting on your Being as incomprehensible triune personal spirit.

We confess that we are far too lackadaisical about reflecting seriously on who and what you are.

We stand before you with great shamefacedness, confessing that there are large times in our lives when we don't think much about you at all, because we are proud, self-sufficient, and presumptuous.

And all too often when we do think about you, our thoughts are so shallow and trite that we actually think that we can fully comprehend you, and thereby we dishonor you, the great, incomprehensible, and awesome God.

Forgive us, Father, for our frivolousness, our giddiness, our silliness, our laziness, and help us all to be done with lesser things and to grow spiritually this semester as we meditate thoughtfully upon your tri-personal noncorporeal Being.

May our studies about you every single day of our lives become for us a great and marvelous instrument of grace to mold us more and more into the likeness of Jesus Christ, in whose great and wonderful name we pray, Amen.

Second Address

'Infinite in His Being'

Jacob left Beersheba and went toward Haran. And he came to a certain place and stayed there that night, because the sun had set. Taking one of the stones of the place, he put it under his head and lay down in that place to sleep. And he dreamed, and behold, there was a ladder set up on the earth, and the top of it reached to heaven. And behold, the angels of God were ascending and descending on it! And behold, the Lord stood above it and said, 'I am the Lord, the God of Abraham your father and the God of Isaac. The land on which you lie I will give to you and to your offspring. Your offspring shall be like the dust of the earth, and you shall spread abroad to the west and to the east and to the north and to the south, and in you and your offspring shall all the families of the earth be blessed. Behold, I am with you and will keep you wherever you go, and will bring you back to this land. For I will not leave you until I have done what I have promised you.' Then Jacob awoke from his sleep and said, 'Surely the Lord is in this place, and I did not know it.' And he was afraid and said, 'How awesome is this place! This is none other than the house of God, and this is the gate of heaven' (Gen. 28:10-17).

Introduction

I greet you again in the name of our infinitely worthy Lord and Savior, Jesus Christ. May he multiply his grace and peace to you today. And may the God of love and peace be with you.

As we saw in our first address the *Westminster Shorter Catechism* begins its description of God by employing the word 'spirit' to describe the God of Christianity – God is a Spirit' – a statement we suggested that probably should be phrased, in light of the context of the biblical verse from which it is drawn (John 4:24), 'God is spirit,' that is to say, God is (tri)personal and noncorporeal, and therefore his essential nature is not and will never be fully comprehensible to us. The *Shorter Catechism* then modifies that phrase with three adjectives: 'infinite, eternal and unchangeable.' That is to say, in his existence as 'spirit' God is infinite, eternal, and unchangeable spirit. A prepositional phrase follows these adjectives, introduced by the words 'in his', that modifies in turn these adjectives. And the seven objects of the preposition 'in', namely, 'being, wisdom, power, holiness, justice, goodness, and truth' – are each in turn qualified by these adjectives.

What this descriptive definition of God intends to declare, then, is this: that the triune God of the Bible and of biblical Christianity exists as a (tri)personal noncorporeal Being who is

infinite, eternal, and unchangeable in his being,
infinite, eternal, and unchangeable in his wisdom,
infinite, eternal, and unchangeable in his power,
infinite, eternal, and unchangeable in his holiness,
infinite, eternal, and unchangeable in his justice,
infinite, eternal, and unchangeable in his goodness, and
infinite, eternal, and unchangeable in his truth.

Before we take up the topic of today's address, I think it is necessary to make three observations about the *Shorter Catechism*'s definition of God.

First, it is not the noun 'spirit' *per se* that distinguishes God absolutely from the creature in the *Catechism*'s definition since angels too are 'spirit' beings, albeit created finite beings, who are also personal noncorporeal beings (Heb. 1:14). Nor is it the last seven nouns that distinguish God from the angels or from mankind since what they designate may be and are used to describe both angels and humankind. No, it is the noun 'spirit' in the sense that we enunciated in our first address and the three adjectives in the definition, 'infinite, eternal, and unchangeable,' that distinguish God in the absolute sense from both angels and the human creature who among all creation is uniquely the *imago Dei*. Of course, only God as *divine* spirit possesses the seven nouns that the *Catechism* employs in the infinite, eternal, and unchangeable sense.

Second, when the *Shorter Catechism* speaks of God's infinite, eternal, and unchangeable being, wisdom, power, holiness, justice, goodness, and truth, it is speaking of attributes that comprise what the Scriptures sum up by the one word 'glory'. The *Catechism* is actually describing the *glory* of God by its definition of God, that is to say, *God's glory is the sum total of all of his attributes*, which is to say that the glory of God is just *the inescapable weight of the sheer intrinsic 'Godness' of God*. And for the creature, whether angel or man, to seek to arrogate to himself any one of God's attributes and thereby to attempt to become 'like God' as did Adam (see Genesis 3:5, 22) is to attack the very glory of God by attempting to make himself equal with God. Or for the creature to seek to deny to him any one of his attributes is also to attack the glory of God for it would deny to him that without which he would no longer be God. Or for the creature to ascribe to him any attribute that he himself does not expressly declare he possesses is equally to attack his glory for such an attribution will be inevitably erroneous and implies that the creature knows God as well as God knows himself and knows him apart from revelation, which is an idolatrous absurdity and impossibility. Therefore, it is absolutely essential – indeed, it is a vital imperative for our spiritual health – that we who desire to know what God is like should always listen carefully to God's description of himself in Holy Scripture alone, submit our hearts to that description without murmuring against it, endeavor to live our lives in accordance with it, and worship him in a way that befits his revealed perfections, that is, with reverence and awe. And speaking of worship, I want to state categorically that, in my opinion, the intrusion into the contemporary church of the superficial, flippant worship styles that abound everywhere today, with their applause for the church's 'performers' and their sappy contemporary music, is not and should never have been regarded as simply a matter of 'cultural preference'. Rather, as an infusion of the popular culture into the church it is a symptom of what A. W. Tozer describes in his book, *The Knowledge of the Holy*, as

> the loss of the concept of [the] majesty [of God] from the popular religious mind. The Church has surrendered her once lofty concept of God and has substituted for it one so low, so ignoble, as to be unworthy of thinking, worshiping men....
>
> The low view of God entertained almost universally among Christians [today] is the cause of a hundred lesser evils everywhere among us. A whole new philosophy of the Christian life has resulted from this one basic error in our religious thinking.
>
> With our loss of the sense of majesty has come the further loss of religious awe and consciousness of the divine Presence. We have lost our spirit of worship and our ability ... to meet God in adoring silence. Modern Christianity is simply not producing the kind of Christian who can appreciate or experience ... life in the Spirit.

The words, 'Be still, and know that I am God,' mean next to nothing to the self-confident, bustling worshiper in this ... century.[1]

This is a dreadfully serious situation due to the fact that idolatry does not consist merely in bowing in adoration before man-made images. The essence of idolatry, as Tozer reminds us, is 'the entertainment of [any] thoughts about God [as true] that are not worthy of him'.[2] And the major cause of this 'loss' and its resultant idolatry is the failure of preachers to preach on the biblical attributes of God, thereby allowing their people by their silence to acquire and entertain thoughts about God that the Bible does not endorse. I also believe the debate that rages in the church today over worship styles – whether worship should be 'traditional' or 'contemporary', 'liturgical' or 'non-liturgical', formal or 'revivalistic' – would disappear overnight if the church at large recovered 'her once lofty concept' of the majesty of the living God. Were that to occur, many worship leaders would know great shamefacedness because of their shallow, self-willed, irreverent styles of worship. For the triune God of Holy Scripture is an absolutely sovereign, transcendently holy, infinitely righteous, incomprehensible Deity – perfections that ought to inspire awe, humility, and reverence in the creature. But he will not be known as such – or served as such – by a people fed with inane choruses, poorly written gospel tunes, silly unscriptural prayers, and mediocre revivalistic preaching. God is to be worshiped with renewed minds. Faith in him requires understanding, and that understanding grows primarily in our congregations as they are nourished by the singing of the biblical psalms and doctrinally sound hymns, by serious prayers of adoration, confession, thanksgiving, and supplication, and by the solid preaching of our

---

[1] A. W. Tozer, *The Knowledge of the Holy* (New York: Harper & Row, 1961), 5.

[2] Tozer, *The Knowledge of the Holy*, 10.

Reformed public worship services. Therefore, we cannot adopt forms of worship that are *theologically* shallow and expect to gain or to retain a biblically sound understanding of God. Hence the antidote to all the problems in contemporary worship will be found in the church's recovery of the awesome majesty of God. As this is being accomplished, the quality and content of the music in our public worship will become different, the content of the public prayers in our public worship will become different, and the preaching in our public worship will become different. And as a result Christians' lives will *become* different!

Third, as we urged in our first address, we must continually bear in mind as we discuss the attributes of God that what we affirm throughout of God *per se* we are affirming equally of God the Father, God the Son, and God the Holy Spirit. That is to say, the *Shorter Catechism* definition of God is a definition of the *triune* God, the three persons of which are, as the sixth answer of the *Shorter Catechism* declares, 'one God, the *same in substance, equal in power and glory.*'

Let us now invoke the blessing of this triune God upon what we say about the attribute of God that is the subject of this morning's address.

Prayer:
Almighty and triune God – Father, Son, and Holy Spirit – who both dwells in that transcendently holy light that no man can approach in his natural state and live and keeps covenant to the thousandth generation of those who love you:

This morning we thank you that we can know you savingly – the infinite personal God – even in the midst of our knowledge of our own unworthiness and sin, and even as we know that, when the desires of your great heart have been so freely opened to us, we have been so slow to worship you in spirit and in truth, with reverence and with awe.

Today we thank you for the mighty truths that you will flash, even if only momentarily, before our eyes from Holy Scripture. We pray for your gracious presence in our lives, that, drawn by the sweetness of your grace and the bliss of your beauty, we may turn our eyes and hearts away from the deceptive and dying, but oh so alluring, lights of this world. May we know you enough to long after you, and longing for you, may we learn to know you even better. Indeed, grant us such heart desire for you that our greatest passion in life will be to know you better than we know anyone or anything else in this world and to enjoy you more than we enjoy anyone or anything else in this world – more than our spouses, more than our children, more than our homes, more than our jobs.

Give us while we appear before you now, acknowledging the depth and the greatness of our own unworthiness and of our many sins and shortcomings, the awareness of the great ocean of your presence sweeping over us. Be with us throughout these chapel times as we think about your glorious attributes. Remove our ignorance, grant us understanding that you are the Lord who is kind, just, and righteous, who delights in these things. We ask all this through Jesus Christ, our Lord. Amen.

* * *

In this address I want us to consider God's infinity in being, that is, his omnipresence. Listen now, in addition to the passage we read earlier that teaches God was present with Jacob though he was unaware of it, to the following selection of verses that teach this divine attribute:

1 Kings 8:27: '...will God really dwell on the earth? The heavens, even the highest heaven, cannot contain you. How much less this temple I have built!'

Psalm 139:7-10: 'Where can I go from your Spirit? Where can I flee *from your presence*? If I go up to the heavens, *you are there* ; if I make my bed in the depths, *you are there.* If I rise on the wings of the dawn, if I settle on the far side of the sea, even there your hand will guide me, your right hand will hold me fast.'

Proverbs 15:3: 'The eyes of the LORD are *everywhere* [*b^ekol māqôm*, 'in every place'], keeping watch on the wicked and the good.'

Obadiah 4: '"Though you [Edom] soar aloft like the eagle, though your nest is set among the stars, from there I will bring you down," says the LORD.'

Amos 9:2-4: 'Though [apostate Israel should] dig down to the depths of the grave, from there my hand will take them. Though they climb up to the heavens, from there I will bring them down. Though they hide themselves on the top of Carmel, there I will hunt them down and seize them. Though they hide from me at the bottom of the sea, there I will command the serpent to bite them. Though they are driven into exile by their enemies, there I will command the sword to slay them.'

Jeremiah 23:23-24: '"Am I only a God nearby," declares the LORD, "and not a God far away? Can anyone hide in secret places so that I cannot see him?" declares the LORD. "Do not I fill heaven and earth?" declares the LORD.'

Ezekiel 8:12: '[The Lord] said to me, "Son of man, have you seen what the elders of the house of Israel are doing in the darkness, each at the shrine of his own idol? They say, 'The LORD does not see us; the LORD has forsaken the land.'"'

Acts 17:27-28: 'God ... is not far from each of us. For in him we live and move and have our being.'

The doctrine
I think it is entirely appropriate to suggest that in the context of the *Shorter Catechism* definition of God it is

rather certain that by its description of God as 'infinite in his Being' the framers of the *Catechism*, because they say nothing about God's attribute of omnipresence anywhere else in their definition, intended to teach that God is *omnipresent*, that is to say, that God transcends all spatial limitations and is immediately and entirely present in every square inch of his creation and therefore that everything and everybody are immediately in his presence.

Some philosophical theologians have inferred God's attribute of omnipresence from his attributes of omnipotence and omniscience. For example, Richard Swinburne argues:

> A person who is omnipotent is able to bring about effects everywhere by basic actions. One who is omniscient at a certain time has justified true beliefs about things which are going on anywhere at any time.... An omniscient being does not depend for his knowledge on the correct functioning of intermediaries. Hence an omnipotent and omniscient person ... is of logical necessity an omnipresent spirit.[3]

While such reasoning has perhaps some value in that it shows the coherence of God's attributes, the Christian is not shut up to a logical inference as the ground for his doctrine of God's omnipresence. As the several Scripture verses we cited show (and we could have cited ten times as many more), the doctrine is directly and explicitly taught in Scripture.

Now what exactly are we saying when we say that God is *omni*present? We are saying not only that all things are immediately in God's presence, which is true enough, but also that God himself is present with his whole Being in every place outside of himself. To put it as simply as I know how: *God is everywhere; all things*

---

[3]Richard Swinburne, *The Coherence of Theism* (Oxford: Clarendon, 1977), 222.

are immediately in his presence. Never do we have any privacy; never have we had a private conversation; his presence is inescapable. Everywhere *there* is God – his Being, his self-revelation, his sovereignty, his activities, his prerogatives, his scrutiny.[4] He is in *all* the particulars of creation, in *all* the events of providence, and in *all* his works of grace. And try as they might, even self-acclaimed atheists cannot escape him for in their hearts they know God. Robert Browning in his poem, 'Bishop Blougram's Apology' (lines 173-97), poetically yet powerfully states the atheists' problem in this regard:

> And now what are we? unbelievers both,
> Calm and complete, determinately fixed
> Today, tomorrow, and forever, pray?
> You'll guarantee me that? Not so, I think!
> In no wise! All we've gained is, that belief,
> As unbelief before, shakes us by fits,
> Confounds us like its predecessors. Where's
> The gain? how can we guard our unbelief,
> Make it bear fruit to us? – the problem here:
> *Just when we are safest, there's a sunset touch,*
> *A fancy from a flower-bell, someone's death,*
> *A chorus-ending from Euripides, –*
> *And that's enough for fifty hopes and fears*
> *As old and new at once as Nature's self,*
> *To rap and knock and enter in our soul,*
> *Take hands and dance there, a fantastic ring,*
> *Round the ancient idol, on his base again, –*
> *The grand Perhaps!* We look on helplessly.
> There the old misgivings, crooked questions are –
> This good God, – what he could do, if he would,
> Would, if he could – then must have done long since:
> If so, when, where, and how? Some *way* must be, –
> Once feel about, and soon or late you hit
> Some sense, in which it might be, after all.
> Why not, 'The Way, the Truth, the Life?'

---

[4] I am employing some of Donald Macleod's language here, taken from his *Behold Your God* (Ross-shire: Christian Focus, 1990), 65.

No, self-avowed atheists cannot escape God because, as Calvin says, 'God himself has implanted in all men a certain understanding of his divine majesty,' with the result that 'a sense of deity [is] inscribed in the hearts of all'[5] – a haunting awareness that self-acclaimed atheists never lose – for 'however much they struggle against their own senses, and wish not only to drive God thence but also to destroy him in heaven, their stupidity never increases to the point where God does not at times bring them back to his judgment seat.'[6]

But while God is in every specific place, yet neither is he confined by any of these places, for no matter how expansive they may be, they cannot confine him (Solomon, you will recall, declared in his dedication prayer: '...heaven, even the highest heaven, cannot contain you,' 1 Kgs. 8:27), nor does he relate the same way to every place outside of himself but rather he relates and acts differently depending upon the place under consideration. Berkhof rightly declares that God is not present

in the same sense in all His creatures. The nature of His indwelling is in harmony with that of His creatures. He does not dwell on earth as He does in heaven, in animals as He does in man, in the inorganic as He does in the organic creation, in the wicked as He does in the pious, nor in the Church as He does in Christ. There is an endless variety in the manner in which he is immanent in His creatures....[7]

But what about hell? Is God present in hell? Is not what makes hell the place that it is the very absence of God? And does not Paul teach in 2 Thessalonians 1:9 that

---

[5]John Calvin, *Institutes*, 1.3.1.

[6]Calvin, *Institutes*, 1.4.2. See also *Institutes*, 1.3.3; 1.4.1, 4, in which Calvin speaks of this 'light of nature' in men as the *sensus divinitatis*, *sensus deitatis*, and *semen religiosus*.

[7]Louis Berkhof, *Systematic Theology* (New combined edition; Grand Rapids: Eerdmans, 1996), 61.

those who suffer eternal perdition will be *excluded* from the presence of the Lord? Yes, Paul says this, but I am quite certain that he intended their exclusion to be an exclusion away from the *approving* presence of the Lord and not from the presence of the Lord *per se*, for John informs us in Revelation 14:10 that the impenitent 'will be tormented in fire *in the presence of* [*enōpion*] the holy angels and *in the presence of* [*enōpion*] the Lamb.' Paul's statement illustrates what I mean when I say that God acts differently depending upon the place of his manifested presence. In hell God manifests his presence but in a *disapproving* manner; he is present there as a condemning Judge. And throughout eternity the impenitent sinner must always behold, as doubtless the most solemn aspect of hell itself, what C. S. Lewis refers to somewhere as the disapproving, lidless, unblinking eye of the wrathful God reproachfully staring at him. So we should affirm,

♦ first, that at all places of his manifested presence outside of himself he is *present to sustain*, as in the case of Christ's upholding the *entire* universe even as he hung upon the Tree (Heb. 1:3; see Col. 1:17); if God for even a nano- or one billionth part of a second should withhold his sustaining presence from this universe it and everything in it would in that instant collapse and disappear.

♦ second, that at some places of his manifested presence outside of himself he is *disapprovingly present to punish sin*, as at the Genesis flood, the destruction of Sodom and Gomorrah, supremely at Calvary, the destruction of Jerusalem in AD 70, and finally in hell; and

♦ third, that at still other places of his manifested presence outside of himself he is *present to bless*. Particularly in this category – 'present to bless' – it pleased God to dwell *incarnationally* in Jesus Christ (Col. 2:9) for us men and for our salvation, to manifest his *indwelling* presence in believers in and by the person of the Holy Spirit (Rom. 8:9-10), and to be near his own in their times of trial and trouble. Psalm 46:1 tells us: 'God is our refuge and strength, a help in trouble found ever [to be],' and his throne is a throne of grace that we may receive mercy and find grace to help in time of need' (Heb. 4:16). He is also with us at death: 'Even though I walk through the valley of the shadow of death,' David declared, 'I will fear no evil, for you are with me' (Ps. 23:4), and God himself has promised us: 'When you pass through the waters, I will be with you; yes, when you pass through the waters, they will not sweep over you' (Isa. 43:2). And in the place the Bible calls 'the new heaven and new earth' God has chosen fully, ultimately, and finally to manifest his approving presence to his children. This 'present to bless' category, as Donald Macleod demonstrates,

pervades Scripture and is set forth in terms of virtually every preposition human language has to offer. God is *with* [*meth*] us (Matthew 28:20), *around* [*sābhîbh*] us (Psalm 34:7), *in* [*en*] us (John 14:17), *in the midst of* [*bᵉqirbāh*] us (Psalm 46:5), *behind* [*āchôr*] us (Psalm 139:5), *underneath* [*mittachath*] us (Deuteronomy 33:27), [*over* (*episcopon*) us (1 Peter 2:25) – RLR], *near* [*qᵉrōbhô*] us (Psalm 148:14), and *before* [*emprosthen*] us (John 10:4).[8]

But in whatever respect he is in all these places, *he is wholly there* – as much in empty space as in every molecule of the solid granite mountain that contains no crack or fissure at all, as much in the lowest hell as in the highest heaven, as much among the sinful hosts of demons and men as among the blissful choir of immaculate angelic singers who never displeased him,

---

[8]Donald Macleod, *Behold Your God*, 66.

for 'in him we [and all other created existences] live and move and have our being' (Acts 17:28).

I must now make two cautionary comments before we proceed farther, the former concerning two errors held by unbelievers, the latter concerning an error held by some evangelicals. The first is this: the doctrine of God's omnipresence must not be so construed as to *identify* God with his creation as in pantheism. Nor should it be so construed, as do panentheistic process theologians such as Charles Hartshorne and John B. Cobb, Jr., as to identify God with the alleged impersonal, moving evolutionary 'force' in the world that is itself undergoing self-development and growth with the world being construed as his 'body'. The two facts of God's 'personalness' and a real creation by him 'in the beginning' preclude such constructions. The biblical teaching of the Creator/creature distinction, therefore, is the guardian 'watchdog' doctrine against all pantheistic and panentheistic constructions of the biblical God. While God, true enough, is everywhere present and active in all things outside of himself – this is Christian theism's doctrine of the divine *immanence* – he as the one *uncreated* Being stands off ontologically over against the *created* universe and is essentially distinct from it – this is Christian theism's doctrine of the divine *transcendence*.

My second word of caution is this: the fact of God's omnipresence precludes taking literally the biblical descriptions of God's 'ascendings' and 'descendings', his 'comings' and 'goings'. God, being everywhere present, does not literally 'come from' or 'go to' specific places. Where such language is employed in Scripture, as in Genesis 11:5 and Isaiah 64:1-2, it must be recognized for what it is – metaphorical language indicating or invoking a special *manifestation* of God's working presence either in judgment or in grace. And since all that we say about God's nature *per se* is equally true with regard to each of the persons of the triune Godhead, this conclusion has special implications with regard to the meaning of both God the Son's Incarnation and God the Holy Spirit's 'coming' into the world at Pentecost. Permit me to work this out a little more in detail.

Being omnipresent as God, God the Son did not literally 'come' into the world two thousand years ago in the sense of coming to a place where he as God was not present before. Nor should the event of the Incarnation be interpreted to mean that the Second Person of the Godhead divested himself of his divine attribute of omnipresence when he assumed our humanity. On more than one occasion in my role as invited lecturer I have asked gatherings of evangelical pastors the following question: 'After the Incarnation had occurred, did the Second Person of the Holy Trinity still possess the attribute of omnipresence or was he confined to the human body of Jesus?' More of them than I would like to report opted for the latter construction, arguing that the very word 'incarnation' means 'in flesh'. Of course, if their choice were true it would mean that God the Son divested himself of his attribute of being always and everywhere immediately present in his created universe. But divine attributes are not characteristics of God that are separate and distinct from his essence that he can lay aside like one might remove a garment of clothing at the end of a busy day and still be the same Being. To hold that God the Son actually divested himself in his incarnate state of humiliation of even one divine attribute is tantamount to contending that he who 'enfleshed' himself as Jesus of Nazareth, while perhaps 'more than man', is not quite God either. And Bishop Moule pointed out long ago that a Savior not quite God 'is a bridge broken at the farther end'.

We must, therefore, construe the event of the Incarnation as an event of addition, *not* subtraction: Without ceasing to be all that he is as God, God the Son took into union with himself something he had never possessed before – a human nature.[9] The event of the Incarnation means to convey the fact that God the Son uniquely *manifested* himself to the world and to men in and by his personal presence in human flesh. It intends to affirm that God the Son, through the instrumentality of the miraculous virginal conception, took into union with himself our human nature in such a real and vital sense that we properly declare that Jesus of Nazareth was and is not only fully human but also fully God manifest in the flesh. We must not for a second, therefore, intend to suggest that the Son of God somehow divested himself of his omnipresence when he became a man. Cyril of Alexandria, who led the orthodox opposition to Nestorius at the Council of Ephesus in AD 431, in a letter to Nestorius wrote:

[The eternal Word] subjected himself to birth for us, and came forth man from a woman, *without casting off that which he was*; ...although he assumed flesh and blood, *he remained what he was*, God in essence and in truth. Neither do we say that his flesh was changed into the nature of divinity, nor that the ineffable nature of the Word of God was laid aside for the nature of the flesh; for he is unchanged and absolutely unchangeable, *being the same always*, according to the Scriptures. For although visible and a child in swaddling clothes, and even in the bosom of his Virgin Mother, he *filled all creation as God*, and was a fellow-ruler with him who begat him, for the Godhead is without quantity and dimensions, and cannot have limits.[10]

---

[9]God the Son did not take into union with himself a human *person*. I address this doctrine, known as the *anhypostasia* ('no person'), in my *A New Systematic Theology of the Christian Faith*, 610-13.

[10]Cyril of Alexandria, from the 'Epistle of Cyril to Nestorius with the XII Anathematisms,' in *A Select Library of Nicene and Post-Nicene Fathers of the Christian Church*, edited by Philip Schaff and Henry Wace (Second series; Grand Rapids: Eerdmans, 1956), 14:202, emphasis supplied.

Some twenty years later, in AD 451, the Council of Chalcedon, whose creedal labors produced the Christological definition that with its four great adverbs of negation fixed the orthodox boundaries of all future discussions, declared that Jesus possessed

two natures *without confusion* [*asynchytōs*], *without change* [*atreptōs*], *without division* [*adiairetōs*], *without separation* [*achōristōs*], the distinctiveness of the natures being by no means removed because of the union, but the properties of each nature being preserved.

John Calvin was hardly heterodox, then, as the radical Lutherans of the Reformation sarcastically charged by their contemptuous *extra-Calvinisticum* ('that extra-Calvin thing'),[11] when he wrote:

Another absurdity ... namely, that if the Word of God became incarnate, [he] must have been confined within the narrow prison of an earthly body, is sheer impudence! For even if the Word in his immeasurable essence united with the nature of man into one person, *we do not imagine that he was confined therein.* Here is something marvelous: the Son of God descended from heaven in such a way that, *without leaving heaven*, he willed to be born in the virgin's womb, to go about the earth, to hang upon the cross, yet *he continually filled the earth even as he had done from the beginning.*[12]

---

[11]Lutheran Christology with its doctrine of the *communicatio idiomatum* ('communication of attributes'), the underpinning of its doctrine of the real presence of Christ's body and blood in the Lord's Supper, is heterodox here. Reformed Christology, espousing the *communio idiomatum* ('communion of attributes') in the unity of Christ's person, views the Lutheran view as a rejection of Chalcedon's great adverbs 'without confusion' and 'without change'. See Richard A. Muller, 'communicatio idiomatum,' *Dictionary of Latin and Greek Theological Terms* (Grand Rapids: Baker, 1985), 72-4.

[12]John Calvin, *Institutes*, 2.13.4, emphasis supplied.

And the *Heidelberg Catechism* grants explicit Reformed creedal status to this position when it declares in Question 48:

> Since [Christ's] Godhood is illimitable and omnipresent, it must follow that it is beyond the bounds of the human nature it has assumed, and yet none the less is in this human nature and remains personally united to it.

The same must be said about the Holy Spirit's 'coming' at Pentecost. He did not 'come' into the world on the Day of Pentecost in any sense that would suggest that he was absent from this world in the Old Testament or that he left some earlier location and came to the upper room where he had not been before. Rather, his personal presence was simply uniquely *manifested* in the upper room at Pentecost – his manifested presence there intending to teach us, not something about him, I must be quick to point out, but something about the One who sent him: In the simple words of C. H. Dodd, '...the Holy Spirit *in* the Church is the sign of Christ's present power and glory [*in* heaven].'[13]

Application
Well, dear friends, this is enough theological exposition for this address. It is now time for some practical applications of what we have said about God's omnipresence to our everyday Christian experience. I would suggest, and I will try to be brief, that the fact of God's omnipresence has several specific points of application to aid us as we live out our Christian witness in and before this watching world.

First, our knowledge of God's personal and immediate presence always with us should be an encouragement to us in times of trouble – in times of extraordinarily difficult duties, in times of poverty, in times of deep

---

[13]C. H. Dodd, *The Apostolic Preaching and Its Developments* (London: Hodder & Stoughton, 1936), 42, emphasis supplied.

affliction, in times of sickness, pain, and death. When nurses and friends must from very weariness leave our bedside, he remains still with us. The psalmist rightly states, as previously noted, 'God is our refuge and our strength, a help in trouble found ever [to be]' (Ps. 46:1). Such knowledge assures us that our God is a God who is near and not a God who is far away from us, that he knows our condition, having even ordained it, and is working out his perfect will in and by it for his glory and our ultimate good, which good, by the way, is not what we may think is good but rather our conformity to Jesus Christ.

Second, our knowledge of his personal and immediate presence always with us should be an encouragement to our prayer life. When we pray to the omnipresent God we do not have to shout to be heard by him. He is here – in our prayer closets, in our bedrooms in the night seasons – nearer to us than the breath we breathe, and he hears our every whisper, indeed, he knows the thoughts, the longings, the agonizings of our heart even before we verbalize them. And if the object of our prayer is a loved one living ten thousand miles away on the other side of this earthly globe, because we know that God is with him or her as well, we can ask our heavenly Father here to care for and to protect our loved one there and to provide our loved one's needs and we know that he is able in that very moment to do so according to his good pleasure.

Third, our knowledge of his personal and immediate presence always with us should be a restraint upon our bent to sin. For example, I have more than once reminded young couples from my pulpits (urging adults to heed my words as well) that they must not think, if they park on some desolate lane on some dark, moonless night and climb into the back seat of the car, that they are alone. No indeed, someone else is there with them, watching them, and observing their activity. The young man and the young woman who have illicit sex on that back road are committing an act that is as public to God as if they were committing it before their parents at high noon on Broad Street. As David says in Psalm 139:11-12:

> If I say, 'Surely the darkness shall fall on me,' even the night shall be light about me; indeed, the darkness shall not hide from you, but the night shines as the day; the darkness and the light are both alike to you.

It is regrettable that David forgot that fact, for if he had taken seriously what he teaches us here, he would not have committed adultery and murder. Believe me, dear friends, if you and I took seriously for one day the fact of God's omnipresence – that we are immediately in his presence and that he knows our every thought, hears our every word, and observes our every action – our lives would be different during that day from what they normally are. We would cease our foolish levity and our unclean mirth and silly jesting; we would take careful heed where we went and what we did; we would make sure our recreation and our amusements were free from sin; we would be more careful regarding what we read and what we viewed on television. And right here I must say that I suspect that many a preacher could have saved himself from the disgrace of discovered immorality and dismissal from the ministry if he had taken seriously the fact of God's *personal* presence in his home and had not fallen into the tragic habit of feeding his sensual appetite by watching pornographic movies or surfing the pornographic websites on the internet late at night while his wife was asleep. If we take seriously the fact that the infinite personal God is ever with us, would we dare to sin in his presence? Would we dare to ignore his will for us? If you know he is present, then

> let your weaker passions dare
> consent to sin, for God is there.

But while the fact of his personal and immediate presence always with us means that we do not have to go to some particular geographic place in order to worship him since we can worship and adore him and call upon him for his care and provision wherever we are simply because he is there, we must not permit our knowledge of this truth to supersede his insistence that we should not forsake the assembling of ourselves together, as is the habit of some, in order to encourage one another and to stir one another up to love and to good works, and to do this all the more as we see the Day of Judgment drawing near (Heb. 10:25). And when we do assemble to worship him, we must worship him 'with reverence and awe' (Heb. 12:28), keeping constantly in mind the realization that God is the primary observer of our worship.

Fourth and finally, to anyone here who is seeking to hide from God because you suspect that he does not approve of your lifestyle – and over the years I have known some pastors and seminarians in that state of affairs – I can only say that you have to realize that it is totally, utterly irrational thinking on your part to try to hide from him or to fly from him:

> Where can you hide, where can you flee?
> There is no place he does not see.
> No distant grave, no foreign place
> can bar you from his searching face.
> You cannot be obscured by night;
> his Spirit pierces dark with light.

You cannot escape him. No matter where you go, no matter how hard you try to avoid confronting him, he is there, *always* there. You have no privacy from him. And the only *rational* thing to do is to bow before his inescapable presence and to close with and to make peace with him.

Well, these are only some suggestions regarding the doctrine's applicatory significance. You may think of others. But these are sufficient to make plain that God's attribute of omnipresence is not an impractical bit of revealed information, and that if we would be the Christians, particularly the Christian preachers and teachers, that God would have us be, we must know this doctrine, both in its content and in its practical implications as well. In sum, we must be able really to mean it when we sing:

Lord, thou hast searched me, and dost know
where'er I rest, where'er I go;
thou knowest all that I have planned,
and all my ways are in thy hand.

Where can I go apart from thee,
or whither from thy presence flee?
In heav'n? – it is thy dwelling fair;
in death's abode? – lo, thou art there.

If I the wings of morning take,
and far away my dwelling make,
the hand that leadeth me is thine,
and my support thy pow'r divine.

If deepest darkness cover me,
the darkness hideth not from thee;
to thee both night and day are bright,
the darkness shineth as the light.

Let us pray:
Almighty God – you who are the King eternal, the blessed and only Potentate, the King of kings and Lord of lords who alone has immortality; you who are invisible, dwelling in unapproachable light, whom no man has seen or can see; who alone are wise – today we worship and adore you for your perfection of omnipresence.

We confess that we have not lived in accordance with your teaching about your omnipresence as faithfully as we should have.

We have all too often sought out many of our own silly inventions, such as Adam did with his fig-leaf apron and such as David did with murder – to hide our sin from your presence rather than to turn to you in humility and penitence.

We have all too often hewn out for ourselves broken cisterns that can hold no water to satisfy our spiritual thirst, and we have all too often turned away from you who alone are the fountain of living water.

We acknowledge today that you have made us for yourself, and that our souls are ignorant and restless until you fill them with that knowledge of your presence that alone brings eternal felicity, hope, and rest.

So grant us throughout this day, throughout every day this week, and throughout the rest of our lives that vital awareness of your presence that will keep us from sin, that will motivate us to holy living, that will encourage and console us, that will give us hope and rest.

This we pray in Jesus' glorious name. Amen.

THIRD ADDRESS

'ETERNAL IN HIS BEING'

LORD, you have been our dwelling place throughout all generations. Before the mountains were born or you brought forth the earth and the world, from everlasting to everlasting you are God (Ps. 90:1-2);

For those God foreknew he also predestined to be conformed to the likeness of his Son, that he might be the firstborn among many brothers. And those he predestined, he also called; those he called, he also justified; those he justified, he also glorified (Rom. 8:29-30);

Praise be to the God and Father of our Lord Jesus Christ, who has blessed us in the heavenly realms with every spiritual blessing in Christ. For he chose us in him before the creation of the world to be holy and blameless in his sight. In love he predestined us to be adopted as his sons through Jesus Christ, in accordance with his pleasure and will – to the praise of his glorious grace (Eph. 1:3-6a).

Introduction

Good morning once again, beloved colleagues and seminarians. I greet you in Jesus' blessed name. I've been praying and asking God to fill us all with the knowledge of himself through this series of addresses on his attributes. And I have been praying this in order that we all may live lives worthy of the Lord and may please him in every way (Col. 1:9-10).

I think that I have already said enough in the two previous addresses for you to realize that when we talk about God's attributes we are talking about his glory. I cannot emphasize this too much. I remember sitting years ago in the classroom of Martin Franzmann, the brilliant New Testament professor at Concordia Seminary in St. Louis, Missouri, and one of only five conservative professors who remained at the seminary when about fifty liberal professors walked out and formed what they called 'Seminex', the 'seminary in exile' – I think it was in his course entitled 'Man in Adam' in which we worked exegetically through a lengthy list of selected New Testament passages that teach something about fallen mankind – when the subject of God's glory came up. I raised my hand and asked him, 'Professor Franzmann, what is the glory of God? It is a phrase we all use a great deal, but exactly what is it?' Without pausing a second, doubtless because he knew that the Hebrew word translated 'glory' is *kābôdh*, literally meaning 'heaviness' of 'weightiness' (and also more than likely too because he had been asked that question many times before in his long professorial tenure), he responded: 'Dear brother, God's glory is just the inescapable "weight" of the sheer intrinsic godness of God.' I've never forgotten Professor Franzmann's definition and have used it many times in my classrooms over the years. This is the reason I defined God's glory in my last address as the inescapable weight of the sum total of all of his attributes.

Now because God's attributes are his glory, the Bible, as a special application of this fact, often substitutes the word 'glory' for specific attributes of God, the particular attribute the writer has in mind having then to be determined from the context in which the word 'glory' occurs. A few examples of what I mean will illustrate this feature in the biblical text.

Exodus 15:11: 'Who among the gods is like you, O LORD? Who is like you – majestic in holiness, *awesome in glory* [th*e*hillôth], working wonders?' Within the context of Exodus 15 it is evident that God's 'glory' here speaks of his power.

Exodus 33:19: When Moses asked the Lord to show him his glory, his kābôdh, the Lord replied: 'I will cause all my goodness to pass in front of you, and I will proclaim my name, the LORD, in your presence. I will have mercy upon whom I will have mercy, and I will have compassion on whom I will have compassion.' Then the Lord declared that his 'glory' would pass by. Apparently, by the word 'glory' in this context God intended his attribute of sovereign goodness, that is, the goodness of his mercy and compassion that he sovereignly administers as he wills.

1 Samuel 15:29: 'He who is the Glory [nētsah] of Israel does not lie or change his mind.' The word 'glory' here is a synonym for God as the truthful and immutably faithful one.

Psalm 19:1: 'The heavens declare the glory of God.' By 'glory' here David doubtless intended God's wisdom and power (see the occurrences of 'glory' in this sense also in the contexts of Psalms 8:1-3; 104:24-31; and Romans 1:20-21).

Isaiah 6:3: The seraphs' antiphonal cry, 'Holy, holy, holy is the LORD Almighty; the whole earth is full of his glory,' almost certainly intends God's majestic transcendent holiness that is present and manifest throughout the entire world.

Romans 3:23: In his sentence, 'All sinned [in Adam] and are continually falling short of the glory of God,' Paul's word 'glory' refers particularly to God's righteous purity as exhibited in the righteous ordinance (see dikaiōma, Rom. 1:32) of his law.

71

Romans 6:4: Paul's sentence, 'Christ was raised from the dead through the glory of the Father,' speaks by its word 'glory' particularly of God the Father's power and covenant fidelity to his Son.

Ephesians 1:6, 12, 14: Because Paul speaks of 'the praise of the glory of his grace' in Ephesians 1:6, he most likely intends by his shorter expression 'to the praise of his glory' in 1:12 and 1:14 the same idea. So in the last two references Paul's word 'glory' refers specifically to the grace of God.

As I pointed out in our last address, our *Shorter Catechism* then is really just describing and extolling by its list of God's several attributes the 'glory' of the triune God. Today we consider his glorious attribute, 'eternal in his being,' but before we begin let us first pray for God's blessing.

Prayer

Everlasting Father, Ancient of Days, may your Spirit move upon our hearts as we consider now your eternality as taught us by your Word to us from another world. May he so direct our thinking that your Word will truly become our sole authority in this matter and may he empower us to resist whatever men may have taught that is not in accord with your infallible Word. As we listen now to your Word, help us to

> think of it carefully,
> study it prayerfully,
> deep in our hearts let its oracles dwell;
> ponder its mystery,
> slight not its history,
> for none ever loved it too fondly or well.

This I ask in that name that charms the angels of heaven and strikes fear in the hosts of darkness, even the name of the eternal Son of God, Jesus Christ, our Lord. Amen.

* * *

Introduction

Our true and certain knowledge of God, as we saw in our first address, is totally dependent on divine revelation (1 Cor. 2:11). True, all men know in their hearts that 'God is there' because of his works of creation *outside* of them (Ps. 19:1) and the light of nature *within* them (John 1:9; Rom. 1:20) so that, in fact, there are no true atheists. But due to mankind's fallen condition the race has suppressed its knowledge of the true God by its godlessness and unrighteousness (Rom. 1:18) with the result that its knowledge of him has become greatly twisted, perverted, and garbled – so much so that fallen mankind even 'changed the glory of the incorruptible God into an image made like corruptible man and birds and four-footed beasts and creeping things' and then 'worshiped and served the creature rather than the Creator' (Rom. 1:23, 25). Paul's is a profound description of all mankind in its fallenness, and it would be descriptive of us in this chapel this morning as well had God's intrusive, incursive, irresistible grace and love not come into our lives. Therefore, if we are to know what God is really like, we must submit and pay close heed to God's propositional revelation of himself in Holy Scripture alone; otherwise, what we claim we know will be fallacious and not true knowledge of God at all. This is what we will attempt to do today as we consider God's attribute of eternality.

Texts

Now what does our *Catechism* mean when it tells us that our God is 'eternal in his Being'? Well, at the very least it means – to use a colloquial expression – that the eternality of God includes the limitless duration of 'both halves' of eternity – that 'half' that was *before* the creation of this universe and that 'half' that includes both the duration of this present universe and the universe that will exist forever *after* its eschatological restoration, that is to say, that God *unendingly* exists in 'both directions'. In sum, our God is the 'everlasting' God; he knows no limitations with respect to temporal duration in either direction. He has *always* existed in the past, exists *now* in the present, and will *always* exist in the future. He never began to be, he knows no growth or age, nor will he ever cease to be. The following verses of Holy Scripture bring this attribute of God's 'always there-ness' clearly before us for our instruction, contemplation, and spiritual edification:

Genesis 21:33: After Abraham planted a small *evergreen* tree as a symbol of his faith, he called on the name of the Lord, the *eternal God* (*ēl 'ôlām*).

Psalm 29:10: '...the LORD sits as King *forever* [*le'ôlām*].'

Psalm 45:6: 'Your throne, O God, will last *forever and ever* [*ôlām wā'edh*].'

Psalm 90:2: '*Before* [*beterem*] the mountains were born or you had formed the earth and the world, even *from everlasting to everlasting* [*mē'ôlām 'adh 'ôlām*] you are God.' This verse makes two assertions: first, the Lord was God *before* he created the world, and second, his divine existence extends from the unlimited past into the unlimited future.

Psalm 102:25-27: 'In the beginning [Heb.: *lephānîm*, 'of old'; Gr.: *kat' archas*, 'from [the] beginning'] you laid the foundations of the earth, and the heavens are the work of your hands. They will perish, but you *remain* [*tha"môdh*]; they all will wear out like a garment. Like clothing you will change them and they will be discarded. But you *remain the same* [*'attāh hū'*], and *your years will never end* [*ûshenôthe(y)kā lō' yittāmmû*]. (Hebrews 1:10-12 applies this passage to God the Son, the Second Person of the Holy Trinity.)

Isaiah 40:28: 'The LORD is the *everlasting God* [*ʾelōhēy 'ôlām*].'

Isaiah 57:15: Here Yahweh as the 'high and lofty one' describes himself as 'continually dwelling forever' [*shōkēn 'adh*].'

Jeremiah 10:10: 'The LORD is the true God; he is the living God and the *everlasting king* [*melek 'ôlām*].'

John 1:1-3: 'In the beginning [of everything else] the Word [already continually] was, and the Word was [already continually] with God, and the Word was [already continually] God. The same was [already continually] in the beginning with God. All things were created by him, and without him was not anything made that was made.' My four insertions of the words 'already continually' are based upon the force of the imperfect *ēn*, that occurs four times in 1:1-2.

Ephesians 3:21: 'To him be glory ... *throughout all ages, world without end* [the Greek is quite interesting here: *eis pasas tas geneas tou aiōnos tōn aiōnōn*, literally saying: 'unto all the generations of the age of the ages'].'

1 Timothy 1:17: 'Now to the *King eternal* [*basilei tōn aiōnōn*] ..., be glory *for ever and ever* [here the Greek literally reads: *eis tous aiōnas tōn aiōnōn*: 'unto the ages of the ages'].'

Hebrews 7:25: 'He is able to save to the uttermost those who come to God through him, *since he ever lives* [*pantote zōn*] to make intercession for them.'

Hebrews 13:8: 'Jesus Christ is the same yesterday, today, and *forever* [*eis tous aiōnas*].'

The doctrine
As I just said, these verses clearly ascribe everlastingness to God. This in itself is a great concept to contemplate and it surely should humble us because none of us

can comprehend a self-conscious, self-determining, tri-personal, non-corporeal Being who never began to be, who is still there at the point where our finite capacity to comprehend his everlasting past collapses from mental exhaustion, who has always existed and who at the beginning of the creation of this universe and everything in it already continually was, and who will always continue to be forever.

But do these verses intend anything more? What is not clear is that his everlastingness should also be understood with most classical Christian thinkers such as Augustine and Aquinas as involving the idea of timelessness. In his discussion of God's eternality in his *Systematic Theology*, Louis Berkhof makes the following, in my opinion, highly significant observation: 'The form in which the Bible represents God's eternity is simply that of duration through endless ages,'[1] that is, simple, pure, unadulterated everlastingness. The following is only a partial typical listing of such statements:

Psalm 10:16	'The LORD is King forever and ever.'
Psalm 41:13	'Praise be the LORD ... from everlasting to everlasting.'
Psalm 48:14	'This God is our God forever and ever.'
Psalm 90:2	'...from everlasting to everlasting you are God.'
Psalm 93:2	'You are from everlasting [*mē'ôlām*].'
Psalm 102:12	'You, O LORD, sit enthroned forever; your renown endures through all generations.'
Psalm 103:17	'...*from everlasting to everlasting* [*mē'ôlām we'adh 'ôlām*] the

---

[1]Louis Berkhof, *Systematic Theology* (New combined edition; Grand Rapids: Eerdmans, 1996), 60.

	LORD's love is with those who fear him.'
Psalm 106:48	'Praise be the LORD ... from everlasting to everlasting.'
Psalm 119:142	'Your righteousness is an everlasting righteousness.'
Isaiah 54:8	'...with everlasting kindness I will have mercy.'
Habakkuk 1:12	'Are you not *from everlasting* [*miqqedem*], O LORD my God.'
Philippians 4:20	'...to our God ... be glory for ever and ever.'
2 Timothy 4:18	'To [the Lord] be glory forever and ever.'
Revelation 4:10	'[They] worship him who lives forever and ever' (see Rev. 10:6; 15:7).
Revelation 11:15	'He shall reign forever and ever.'

So Berkhof is certainly correct when he states: '...the form in which the Bible represents God's eternity is simply that of duration through endless ages.' But then Berkhof immediately aborts the significance of this statement with his following remark: 'We should remember, however, that in speaking as it does the Bible uses popular language, and not the language of philosophy.'[2] Is there a problem with the Bible not using the language of philosophy here? I do not think so. Our reaction to his caveat should be, in my opinion, that it is simply *sheer dogmatism* on Berkhof's part to assert that the Bible is using 'popular language' here, implying that the *real* truth of the matter is something else, and that to arrive at this 'something else' one must appeal to the categories of philosophy to discover it. Without intending to be snide, I must ask, how does Berkhof know this? Did he receive some extra-biblical revelation that informed him of this? Of course not!

---

[2]Berkhof, *Systematic Theology*, 60.

His comment, of course, reflects, as I have already suggested, the influence of Augustine and others who have argued that time, by definition, is the *succession of ideas in a finite mind*, and since God being omniscient allegedly has no such succession in his mind, he is therefore 'timeless', whose timeless existence is to be viewed as qualitatively separate and distinct from what is described as created temporal existence.[3] Gordon H. Clark, following Augustine's lead, declares:

> If there is a succession of ideas in God's mind, then the ideas that succeeded today were not present yesterday [in my opinion, this is a rare *non-sequitur* on Clark's part], and presumably some of yesterday's ideas have passed by [in my opinion, another and apparently not quite as rare *non-sequitur* on Clark's part]. But this means that God did not know all things yesterday, neither is he omniscient today [this is a false conclusion based upon the preceding *non-sequiturs*].
>
> Is it not clear [Clark continues] that a temporal succession of ideas in God's mind is incompatible with omniscience? Man is not omniscient precisely because his ideas come and go [What is happening to Clark here? This is only partly true; man is not omniscient primarily because he is a finite creature]. Man's mind changes from day to day; God is omniscient, immutable, and *therefore* eternal.[4]

---

[3]Augustine's analysis of time, in which he urges that time is a subjective idea in a finite mind, may be found in his *Confessions*, book 11, chapters 11–30. There Augustine declares that time is 'extendedness' existing in the finite mind: 'It is in you, O mind of mine, that I measure the periods of time. Do not shout me down that it exists [he means here, 'objectively'].... In you ... I measure the periods of time' (chap. 27; see also book 13, chap. 16). Accordingly, in his *De Diversis Quaestionibus ad Simplicianum*, II, ii, 2, he affirms: 'If God's knowledge even embraces events themselves, they are not future to him, but present; and on this account foreknowledge [*praescientia*] can no longer be spoken of [with reference to God], but only knowledge [*scientia*].' In other words, the distinction between knowledge and foreknowledge is not in God but only in us.

Note Clark's 'therefore' in his last sentence: 'God is omniscient, immutable, and *therefore* eternal.' Aside from the twin facts that the Augustinian view as he represents it seems, first, to make God's eternality, viewed in terms of timelessness, more an *inference* from God's attributes of omniscience and immutability than a *revealed* attribute of God's Being as such, and second, says nothing by its definition of God's eternality as timelessness about God's *everlastingness* about which the Bible often speaks, it seems again to me to be sheer dogmatism to declare, because God is omniscient, that there can be no consciousness of successive duration in his mind relative to his own existence. Robert Lewis Dabney of Union Theological Seminary in Virginia observes:

...if ... the divine consciousness of its own existence has no relation to successive duration, I think it unproved, and incapable of proof to us. Is not the whole plausibility of the notion hence; that divines ... infer: Since all God's thoughts are ever equally present with Him, He can have no succession of His own consciousnesses; and so, no relation to successive time. But the analysis is false ... and does not prove the conclusion as to God, if correct.... In all the acts and changes of creatures, the relation of succession is actual and true. Now, although God's knowledge of these as it is subjective to Himself, is unsuccessive [I take him to mean here that God does not first learn about them and know them as the creature acts out these changes], yet [his knowledge] is doubtless correct, i.e. true to the objective facts. But these [objective facts] have actual succession. So ... the idea of successive duration must be in God's thinking. Has He not all the ideas we have; and infinitely more? But if God in thinking the objective, ever thinks successive duration, can we be sure that His own consciousness of

---

[4]Gordon H. Clark, 'Time and Eternity,' *Against the World: The Trinity Review,* 1978–1988 (Hobbs, New Mexico: Trinity Foundation, 1996), 79.

His own subsistence is unrelated to succession in time? The thing is too high for us. The attempt to debate it will only produce one of those 'antinomies' which emerge, when we strive to comprehend the incomprehensible.[5]

I concur with Dabney's analysis but, for biblical reasons to be noted shortly, not with his agnostic conclusion.

Charles Hodge of Princeton Seminary also writes agnostically regarding whether God experiences succession in thoughts and acts within himself: 'When we are ignorant, it is wise to be silent. We have no right to affirm or deny, when we cannot know what our affirmations or denials may involve or imply.... We know that God is constantly producing new effects...; but we do not know that these effects are due to successive exercises of the divine efficiency.' But having said this, Hodge then seems to reverse himself:

> ...so far as thinking and acting involve succession, succession must belong to God. There are mysteries connected with chronological succession, in our nature, which we cannot explain.... If unable to comprehend ourselves, we should not pretend to be able to comprehend God.'[6]

Hodge does not write here with the clarity that we have come to expect from him. But this much is certain: He certainly denies that succession is applicable to God with regard to *creaturely* events:

> They are ever present to the mind of God. ...with [God] there is *no distinction* between the present, past, and future, but *all things are equally and always present to Him*. With Him duration is an *eternal now*'; again,

---

[5]Robert Lewis Dabney, *Lectures in Systematic Theology* (Reprint of 1878 edition; Grand Rapids, Zondervan, 1972), 40.

[6]Charles Hodge, *Systematic Theology* (Reprint; Grand Rapids: Eerdmans, n.d.), I:388-9.

'to Him there is neither past nor future ... the past and the future are always and equally present to Him [as an eternal now]'; and still again, 'to Him there is neither past nor future, *neither before nor after.*'[7]

Such statements, it seems to me, are not only unfounded biblically but also have three major problems: First is the inherent contradiction in saying that for God duration is an 'eternal present' or an 'eternal now' with 'neither past nor future', 'neither before nor after', because the words 'present' and the temporal 'now' have significance only in the ordering category that includes past and future as well. Nicholas Wolterstorff makes this point in his discussion of Augustine's argument for God's timelessness:

> In order for something to be timeless, none of these ordering relationships [past, present, or future] can be applicable to that being. If a being is truly timeless, it should be impossible for it to exist *simultaneously* with anything else, or *before* anything else, or *after* anything else. Once it is established that a being does occupy one of the ordering relations, then that being is clearly temporal.[8]

Second, if Hodge's words are taken literally, they reduce to zero significance the temporal aspect in every finite Hebrew, Aramaic, and Greek verb form God employs in his revelational description to us of his thoughts, words, and actions, and virtually transforms them all in meaning into *timeless* participles, a reductionistic transformation that you Hebrew and Greek students struggling to master the intricacies of these verb systems might well be willing to endorse – but I caution

---

[7]Charles Hodge, *Systematic Theology*, I:388, 385, 386, 538.

[8]See Wolterstorff's entire argument in 'God Everlasting,' in *God and the Good*, edited by C. Orlebeke and Lewis Smedes (Grand Rapids: Eerdmans, 1975), 181-203 (emphasis supplied).

you, if you start parsing all your verb forms as timeless participles you'll fail your language courses.

Third, Hodge's words, '...to [God] there is ... *neither before nor after,*' also reduce to zero significance the preposition 'before' in such Old Testament verses as Psalm 90:2 ('*Before* the mountains were brought forth ... you are God') and Jeremiah 1:5 ('*Before* I formed you in the womb I knew you') and the preposition 'after' in such Old Testament verses as Joshua 24:5 ('... I plagued Egypt.... *Afterward* I brought you out') and Jeremiah 12:15 ('...it shall be, *after* I have plucked them out, that I will return'), as well as the significance in the New Testament of

♦ the preposition *pro*, in Jesus' statement: '...you loved me *before* the foundation of the world' in John 17:24;

♦ the preposition *pro*, prefixed to the noun *prognōsei* ('*fore*knowledge') in Acts 2:23 and the '*pro*-verb' *proōrisen* ('*pre*destined') in Acts 4:28;

♦ the two great '*pro*-verbs,' *proegnō* ('he *fore*knew') and *proōrisen* (this latter verb occurs twice) ('he *pre*destined') in Romans 8:29-30;

♦ the *pro*, in Ephesians 1:4 ('he chose us ... *before* the creation of the world'), the *proorisas* ('having *pre*destined') in Ephesians 1:5, and the *prooristhentes* ('having been *pre*destinated') in Ephesians 1:11;

♦ the *mēpō* ('*before* the twins were born, God told her') in Romans 9:11; and finally,

♦ the *pro* ('*before* the times of the ages') in 2 Timothy 1:9.[9]

---

[9]In my opinion, it is not sufficient as a rebuttal here to declare as does John M. Frame, *No Other God: A Response to Open Theism* (Phillipsburg, N.J.: Presbyterian & Reformed, 2001): '...atemporalists appropriately reply that some word such as *before* is almost a necessity of language' (148, fn. 19), and that 'the 'before' is, of course, from our temporal point of view' (146, fn. 17), because these *pro*'s

Is not God informing us by such statements that he had an 'eternal purpose' (Eph. 3:11) for the world *before* he created the world?  And does this not mean that *before* he created the world, if an angel had asked him about the 'when' of the world's creation, as the God of truth he would have had to say: 'I have not yet created the world. Its creation is yet in the *future*'? And would he not have to say now, as the same God of truth, 'I *have* created the world; its creation is a thing of the *past*'? Are we to understand all these biblical statements simply as anthropomorphic metaphors actually signifying nothing temporal for God, metaphors that the Holy Spirit employed because of the weakness of our finite ability to conceptualize God's timeless eternality? I say no, and I think the fact of a *real* creation out of nothing at the beginning of all created things in the distant past, at which moment God already continually was, *requires* that we say so.

For these three reasons the ascription to God of the attribute of 'timeless' eternality understood as the absence of a divine consciousness of successive duration with respect to his own existence should not be maintained. It is inconsistent and cannot be supported from Scripture. It is, at best, a philosophical inference and, I think, a fallacious one at that. And it implies that I know something – the idea of succession with respect to my existence – that God does not know.

On the other hand, the Christian should not endorse without careful qualification the idea that time is an aspect of God's eternality. It all depends on one's definition of time. For example, if 'time' should be thought of as an *objective* succession of moments existing independently and apart from *all* minds, it would suggest that something independent of and in addition to God is moving history forward, and thus a shadow is cast upon God's sole sovereign Lordship over

---

('before') are describing, not *my* temporal perspective, but *God's* revealed activity prior to the creation of the world.

time and history. But if one were to adopt a definition such as that of J. Oliver Buswell, Jr. by which time is defined as the 'mere abstract [that is, ideational] possibility of the before and after relationship in sequence',[10] that is to say, if time is defined as the *idea* in a knowing mind of the before and after relationship in durational sequence, then there is no problem, in my opinion, in urging that time eternally resides in the mind of God and is descriptive, on the one hand, of the relationship between his thoughts and creative actions (the former preceding the latter in durational sequence) and, on the other hand, of his knowledge of the durational relationship between any one of his acts and a second divine act. This would mean that, for God, while he himself ever remains *ontologically* unaffected by durational sequence, and while his thoughts themselves are *eternally* intuited, comprehensive, and teleologically ordered and *not* arrived at chronologically through the discursive process, nevertheless, the concepts of 'before' and 'after' in durational succession are distinct *epistemological* categories as applicable to him as they are to us. This would mean that

♦ he knows that his thoughts on the one hand and his actions on the other are related to each other in the 'before' and 'after' relationship,
♦ he knows that his 'this-world' actions stand related to each other in a temporal durational sequencing, and
♦ he knows the creature's past, present, and future respectively as past, present, and future.

Even Hodge himself was apparently troubled somewhat by his words that I cited earlier, for when he writes later about God's knowledge he makes this better statement:

---

[10]J. Oliver Buswell, Jr., *A Systematic Theology of the Christian Religion* (Grand Rapids: Zondervan, 1962), I:47.

God knows all things as they are, ...the past as past, the present as present, the future as future. Although all things are ever present in his view, yet he sees them as successive in time.[11]

So affirming Buswell's definition still allows the Christian to hold that the everlasting God, while he is at any and every given moment immanent in his world, is still the sovereign Creator and Lord over it, that the world (including its future) is in no sense foreign or unknown to him, and that history – past, present, and future – is the product of his eternal plan, his providential oversight and preservation, and his common and special grace.

I make no apology for what may perhaps have seemed at times in this address to the theologically uninitiated to be simply theological meandering, for in my opinion God's eternality viewed as timelessness, contrary to Ronald H. Nash's opinion that there is 'no reason why theism cannot accommodate itself to either interpretation,'[12] has the three serious negative implications that I discussed earlier and one more that I will mention in a moment. But I admit that this is enough theological perambulation for one address, and it is now time to apply the doctrine of God's eternality to Christian experience.

Application
My first point of application has to do with the issue of theological method. Before everything else, I want us all to acquire a theology of God that will pass *biblical* muster since the Bible is our only rule for faith and practice. It is my opinion that the classical construction of God is sometimes more philosophical and speculative than biblical, a case in point being its philosophical construction of God's eternality as timelessness. In

---

[11]Hodge, *Systematic Theology*, I:397.
[12]Ronald H. Nash, *The Concept of God* (Grand Rapids: Zondervan, 1983), 83.

another area of theology proper, namely, the doctrine of the Trinity, John Calvin had to choose between the theological speculation of the Nicene fathers' 'very God of very God' expression and the *autotheotic* ('God in and of himself') nature of the deity of God the Son. Calvin was, says John Murray,

> too much a student of Scripture to be content to follow the lines of what had been regarded as Nicene orthodoxy.... It is ... to the credit of Calvin that he did not allow his own more sober thinking to be suppressed out of deference to an established pattern of thought when the latter did not commend itself by conformity to Scripture and was inimical to Christ's divine nature.[13]

And in so doing, the great French/Swiss Reformer set for us all – his theological sons and daughters – the highest standard of loyalty to Scripture and the finest example of the theological method that should be employed throughout the entire theological enterprise. I would urge us all to follow in his train, for to be Reformed really means just to be *radically biblical* in all that we believe and teach, and to be 'always Reforming' means that we desire to be more radically biblical tomorrow than we are today. This is what I have attempted to do today with respect to God's eternality viewed as 'everlastingness'. But in order to do *this*, it means that you and I must be dogged – relentlessly so – in our pursuit of acquiring all the tools necessary to do sound exegesis of the biblical text. You students must take seriously every lesson you are given in Hebrew and Greek and you must master every lesson before you move to the next. *Stay up all night if necessary in order to get the points of the lesson down cold in your mind.* And you must also master grammatical/historical hermeneutics, for it is one thing to translate a passage accurately –

---

[13]John Murray, 'Systematic Theology,' in *Collected Writings of John Murray* (Edinburgh: Banner of Truth, 1982), 4:8.

that is only the beginning of arriving at the meaning of the passage – and it is quite another thing entirely to interpret it properly (indeed, if truth be told, I should say that one has not really completed the former task of translation if he has not right along been governed in his translation work by sound canons of grammatical/ historical hermeneutics).

My address today on the doctrine of God's eternality has attempted to model for you this method of listening first and foremost to God's inspired Word that does not hesitate to represent God's eternality simply in terms of everlastingness – a fact, I would remind you again, that Berkhof admits. I would urge us all as well not to hesitate to represent God's eternality in the same way and to teach that God's eternality is to be understood in terms of everlastingness – a concept difficult enough in itself for us to comprehend – rather than timelessness.

My second point of application – and this is the fourth negative implication for God as timeless that I mentioned above – has to do with the precarious implication that a timeless God has for the *locus* of soteriology. If God has neither fore-knowledge nor 'after'-knowledge but only knowledge, that is, if God's 'time words' to us respecting his plan and actions do not mean for him the same as they mean for us and are thus only metaphorical at best and not univocal, then perhaps *for him* Christ *has* not yet come (past tense) and died for our sin; perhaps he never *will* come (future tense), *for he is Deity and therefore allegedly timeless*, which would mean that *for him* you and I are still in our sin and under the wrath and curse of the righteous Judge of all the earth – 'either this, or sin is merely an illusion, and we might as well become Eddyistic idealists and be done with the gospel.'[14] But the everlasting God tells us in his Word that Christ came 'in the fullness of time' (Gal. 4:4; *chronou*) and 'at the proper time' (1 Tim. 2:6; *kairos*), that Christ's first

---

[14]Buswell, *Systematic Theology*, I, 47.

coming took place in the historical past during the reign of Caesar Augustus (Luke 2:1), and that his Son died at Calvary during the reign of Tiberius Caesar when Pilate was governor of Judah and Annas and Caiaphas were Israel's high priests (Luke 3:1-2). All this is past history, and it is past history for God as well as for us. And he tells those of us who have trusted his Son's doing and dying for our salvation that he *has* pardoned us and that 'we *have been* justified by faith' (Rom. 5:1). Thank God that *not only for us but for him as well a real transition from wrath to grace has occurred for us in history!* Thank God that *for God too* the ground of our forgiveness is a matter of past history! Thank God that he *has* blotted out our transgression! Thank God that he remembers our sins no more against us today! Thank God that our *future* and *final* salvation is *nearer* than when we first believed (Rom. 13:11) – not only nearer *for us* but nearer *for God* as well! All this is to say that God takes history seriously. He knows the distinction between the past, the present, and the future, and for him our past is past, our present is present, and our future is future.

My third and last point of application has to do with our assurance of salvation as Christians in the midst of our falls and failings in our Christian walk. Where are you today, dear brothers and sisters; what are *your* failings? Have you fallen in some way today? Doubtless you and I both have, even many times and in many ways about which we are not even aware. For

> if ever it should come to pass
> that sheep of Christ might fall away,
> my fickle, feeble soul, alas,
> would fall a thousand times a day.

Is help anywhere to be had when we fall? And if there is, is it only *temporary* or is it *everlasting*? To this last question God's Word assures us that in spite of our failings we are *everlastingly* secure because our High Priest, who *lives forever,* is *ever* at his Father's right hand interceding *everlastingly* for us. Our High Priest died a 'once for all time' atoning death in history for us that requires no repetition (see the *ephapax*, in Rom. 6:10; Heb. 7:27; 9:12, 25-26, 28; 10:10-14; 1 Pet. 3:18). He sits today at his Father's right hand for us. And as Francis Shaeffer so often reminded us, not only is our God *there* but he has also *spoken* to us – spoken words of *everlasting* mercy and love, words of *everlasting* guidance and direction, words of *everlasting* counsel and consolation that are *forever* settled in heaven. So look up with confidence, my friends. Take heart in the midst of your failings. Your God is *everlastingly* there for you; and because 'his mercy is *everlasting* [*le'ôlām hasdô*]' (Ps. 100:5), because '*from everlasting to everlasting* [*mē'ôlām we'adh 'ôlām*] the Lord's love is with those who fear him' (Ps. 103:17), because 'with everlasting kindness [*behesedh 'ôlām*] [he] will have compassion on you' (Isa. 54:8), because he 'loves you with an *everlasting love* [*'aha'bhath 'ôlām*]' (Jer. 31:3), he 'will *never* [*ou mē*] leave you *nor* [*oud' ou mē*] will he forsake you' (Heb. 13:5; note the *five* Greek negatives in this single verse) but to the contrary will continually 'meet all your needs according to his glorious riches in Christ Jesus' (Phil. 4:19). I have often thought that the lyricist of the hymn verse,

> The soul that on Jesus hath leaned for repose,
> I will not, I will not desert to his foes;
> That soul, though all hell should endeavor to shake,
> I'll never, no, never, no, never forsake,

with its five negatives in the last line, wrote more scripturally than he perhaps realized.

Then Jesus declared: 'The one who comes to me I will *never* [*ou mē*] cast out' (John 6:37-40), and he affirmed: 'My sheep ... will *never* [*ou mē ... eis ton aiōna*] perish ... no one will snatch them out of my hand ... and no one is able to snatch them out of my Father's hand' (John 10:27-29). Moreover, writes Paul, '[the Father] who did not spare his own Son but delivered him up for us all, how shall he not with him also *freely* give us all things' needful for our everlasting salvation (Rom. 8:32), and '[the Father] who is rich in mercy, because of his great love with which he has loved us, even when we were dead in trespasses, made us alive together with Christ (by grace you have been saved)' (Eph. 2:4-5). Therefore, we may be assured that 'he who began a good work in [us] will carry it on to completion until the day of Christ Jesus' (Phil. 1:6). Because '[Christ] is able to save forever those who come to God through him, because he ever lives to makes intercession for them' (Heb. 7:25), Peter can reassuringly write: 'You are kept by the power of God through faith for the salvation ready to be revealed in the last times' (1 Pet. 1:5).

Ah, dear hearts, I know that if God ever savingly loved me at all, then he will love me *forever*. In sum, I know, 'did Jesus once upon me shine, then Jesus is *forever* mine.' And I hope and pray that you know this as well.

Let us pray:
Everlasting Father, ever-living Son, eternal Holy Spirit:

We praise you – the eternal triune God – this morning for your *everlasting* mercies to us; they are new *every* morning.

We praise and thank you that you set your love upon us *before* the creation of the world, and we praise and bless you that our end will be perfect conformity to the likeness of Jesus Christ.

We thank you that you are there, *always* there, for us in the unsettling vicissitudes of life.

And we praise and thank you that you have spoken words of love and comfort to us in your Word that is *forever* settled in the heavens.

As we go about our tasks today may the awesome truth of your *everlastingness* bind us to you, living as we are in a world where 'change and decay in all around we see'.

And may we *consciously* find in you the permanency that we so desperately need and desire, that permanency that can be found nowhere else and in no one else.

This we pray in Christ's name, Amen.

FOURTH ADDRESS

'UNCHANGEABLE IN HIS BEING'

Hear my prayer, O LORD; let my cry for help come to you. Do not hide your face from me when I am in distress. Turn your ear to me; when I call, answer me quickly. For my days vanish like smoke; my bones burn like glowing embers. My heart is blighted and withered like grass; I forget to eat my food. Because of my loud groaning I am reduced to skin and bones....
But you, O LORD, sit enthroned forever; your renown endures through all generations....
In the beginning you laid the foundations of the earth, and the heavens are the work of your hands. They will perish, but you remain; they will all wear out like a garment. Like clothing you will change them and they will be discarded. But you remain the same, and your years will never end (Ps. 102:1-5, 12, 25-27);

Jesus Christ is the same yesterday and today and forever (Heb. 13:8).

Introduction

Good morning, beloved brothers and sisters in Christ: I'm delighted to be with you once again and I count it all joy to continue our series of chapel addresses on the attributes of our great God. It has been a rich blessing for me personally to reflect again upon the attributes of the Christian God, and I want to thank the faculty again for graciously asking me to deliver this series of addresses to you. It is my prayer that God will multiply his grace and peace to you through my words, but only to the degree, of course, that they reflect the truth of Holy Scripture.

As you know, we've been using as our guide the *Shorter Catechism* definition of God, which statement the Westminster Assembly wrote for the church's children and that Charles Hodge opined was 'probably the best [extrabiblical] definition of God ever penned by man'.[1] It really is a remarkable reduction of what the Westminster Assembly's *Confession of Faith* states much more fully about the nature of God. Listen as I read the fuller *Confession of Faith*, Chapter II, articles I-II:

I. There is but one only, living, and true God, who is infinite in being and perfection, a most pure spirit, invisible, without body, parts, or passions; immutable, immense, eternal, incomprehensible, almighty, most wise, most holy, most free, most absolute, working all things according to the counsel of his own immutable and most righteous will, for his own glory; most loving, gracious, merciful, long-suffering, abundant in goodness and truth, forgiving iniquity, transgression, and sin, the rewarder of them that diligently seek him, and withal, most just, and terrible in his judgments, hating all sin, and who will by no means clear the guilty.

II. God hath all life, glory, goodness, blessedness, in and of himself; and is alone in and unto himself all-sufficient, not standing in need of any creatures which he hath made, nor deriving any glory from them, but only manifesting his own glory in, by, unto, and upon them. He is the alone fountain of all being, of whom, through whom, and to whom are all things; and hath most sovereign dominion over them, to do by them,

---

[1]Charles Hodge, *Systematic Theology* (Reprint; Grand Rapids: Eerdmans, n.d.), I:367.

for them, and upon them whatsoever himself pleaseth. In his sight all things are open and manifest, His knowledge is infinite, infallible, and independent [that is, not dependent] upon the creature, so as nothing is to him contingent, or uncertain. He is most holy in all his counsels, in all his works, and in all his commands. To him is due from angels and men, and every other creature, whatsoever worship, service, or obedience he is pleased to require of them.

In this confessional description of God that I just read to you, in my opinion you heard more truth about God than the average Christian hears about the being and character of God from his church's pulpit in a year if not in a lifetime.

Some commentators on the *Confession of Faith*, for example, James Benjamin Green, late professor of systematic theology and homiletics at Columbia Theological Seminary in Decatur, Georgia, suggest that the first two paragraphs depict respectively what God is *ontologically* in himself (*in se*) and what he is *economically* for us (*pro nobis*).[2] But while there appears at first reading to be some basis for this observance, it must be acknowledged, as John Murray, late professor of systematic theology at Westminster Theological Seminary in Philadelphia, observes, that 'so inclusive and yet so compressed are the two sections dealing with the being, attributes, and counsel of God that it is difficult if not impossible to discover the order of thought followed'.[3] Green himself recognizes that the division that he draws between the two paragraphs cannot be rigidly maintained, for he asks rhetorically: 'Does not the second paragraph repeat some ideas expressed in

---

[2]James Benjamin Green, *A Harmony of the Westminster Presbyterian Standards* (Reprint; no publication location: Collins & World, 1976), 26-7.

[3]John Murray, 'The Theology of the Westminster Confession of Faith' in *Collected Writings of John Murray* (Edinburgh: Banner of Truth, 1982), 4:247-8.

the first section?'[4] And the answer, of course, is yes, it does. Donald Macleod, principal and professor of systematic theology in the Free Church of Scotland College in Edinburgh, even states that the *Confession* 'is content [in its first two paragraphs on God] with an almost haphazard list of the perfections ascribed to God in the Bible'.[5]

I am not convinced, however, that these two paragraphs are as haphazardly arranged as they might appear. In my opinion the Westminster divines did intend the first paragraph to describe what God is in himself but brought in also at the end of that paragraph God's reactions toward human beings in order to provide the most complete list of his essential attributes. Then they intended the second paragraph to advance upon the first *in the sphere of authority* by emphasizing God's sovereign dominion over all his works, including angels and men, having the right as the one divine Sovereign to require of them whatever worship, service, or obedience he pleased. In sum, the first paragraph emphasizes what God is as God *in se*; the second paragraph emphasizes what he is as the sovereign Lord of the universe and underscores his divine sovereignty over all creation. It is certainly true that the *Confession of Faith* makes no attempt to classify in any irrefutably distinguishable manner the attributes of God beyond the broad distinction I just mentioned, and certainly not in the manner most favored by Reformed theologians today, namely, that of 'incommunicable' and 'communicable' attributes, since '[that] distinction [is] untenable without further qualification',[6] which qualifications are so condemning in nature that the distinction is reduced to the point of utter uselessness. Nor will we attempt to classify them

---

[4]Green, *Harmony*, 27.

[5]Donald Macleod, *Behold Your God* (Ross-shire, Scotland: Christian Focus, 1990), 20.

[6]Louis Berkhof, *Systematic Theology* (New combined edition; Grand Rapids: Eerdmans, 1966), 56.

either. We will simply continue to follow the simple definition of God that the *Shorter Catechism* provides us. Let us now invoke the blessing of God on this morning's exposition of his attribute of unchangeableness.

Prayer

Our Father and our God: Heartened by your exceedingly great and precious promises to us, we bring our praises, however imperfect, to join in that great song of praise, honor, glory, and blessing being sung in heaven that is directed toward you who, together with your beloved Son and the eternal Spirit, are the thrice-holy God and our Creator and Redeemer.

We have assembled once again in this chapel to learn about you. As we consider today your immutable being and character, help us to handle aright your Word of truth. Seal upon our hearts the truths that we will survey this morning for the benefit of this assembly of seminarians and for the glory and cause of Jesus Christ our Lord. I ask this in his blessed and holy name. Amen.

* * *

This morning we move to a consideration of the *Shorter Catechism's* affirmation that God is 'unchangeable in his being'. Here the *Catechism* affirms the unchangeable nature and character of God, often referred to in the theological literature as his *immutability*. This doctrine affirms that God, ontologically and decretally speaking, does not and cannot change. Such verses as the following, among many that might be cited, provide the biblical basis for this classic Christian conviction:

Texts

Exodus 3:14: 'God said to Moses: "I am who I am"; and he said: "Thus shall you say to the sons of Israel: 'I Am has sent me to you.'"' Before moving on, I should say something about my reason for believing

God's name 'I am' and its cognate name 'Yahweh' speak of God's immutability. I believe Geerhardus Vos is correct when he declares that the name 'I Am' 'gives expression to the self-determination, the independence of God, [that] we are accustomed to call His *sovereignty*, [which is just to say that] the name Jehovah signifies primarily that in all that God does for His people, He is from-within-determined, not moved upon by outside influences. But from this there issues immediately another thought, quite inseparable from it, viz., that being determined from within, and *not subject to change within, He is not subject to change at all.*[7]

Numbers 23:19: 'God is not a man, *that he should lie,* nor a son of man, *that he should change his mind.* Does he speak and then not act? Does he promise and then not fulfill.'

1 Samuel 15:29: 'The Glory of Israel *does not lie or change his mind*; for he is not a man, that he should change his mind.'

Psalm 102:26-27: '[The earth and the heavens] will perish, but *you remain* [*'attāh tha*ᵃ*mōdh*]; they will wear out ... but *you remain the same* [*'attāh hū'*].'

Malachi 3:6: 'For I, the LORD, *do not change* [*lō' shānîthî*]; therefore you, O sons of Jacob, are not consumed.'

Romans 11:29: 'The gifts and callings of God are *irrevocable* [*ametamelēta*].'

2 Corinthians 1:18-20: '...as surely as God is faithful, our message to you is not "Yes" and "No." For the Son of God, Jesus Christ, who was preached among you by me and Silas and Timothy, was not "Yes" and "No," but *in him it has always been "Yes."* For no matter how many promises God has made, they are "Yes" in

---

[7]Geerhardus Vos, *Biblical Theology* (Reprint; Grand Rapids: Eerdmans, 1954), 134.

Christ. And so through him the "Amen" is spoken by us to the glory of God.'

2 Timothy 2:13: 'If we are faithless, he *remains* [*menei*] faithful; for he cannot deny himself.'

Hebrews 6:17-18: 'Because God wanted to make the unchangeable character [*to ametatheton*] of his purpose very clear to the heirs of what was promised, he confirmed it with a [covenantal] oath [see Gen. 15:8-18]. God did this so that, by two *unchangeable things* [*pragmatōn ametathetōn*, namely, his purpose and his covenant oath] in which it is impossible for God to lie, we may be greatly encouraged.'

Hebrews 12:28: '...we receive a kingdom that *cannot be shaken.*'

Hebrews 13:8: 'Jesus Christ is *the same* [*ho autos*] yesterday and today and forever.'

James 1:17: 'Every good and perfect gift is from above, coming down from the Father of the heavenly lights, who *does not change* [*ouk eni parallagē*] like shifting shadows.'

The doctrine

These verses affirm the *immutability* of God's being and the *constancy* of his eternal purpose, which perfections guarantee that God remains always the same living and true God, always faithful to himself, his decrees, and his works. This entire universe is in a state of constant change and flux, and because of Adam's fall, 'change and *decay* in all around we see.' But the one living and true God in his infinite being is *perpetually* the same, and he remains *everlastingly* the same as the great 'Thou who changest not'. There was never a time when he was not, and there will never be a time when he shall cease to be. He cannot change for the better because he is already perfect; and being perfect, he cannot change for the worse. He is altogether unaffected ontologically by anything outside of himself. Neither ontological improvement nor ontological deterioration is possible for him. Whatever were his attributes of old, that they are now, and of each of them as they pass before our viewing we may sing: 'As it was in the beginning, 'tis now, and ever shall be, world without end.'

Now I must issue a caveat. Classical theists have sometimes represented God's immutability in such a sense that they have portrayed him as being virtually frozen in timeless immobility and impassibility. They reason that any movement or feeling on his part such as anger, joy, or grief must either improve his condition or detract from it. But since neither is possible for a perfect being, he remains, to use James I. Packer's characterization of this position, in an 'eternally frozen pose'[8] as *immobile* and *impassible*, that is, inaccessible to and incapable of feelings or emotions.

But this is not the Bible's description of God. The God of the Bible is constantly acting into and reacting to the human condition. In no sense is the God of Scripture insulated or detached from, unconcerned with, or insensitive and indifferent to the joys and miseries of fallen mankind. Everywhere the Bible depicts him both as one who registers grief and sorrow over and displeasure and wrath against man's sin, and as one who in compassion and love has taken effective steps in Jesus Christ to reverse the misery of his elect and even the rest of mankind to a degree. Everywhere Holy Scripture portrays him as entering deeply into authentic interpersonal relations of love with his people and truly caring about them and their happiness. As W. Norris Clarke states, the biblical God is a 'religiously available' God on the personal level.[9]

---

[8]James I. Packer, 'Theism for Our Time' in *God Who Is Rich in Mercy* (Grand Rapids: Baker, 1986), 16.

[9]W. Norris Clarke, 'A New Look at the Immutability of God,' in *God, Knowable and Unknowable*, edited by Robert J. Roth (New

To say then that God is unchangeable or immutable must not be construed to mean that he cannot and does not act. The God of the Bible acts, indeed, acts with passion, on every page of Scripture. In other words, he is not *static* in his immutability; he is *dynamic* in his immutability. But his dynamic immutability in no way affects his 'Godness'. To the contrary, he would cease to be the God of Scripture if he did *not* will and act in the ways the Bible ascribes to him. But he always wills and acts, as Isaiah declared, in faithfulness to his decrees: 'In perfect faithfulness,' Isaiah sings, 'you have done marvelous things, things planned long ago' (25:1). Therefore, Louis Berkhof is correct, in my opinion, when he concludes:

> The divine immutability should not be understood as implying *immobility*, as if there were no movement in God.... The Bible teaches us that God enters into manifold relations with man and, as it were, lives their lives with them. There is change round about Him, change in the relations of men to Him, but there is no change in His being, His attributes, His purpose, His motives of action, or His promises.[10]

Thus, as Jürgen Moltmann has most notably contended in our time,[11] whenever and wherever God's impassibility is interpreted to mean that he is impervious to human pain or incapable of empathizing with human grief we must renounce it and steadfastly distance ourselves from it.[12] For while such is descriptive of Aristotle's concept of God as 'thought thinking thought' and of Buddha, it is in no sense descriptive of the God of Holy

---

York: Fordham, 1973), 44.

[10]Berkhof, *Systematic Theology*, 59.

[11]Jürgen Moltmann, *The Crucified God* (London: SCM, 1974). See also John M. Frame, *No Other God: A Response to Open Theism* (Phillipsburg, NJ: Presbyterian and Reformed, 2001), 180-85.

[12]God's 'passibility' pertains to him only at the level of his tri-personhood, not at the level of his essential deity.

Scripture who as a God of infinite love showed his love to suffering humankind by giving his own Son up to the death of the cross.[13] John R. W. Stott bears testimony to my point here with the following words:

> In the real world of pain, how could one worship a God who was immune to it? I have entered many Buddhist temples in different Asian countries and stood respectfully before the statue of Buddha, his legs crossed, arms folded, eyes closed, the ghost of a smile playing round his mouth, a remote look on his face, detached from the agonies of the world. But each time after a while I have had to turn away. And in imagination I have turned instead to that lonely, twisted, tortured figure on the cross, nails through hands and feet, back lacerated, limbs wrenched, brow bleeding from thorn-pricks, mouth dry and intolerably thirsty, plunged in God-forsaken darkness. This is the God for me! He laid aside his immunity to pain. He entered our world of flesh and blood, tears and death. He suffered for us.... There is still a question mark against human suffering, but over it we boldly stamp another mark, the cross which symbolizes divine suffering. 'The cross of Christ ... is God's ... self-justification in such a world' as ours.[14]

When our *Confession of Faith* declares then that God is 'without ... passions' it means that he has no *bodily* passions such as the need to satisfy hunger or the desire to fulfill himself sexually. We do however affirm that God is impassible in the sense that the creature cannot *inflict* suffering, pain, or any sort of distress or discomfort upon God against his will. Insofar as God enters into such experiences, it is always the result of *his* deliberate voluntary decision. God's experiences do not come upon him as ours come upon us. Ours come upon us often

---

[13]We will say more about God's love in the ninth address.

[14]John R. W. Stott, *The Cross of Christ* (Downers Grove, Illinois: InterVarsity, 1986), 335-6.

unforeseen, unwilled, unchosen, and forced upon us against our wills. His are foreknown, willed, and chosen by him and are never forced upon him *ab extra* apart from his determination to accept them. In short, God is never the creature's *unwilling* victim. Even when Jesus hung upon the cross his suffering was according to the predeterminate counsel and foreknowledge of God (Acts 2:23). And he himself said, you will recall: 'No one takes [my life] from me, but I lay it down of my own accord. I have authority to lay it down and authority to take it up again. This ... I received from my Father' (John 10:18).

A threefold response to an objection

Someone may be asking here, with regard to God's decretal immutability, if God always acts in accordance with his predetermined eternal purpose that is unalterably fixed, how are we to explain the fact that the Scriptures will speak of God as being 'grieved' over some prior action on his part (Gen. 6:5-7; 1 Sam. 15:11) or of his 'changing his mind' with regard to a certain stated course of action or seemingly expressing a willingness to chart a new course of action (Exod. 32:9-10; Jonah 3:3-5, 10)? If such grief and alteration of mind are aspects of his *dynamic* immutability, what then does his *immutability* mean? Hasn't it been reduced in meaning to zero? How do these scriptural data square with the Bible's and Reformed theology's teaching of the unalterable fixity of God's eternal decree?

I will make a threefold response and will be brief in doing so. First, where, upon a superficial reading, the biblical text might seem to suggest that God arbitrarily alters his course of action away from a previously declared course of action, one should understand this so-called 'new course' as only his settled, *immutably certain* response to a change in the human response to him and to his holy laws, in accordance with the principle of divine conduct that he enunciated respectively in Jeremiah 18:7-10 and Psalm 18:25-27:

> If *at any time* I announce that a nation or a kingdom is to be uprooted, torn down and destroyed, and if that nation I warned repents of its evil, then I will relent and not inflict on it the disaster I had planned. And if *at another time* I announce that a nation or kingdom is to be built up and planted, and if it does evil in my sight and does not obey me, then I will reconsider the good I had intended to do for it.

> To the faithful you show yourself faithful, to the blameless you show yourself blameless, to the pure you show yourself pure, but to the crooked you show yourself shrewd. You save the humble but bring low those whose eyes are haughty.

In other words, God *always* acts the same way toward moral good and the same way toward moral evil. The things he loved in Abraham's day he still loves today and will love forever; the things he hated in Abraham's day he still hates today and will hate forever. The world's morality may, does, and shall in the future deteriorate. But God's immutable standard of morality, summarily declared *in stone* in the Ten Commandments, will never change. And he will always respond to men's morality or immorality the same way. In every relationship he has with mankind, the immutable moral fixity of his character is and will be evident. And because this is so self-evidently true, as he himself declared, God did not deem it necessary when he inspired the Scriptures to attach to every promise he made or to every prediction of judgment he issued the corresponding conditions for weal or woe. His stated principle of conduct is always operative, and if the biblical interpreter does not realize this he may conclude wrongly that God has broken a promise or has failed to carry out a predicted judgment when in reality he is acting according to his declared principle of conduct.

The second thing I would say is this: God being the God of infinite goodness that he is, we should not be surprised at all to read that, in response to the evil of those who refuse to obey him, he could be grieved that he had made them. In fact I would argue and will argue in Lecture Nine that, God being the God that he is, it would be very strange if we did not hear him say that man's sin and evil were sources of great grief to him. God himself declared, you will recall: 'I take no pleasure in the death of the wicked, but rather that they turn from their ways and live' (Ezek. 33:11). Just as God, because he is holy, cannot look upon man's sin with any degree of approbation (Hab. 1:13), so also, because he is good, he cannot look upon the sinner's doom with the slightest degree of positive pleasure. The creature's obedience *always* brings him joy; the creature's disobedience *always* grieves him, and he does not hesitate to tell us so. When a sinner repents there is *always* joy in the presence of the angels (Luke 15:7, 10); when a child of God falls into sin the Holy Spirit is *always* grieved (Isa. 63:10; Eph. 4:30), and he does not hesitate to tell us so. So what many interpreters would assert are examples of the *mutability* of God's purpose are in actuality remarkable examples of God's *fixed character* and *immutable purpose* to relate himself correspondingly to men precisely in accordance with their attitude toward him and his wise and holy precepts.

Third, with respect to God's threat to destroy Israel and to 'begin anew' with Moses in Exodus 32:9-10, while God's anger against Israel was real and in no sense feigned, God knew that his threat to destroy Israel would not be actualized because, as his words to Moses, 'Leave me alone that...,' indicate, Moses stood before him as Israel's mediator and God knew that Moses would intercede on Israel's behalf. By determining that his response to Israel's rebellion would turn on Moses' mediation (for other instances of biblical mediation see Gen. 18:22-23; 19:29; Job 1:4-5; Ezek. 22:30; Amos 7:1-6) God was teaching everyone thereafter, including us 'on whom the fulfillment of the ages has come' (1 Cor. 10:11), by this incident that he *always* relates himself to his covenant people salvifically through a mediator. By his mediation in Exodus 32:13, 30-32 Moses was signifying the central redemptive principle of all biblical salvation through mediation, and in so doing his mediation became by divine design an Old Testament type of Christ's mediatorial work. So what some might perceive as an example of the *mutable* character of God's purpose is in actuality a remarkable example of God's *immutably* fixed purpose to relate himself to his people *always* on the basis of the intercession of an appointed mediator.

To one who might ask: 'But didn't he know, before he created them, that mankind would disobey him and cause him grief? And if he did, why did he, if he is a God of compassion, create the human race in the first place if he knew that it would disobey him and cause him grief, resulting in his hostility toward them and, in the case of the non-elect, their eternal pain and anguish?' – to that one's first question I would answer: 'Yes, surely!' And to his second question I would note that before he finds fault with God's wisdom, love, and justice *vis à vis* the world that *actually* exists, he must be able to show that another world into which evil could not and would not come to actuality would, first, be richer than or at least just as rich in moral and spiritual values as this actual world, second, would better accomplish or at least accomplish God's same end, namely, the glorification of his beloved Son as the 'Firstborn' among many redeemed brothers and sisters (Rom. 8:29) to the glory of God the Father (Phil. 2:11) as well as the magnification of God's 'many-faceted wisdom' exhibited in and by the church (Eph. 3:10) and the riches of his grace (Eph. 1:6, 12, 14), and third, would more accord with or at least be in harmony with and revelatory of the entire range of his divine attributes. This God's critic cannot do. So in light of God's declared eternal purpose to save an elect to be his Son's bride to the glory of God the Father and to the praise of his glorious grace, we must conclude that *this is the best of all possible worlds to accomplish the divine end,* and that any other imaginary world in which sin and its consequences are absent fails both to meet these criteria and to justify itself.

But enough of theologizing. Let's turn our attention now away from our exposition of this doctrine to some applications of it for our lives and the lives of men in general. I want to make three such applications.

Application
I am aware when I say what I am now about to say that I am getting ahead of myself somewhat in this series but I think the following things needs to be said in order to drive home my first point of application:

Was God *all-wise* when he laid the foundations of the earth, when he spoke and the mountains and seas appeared? The Bible says he was. Then because he is immutable he is precisely the *same* all-wise God today in his dealings with you and will remain so forever. He is not less skillful. Neither has he become mentally senile nor does he have less knowledge now.

Was he *mighty* when he spoke this world into existence out of nonexistence? The Bible says he was. Then because he is immutable he is precisely the *same* mighty God today in his dealings with you and will remain so forever. The arm of his strength has not palsied in the slightest; he is the *same* infinite Colossus of might today, and the strength of his power has not been sapped in the slightest degree.

Was he *just and holy* in the past when he destroyed the antediluvian world by the Genesis flood, when he rained fire and brimstone from heaven on Sodom and Gomorrah, when he poured out his destructive plagues upon Egypt? The Bible says he was. Then because he is immutable he is precisely the *same* just and holy God today in his dealings with you and will remain so forever. What he hated when he sent the Flood he still hates and what he loved then he still loves. What he hated when he destroyed Sodom and Gomorrah he still hates and what he loved then he still loves.

Was he *truthful* in the past when he bound himself by covenant oath to save his elect? The Bible says he was. Then because he is immutable he is precisely the same truthful God today in his dealings with you and will remain so forever. His veracity is immutable; his Word is 'forever settled in the heavens' (Ps. 119:89).

Was he *good and kind, generous and gentle, benevolent and plenteous in mercy and pity, full of steadfast lovingkindness, and forgiving* in the past when again and again he forgave backsliding Israel for its sins? The Bible says he was. Then because he is immutable he is precisely the *same* good, kind, generous, gentle, benevolent, forgiving God today in his dealings with you, plenteous in mercy, full of lovingkindness, and will remain so forever. As we saw in the previous lecture, his love is everlasting (Jer. 31:3), and his mercies will never cease to be, for they too are everlasting (Ps. 100:5).

Did he have a *plan of redemption* before the creation of the world that included you and me? The Bible says he did. Then because he is immutable he has precisely that *same* plan of redemption today that involves us and he will have it forever. You and I are still beneficiaries of it. Not one of its stipulations will he ever alter. Did he make *us* any promises in that plan? The Bible says he did. Then those promises are still binding upon him today and shall be binding upon him forever, for by 'two immutable things' – his eternal purpose and his binding covenant oath – he has confirmed and sealed his Word. His promises are not 'Yes and No,' affirms Paul. They are

'Yes,' and the gospel declares the 'Amen!' (2 Cor. 1:19). In sum, bring before me any attribute of God you choose and I will write on it *semper idem* – 'always the same.' And you, my brothers and sisters, knowing and trusting this one living and true God who is 'always the same', can sing with complete confidence:

'Great is thy faithfulness,' O God my Father,
there is no shadow of turning with thee;
thou changest not, thy compassions, they fail not;
As thou has been thou forever wilt be.

If truth be told, it is only such a God – *our* God – who *can* be known and trusted! A mutable god can never be really known or trusted, for it changes. What such a god is today it will not be tomorrow. What it says is true today may not be true tomorrow. What it says it will do can never be relied upon.

Given then these implications, I launch now my second point of application with this question: In what does *your permanency* in our most holy Faith reside? Peter thought it resided in him and he assured the Lord that though all the other disciples would forsake him, yet he would never forsake him. He was wrong, of course. All of us are all too aware of his miserable failure. So I ask again, wherein does your permanency in the Faith reside? In *your* fidelity to Christ? In *your* love for God? Hardly! Your fidelity and your love are much too fickle, much too similar to the unstable waters of 'the troubled sea when it cannot rest' (Isa. 57:20). In what then does it reside? Well, what declares the Scripture? 'I, the LORD, do not change; therefore you, O sons of Jacob, are not consumed.' If God were a God who 'changed like shifting shadows', we who in our natural state of sin are even now still rightly faggots for eternal fire would be consumed. No earthly father in this world would ever endure the rebellion of his children had his sons and daughters provoked him even a nano-nano-amount as much as God has been provoked by us, the sons of Jacob. Even in the state of grace our best works are 'mixed with so much weakness and imperfection, that they cannot endure the severity of God's judgment,' are in themselves 'blameable and reprovable in his sight' (*Westminster Confession of Faith*, XVI.V, VI), and are accepted by God as 'good' only because, being ourselves 'in Christ', God imputes also to our works the righteousness of his Son. So our permanency in the Faith ultimately resides in none of our achievements or doings.

That which stands this very hour between us and hell's everlasting lake of fire is the impregnable wall of 'the immutability of God's decree of election, flowing from the free and unchangeable love of God the Father, ...the efficacy of the merit and intercession of Jesus Christ, the abiding of the Spirit, and of the seed of God within [us], and the nature of the covenant of grace' (*Westminster Confession of Faith*, XVII.II). Though we prove unfaithful, God 'remains faithful; for he cannot deny himself' (2 Tim. 2:13). Our permanency in the Faith resides then in the immutable faithfulness of God to us. For reasons in himself and for none in us God set his love upon his chosen ones before the creation of the world and predestined us to become conformed to the image of his Son that his Son might be the Firstborn among many brothers and sisters and all to the praise of his glorious grace. And '[we] whom he predestined, [even we, the *same* group he predestined, not another group, not a part of this group] he also called, and [we] whom he called, [even we, the *same* group he called, not another group, not a part of this group] he also justified, and [we] whom he justified, [even we, the *same* group he justified, not another group, not a part of this group] he also glorified' (Rom. 8:29-30). So we who are in Christ are already seated with God on his throne in heaven, as far as God's immutable determinations are concerned (Eph. 2:6)! Which is just to say that in the immutable mind of God he sees us as already glorified. The tight, inflexible syntax of Romans 8:29-30 is such that it brings before us an unbreakable 'golden chain' of actions on God the Father's part that connects eternity past with eternity future. As you and I were in his eternal plan before the creation of the world, so we are still permanently in his plan, united as we are to Christ and his high priestly ministry, and so we ever will be. So our permanency in the Faith is rooted in the Father's *immutable* decree, in his Son's *unchanging* priesthood, in the Spirit's *ever-abiding* presence within us, and in the triune God's *perpetual, irrevocable* covenant fidelity. Hence you and I can never finally be lost.

If one child of God could ever eventually perish, then God would not be immutable, and we might well all perish. Then no gospel promise would be certainly true. God's Word would then be untrustworthy, and nothing in it would be worthy of our acceptance. But because God is unchangingly faithful to us, we know that he loves us and will love us forever. And each of us who knows that he is the object of God's eternal, unchanging love can sing: 'Did Jesus *once* upon me shine, then Jesus is *forever* mine.'

Because God is immutable, Christians can know that someday they will enter the renewed heaven and renewed earth that now is subjected to frustration but then will be liberated from its bondage to decay (Rom. 8:20-21) and 'death shall be no more, neither shall there be mourning nor crying nor pain any more' (Rev. 21:4). In our glorified state we will be fully conformed to the moral likeness of the Son of God. We will then fully reflect the holy character of Jesus, the 'second man' and 'last Adam', our wills having been 'made perfectly and immutably free to do good alone, in the state of glory' (*WCF*, IX.V). 'This is the highest end conceivable not only by men but also by God himself. God himself could not contemplate or determine a higher destiny for his creatures.'[15]

---

[15]John Murray, 'The Goal of Sanctification' in *Collected Writings of John Murray*, 2:316.

In our glorified state we will be 'with the Lord forever' (1 Thess. 4:17). There we will rest from our present earthly labors; there we will worship and serve the Lord forever. Doubtless, the fine arts will be present there. Together with angelic choirs and the redeemed church of God, deaf mutes now will then sing great music – I mean truly great music with lyrics by Moses and the Lamb. Paraplegics now will then dance. Since this is so, I am sure we will all experience gladness of heart watching Joni Eareckson Tada dancing joyously with all the saints. Bad music and lyrics that push destructive and abusive lifestyles will not be there. And many current occupations will not be needed there – armies, international spy services, police forces, firemen, lobbyists, lawyers, funeral directors, physicians, dentists, nurses, air conditioning services, furnace services, and street repair services, just to name a few. There will be no crumbling, crime-infested inner cities or ugly drug-infested urban sprawls there. The new earth will be a place of unimaginable beauty and intense activity. It will doubtless also be a massive job-retraining center. But it will never be boring, first, because those who are there want to be there, second, because human selfishness that is a major contributor to boredom, will not be there, and third, because the human body will no longer be vulnerable to weariness and drowsiness.[16] In one phrase, joyous saints will rule forever over the new earth according to their Lord's gracious assignments.

My third point of application is this: If every divine promise of *blessing* is immutable, if our Lord's high-priestly ministry saves to the uttermost and forever all those who come to God through him, if every covenant oath of God is unalterable, so that the salvation of the elect is 'particularly and *unchangeably* designed, and their number so certain and definite, that it cannot be either increased or diminished' (*Westminster Confession*

---

[16]John Gilmore, *Probing Heaven: Key Questions on the Hereafter* (Grand Rapids: Baker, 1989), 169.

of Faith, III.IV), then this mad, insane world must be confronted through what it regards as the 'foolishness' of gospel proclamation with the fact that it is equally true that God is also unchanging *in his threats* and that he will someday judge the secrets of men's hearts through Christ Jesus according to the gospel (Rom. 2:16). John Dick aptly states:

> The Divine immutability, like the cloud [that] interposed between the Israelites and the Egyptian army, has a dark as well as a light side. It insures the execution of His threatenings, as well as the performance of His promises; and destroys the hope [that] the guilty fondly cherish, that He will be all lenity to His frail and erring creatures, and that they will be much more lightly dealt with than the declarations of His own Word would lead us to expect. We oppose to these deceitful and presumptuous speculations the solemn truth, that God is unchangeable in veracity and purity, in faithfulness and justice.[17]

What this means is this: God has immutably declared that he will save only those who trust the saving work of his Son and will consign to perdition those who do not trust the saving work of his Son.[18] So let the unbelieving

---

[17]John Dick, *Lectures on Theology* (New York: Robert Carter, 1852), I, 207.

[18]The New Testament alone teaches the ultimate bifurcation of human destiny in more than fifty passages (Matt. 7:22, 23; 12:41, 42; 13:40-43; 24:51; 25:41-46; Mark 12:9; Luke 13:25-30; 16:19-28; 21:36; John 5:22-30; 12:47, 48; 15:6, 22-25; 16:8-11; Acts 17:31; 24:25; Rom. 1:32; 2:2, 3, 5; 5:16, 18; 14:10; 1 Cor. 5:13; 2 Cor. 5:10; Gal. 6:7; 1 Thess. 4:6; 5:1-10; 2 Thess. 1:5-10; 2:3-12; 2 Tim. 4:1; Heb. 4:12, 13; 6:4-8; 10:26-31; James 2:13; 4:12; 1 Pet. 2:7, 8, 23; 3:12; 4:17, 18; 2 Pet. 3-10; 3:7; 1 John 3:7, 8; Jude 4-6, 13, 15; Rev. 14:7, 9-11, 17-20; 15:1; 16; 19:1-3; 11-21; 20:11-15; 22:15). The New Testament also teaches in numerous passages that those consigned to perdition will experience conscious torment, for example, Matthew 8:12, 29; 13:42; 18:8-9; 22:13; 24:5.1; 25:30; Luke 16:23, 24, 28; Revelation 14:9-11; 20:10.

moralist be as good, as moral, as honest, as upright as he can be, he will still be condemned. For God's declaration will forever stand: 'He only who trusts my Son shall be saved; he who does not trust my Son is condemned already and shall be damned forever' (see John 3:18). This declaration is as unchangeable as God himself. After *ten thousand years* of conscious torment in hell the moralist will still read this divine edict in burning letters above him:

> He only who trusts my Son shall be saved; he who does not trust my Son is condemned already and shall be damned forever.

After *ten billion ages* of anguish in hell have rolled away the man who looked to his own morality in this life for his salvation will still see it emblazoned over the 'great chasm that has been fixed' ['and that shall remain so' according to the verb *estēriktai*, the perfect passive of *stērizō*] (Luke 16:26):

> He only who trusts my Son shall be saved; he who does not trust my Son is condemned already and shall be damned forever.

And when that tormented moralist – perhaps ever hoping in the words of Alfred Lord Tennyson's *In Memoriam*, that 'at last – far off – at last ... winter [will] change to Spring' – thinks that the wheel of eternity must surely have spun out its last thread after it seems that the ages of the ages have passed, after it seems that every particle of what we call eternity must surely have run out, he will still see written in flaming letters burning as brightly as they ever did these words:

> He only who trusts my Son shall be saved; he who does not trust my Son is condemned already and shall be damned forever.

No, dear friends, I get no pleasure in saying it but say it I must: the words of Dante's *Inferno* do indeed apply here to the impenitent and unbelieving: 'Leave every hope, ye who enter here.' The Bible clearly teaches that 'the cowardly, the unbelieving, the vile, the murderers, the sexually immoral, those who practice magic arts, the idolaters and all liars [will have] their place in the lake that burns with fire and brimstone' (Rev. 21:8), that 'nothing impure will ever enter [the new earth], nor will anyone who does what is shameful or deceitful' (Rev. 21:27), and that 'outside are ... those who practice magic arts, the sexually impure, the murderers, the idolaters and everyone who loves and practices falsehood' (Rev. 22:15). My brothers and sisters, may Christ's love constrain us, in view of the dreadful final plight of the unbeliever, to proclaim with power and perseverance to the lost moralists of this world the unsearchable riches of Christ before it is for them everlastingly too late, for once consigned to hell they will be in hell forever and forever.

Well, for the last few minutes we have been working through the Bible's teaching on God's unchanging essence, his immutable character, his unfailing covenant faithfulness, and some of their implications for us. I have prayed all week that God's Spirit would take this address and meet you where you are at this time in your life – in your joys and in your sorrows, in your plenty and in your want, in your encouragements and in your discouragements, in your serenities and in your perplexities. I cannot apply this address directly to you myself – I know that all too well; only the Spirit of God, because he is God and knows your heart, can sovereignly work by and with God's Word in your heart. But what I can do is to urge you all to take seriously the fact of God's immutability both in the certainty of his blessing upon his own and in the certainty of his curse upon the rest of mankind, and, if you are a Christian, to revel in the fact that your God, the unchanging God of Scripture, stands on the bridge of your life as your sure and steadfast Captain. If you are not a Christian I implore you to be reconciled to God through faith in his Son. And I am trusting that the Holy Spirit will take these flashes of truth and illumine your lives hereafter by them. May it begin to be so today for all of us.

Let us pray:
Almighty God, our heavenly Father: We bow before your infinite, eternal, and unchangeable being in this moment, and we praise you for your unchanging covenant faithfulness to us, your frail and all-too-often-faithless, fickle children. Forgive us, merciful Father, for our inexcusable wandering from your ways, our unjustifiable wasting of your gifts, our irresponsible forgetting of your love. Help us to go from this chapel this morning with more confidence in your *unwavering* fatherly love and care than when we entered. And by your grace may we grow in our love for you and be more faithful to you who are our *ever*-faithful, *never*-failing God. We pray in Jesus' name. Amen.

Fifth Address

'Infinite, Eternal, and Unchangeable in His Wisdom'

O Lord, you have searched me and you know me. You know when I sit and when I rise; you perceive my thoughts from afar. You discern my going out and my lying down; you are familiar with all my ways. Before a word is on my tongue you know it completely, O Lord. You hem me in – behind and before; you have laid your hand upon me. Such knowledge is too wonderful for me, too lofty for me to attain....

My frame was not hidden from you when I was made in the secret place. When I was woven together in the depths of the earth, your eyes saw my unformed body. All the days ordained for me were written in your book before one of them came to be. How precious to me are your thoughts, O God! How vast is the sum of them! Were I to count them, they would outnumber the grains of sand. When I awake, I am still with you....

Search me, O God, and know my heart; test me and know my anxious thoughts. See if there is any offensive way in me, and lead me in the way everlasting (Ps. 139:1-6, 15-18, 23-24).

Introduction

Good morning once again, dear brothers and sisters in Christ. I pray that in all respects you are in good health and prospering in your studies here at the seminary, just as your souls are prospering. I regard this opportunity to deliver this series of chapel addresses on the attributes of God as a high honor and privilege, and you may be assured that I am praying that the series will contribute both to the advancement of your knowledge of God and to the improvement of your souls' spiritual health. To that end let us pray together now.

Prayer

All-wise and all-knowing God: We acknowledge before you this morning that to satisfy our spiritual thirst we have in *our* wisdom, thinking we know better than you, all too often hewn out for ourselves broken cisterns that can hold no water, and we have all too often in *our* wisdom, again thinking we know better than you, turned away from you who alone are the fountain of living water. We pray for your pardon for this our folly.

This morning we bow before you in our acknowledged ignorance of your sovereign ways and works and cry to you for illumination. Grant again, we pray, as you have so often done before, that your Holy Spirit may hover over the acknowledged confusion of our hearts as he did over the primeval Genesis chaos and out of our spiritual darkness bring forth light and out of our life's disorder bring forth order, peace, and beauty. We pray that what your Word will give us in this chapel hour this morning will have a lasting positive effect upon our lives and upon our present and future ministries.

I beseech you, Father, to prosper your Word this morning as I attempt to teach this assembly of seminarians something about the 'deeps' of your wisdom and knowledge.

All these things I ask, not because I think we deserve them, but because our mighty Savior, Jesus Christ our Lord, does, in whose name I pray. Amen.

* * *

'Infinite, eternal, and unchangeable in his wisdom.' This morning we want to consider God's wisdom and knowledge. The church of Jesus Christ has always believed and confessed that the one living and true God is infinitely wise – eternally and unchangeably so. And although the *Shorter Catechism* does not mention God's knowledge by word, I am certain that its framers intended that we include within the *Shorter Catechism*'s reference to God's wisdom also his attribute of knowledge since the *Confession of Faith* and the *Larger Catechism* do mention God's knowledge – the former declaring that 'His knowledge is infinite, infallible, and independent [that is, not dependent] upon the creature, so as nothing is to him contingent, or uncertain,' the latter affirming that he 'know[s] all things'.

The Scriptures are replete with these teachings, the following twenty-one passages being just a sampling of the Scripture's fullness on this topic:

Texts

Genesis 16:13: 'You are *a God who sees* ['ēl rǒ 'î].'

1 Samuel 2:3: '...the LORD is *a God who knows* ['ēl dē 'ôth], and by him deeds are weighed.'

1 Samuel 16:7: 'Man looks at the outward appearance ... the LORD looks at the heart.'

Job 23:10: 'He knows the way I take.' (See also Job 9:4; 12:13)

Job 37:16: 'Do you know ... those wonders of him who is *perfect* [tᵉmîm] in knowledge?'

Psalm 33:13: 'From heaven the LORD looks down and sees all mankind; from his dwelling place he watches all those who live on earth – he ... considers everything they do.'

Psalm 90:8: 'You have placed our iniquities before you, our secret sins in the light of your presence.'

Psalm 94:9-11: 'Does he who implanted the ear not hear? Does he who formed the eye not see?... Does he who teaches man lack knowledge? The LORD knows the thoughts of man....'

Psalm 104:24: 'How many are your works, O LORD! In wisdom have you made them all.'

Psalm 139:1-4, 15-16: 'O LORD, you have searched me and know me. You know when I sit and when I rise; you perceive my thoughts from afar. You discern my going out and my lying down; you are familiar with all my ways. Before a word is on my tongue you know it completely, O LORD ... My frame was not hidden from you when I was made in the secret place. When I was woven together in the depths of the earth, your eyes saw my unformed body. All the days ordained for me were written in your book before one of them came to be.'

Psalm 147:5: 'Great is our God ... his understanding is *infinite* ['ên mispār, literally, 'there is no measuring (it)'].'

Proverbs 15:3: 'The eyes of the LORD are everywhere, keeping watch on the wicked and the good.'

Isaiah 40:13-14, 27-28: 'Who has the understanding of the Spirit of the LORD, or instructed him as his counselor? Whom did the Lord consult to enlighten him, or who taught him the right way? Who was it that taught him knowledge or showed him the way of understanding.... Why do you say, O Jacob, and complain, O Israel, 'My way is hidden from the LORD; my cause is disregarded by my God?' Do you not know? Have you not heard? The LORD is the everlasting God, the Creator of the ends of the earth. He will not grow tired or weary, and his understanding is *unsearchable* ['ên hēker, literally, 'there is no searching (it)'].'

Isaiah 46:10: 'I make known the end from the beginning, from ancient times, what is still to come.'

Hosea 7:2: '[The sons of Israel] do not consider in their hearts that I remember all their wickedness; ... they are before my face.'

Daniel 2:22: God 'gives wisdom to wise men, and knowledge to men of understanding. It is he who reveals the profound and hidden things; he knows what is in the darkness.'

John 2:24-25; 21:17: Jesus, in his divine nature as the Second Person of the Godhead, 'knew all men and ... knew what was in man.' And learning this, Peter later declared: 'Lord, *you know all things [panta su oidas]*. You know that I love you.'

Romans 11:33-34: Paul, overcome by the marvel of the intricate inner workings of God's plan to save Jews and Gentiles, exclaimed: 'Oh, the depth of the riches of the wisdom and knowledge of God! How *unsearchable* [*anexeraunēta*] his judgments, and his paths *beyond tracing out* [*anexichniastoi*]! Who has known the mind of the Lord? Or who has been his counselor?'

Romans 16:27: Paul declares that the Christian God is 'the only wise God'.

Hebrews 4:13: 'Nothing in all creation is hidden from God's sight. Everything is uncovered and laid bare before the eyes of him to whom we must give account.'

1 John 3:20: 'God ... *knows everything [ginōskei panta]*,' a statement that in three words says it all!

The doctrine
Clearly, our God is omniscient. God's knowledge – intuited in the sense that he never had to learn anything through the learning process – encompasses all possible and actual knowable data. He knows to perfection and without qualification all things – all things visible and invisible in heaven and on earth; all spirits, thrones, and dominions in heaven and in hell; all matters past,

present, and future; all the thoughts of every mind, all the words of every tongue, and all the activities of every creature living and dead; all their purposes, all their plans, all their relationships, all their complicities, and all their conspiracies; all physical and spiritual causes, all natural and supernatural forces, and all real and contingent motions; all mysteries and all unuttered secrets; all true propositions as true and all false propositions as false, all valid conclusions as valid and all invalid conclusions as invalid – and always has known them and always will know them. And his knowledge is related to his wisdom so that God judiciously employs his knowledge to accomplish perfectly his holy and just ends. This is just to say again that God knows everything and that he employs what he knows wisely with a wisdom that is 'first of all pure; then peace-loving, considerate, *willing to yield* [*eupeithēs*], full of mercy and good fruit, impartial and sincere' (Jas. 3:17).

But while the church of Jesus Christ has always believed and confessed that the one living and true God is infinitely wise and all-knowing, it is the Reformed church alone that includes within its exposition of God's wisdom and knowledge a serious study of God's 'eternal purpose' (Eph. 3:11). Reformed theology, which it is our happy lot to inherit, stresses that God's 'eternal purpose' reflects his infinite, eternal, and unchangeable wisdom that devised perfect ends and achieves those ends by perfect means. God in his infinite wisdom had wise reasons for determining all the ends and all the means to those ends that he did for his creation, even though these ends and means for the most part, if not totally, are inscrutable and hidden to most, if not to all, of his rational creatures.

Let me take you into this matter of God's infinitely wise 'eternal purpose' a bit farther. The fact that God's infinitely wise purpose is *also eternal* and *immutable* means that there was never a moment when God deliberated whether he would create the world or not, for his purpose is eternal and immutable. A God who might have determined not to create this universe is simply not the God of the Bible. This fact also means that there was never a second moment when God deliberated whether he would save some people whom the Bible calls his elect or not, for again his purpose is eternal and immutable. A God who might have determined not to save anyone is not the God of the Bible either. This fact also means that there was never a third moment when he deliberated whether he would save them through Christ's saving work or through some other means, for yet again his purpose is eternal and immutable. A God who might have determined to save his elect by some means other than through his own beloved Son's cross-work is not the God of the Bible either. All of these features of his purpose were eternally and immutably determined! And to suppose that God's eternal, immutable purpose could have been other than it is is to suppose that *God* could be other than he is. But this is impossible since *he is eternally immutable* not only in his Being but also in his purpose. Therefore, God *had* to create the world because he had eternally purposed to do so. He *had* to save the elect because he had eternally purposed to do so. And he *had* to save his elect through Christ because he had eternally purposed to do so. To suppose otherwise is to suppose that God's *eternal* purpose had at some moment a degree of mutability about it that is foreign to the eternal and immutable Being and purpose of God. So much for the debate, then, as to whether Christ's cross work was only hypothetically or absolutely necessary. Christ's cross work was, of course, *absolutely* necessary for the salvation of God's elect, for God's eternal, immutable purpose, among other reasons that could be advanced,[1] rendered it so. Salvation, of course, is still the result of God's free and sovereign grace grounded in

---

[1]See my *A New Systematic Theology of the Christian Faith* (Second edition; Nashville, Tenn.: Thomas Nelson, 1998), 665-6, for five other reasons.

his sovereign good pleasure since no cause external to him forced him to purpose eternally as he did.

Now with regard to the execution of his eternal purpose, his perfect wisdom and knowledge were exhibited in his creative activity in Genesis 1–2. Upon the completion of his creative work God declared that all that he had made was 'very good' (Gen. 1:31). The psalmist, very likely David, exclaims, you will recall: 'How many are your works, O LORD! In wisdom have you made them all' (Ps. 104:24). His wisdom and knowledge also lie behind all his ways as he *providentially executed* in the past, continues *providentially to execute* at the present, and *will providentially execute* in the future his eternal plan throughout present-earth and later new-earth history. And we see God's eternal wisdom especially on *salvific* display in Christ's death at Calvary, for the *crucified* Christ (*note*: not just the Christ but the *crucified* Christ) – who is at the center of all God's ways and works – is, Paul declares, *the* wisdom of God (1 Cor. 1:24), the one in whom are hidden all the treasures of wisdom and knowledge (Col. 2:3) and the one in whom the fullness of the Deity dwells bodily (Col. 2:9). Preaching devoid of the cross – and you aspiring ministers must never forget this if you desire God's blessing on your ministry – is preaching devoid of the divine wisdom, which means, should you ever abandon the cross in your preaching, that your sermons, if they can be called sermons any longer at all, will become sterile, moral platitudes at best by instilling self-righteousness in those who think they are morally good and/or positively harmful dogmas at worst by fostering despair in those who know they are incapable of keeping God's commandments perfectly.

The verses I have cited also clearly teach us that the all-wise God is also all-knowing. At every moment he is cognizant of everything that ever was, now is, or ever shall be. He necessarily knows his own uncreated essence exhaustively, and he necessarily knows his created universe exhaustively – and he knows both intuitively, instantaneously, simultaneously, and everlastingly. His knowledge of himself and of all created things is absolutely comprehensive and eternally 'intuited', that is to say, he never had to learn anything through the learning process because he already knows everything there is to know. He 'never receives from some other source or from his own inventive genius an idea he never previously had' (Gordon H. Clark). He cannot learn more than he knows already for he already knows the limitless infinity of facts that can actually and possibly be known. He knows every detail of every being in the universe – in heaven, on earth, and in hell. Never are his wisdom and knowledge nonplussed; never is he in a quandary about anything. Nothing escapes his notice; nothing is hidden from him, which means, of course, that you have never had a private conversation with anyone in your life nor will you ever have one! So be careful what you think and say.

God has never forgotten anything either. Never will he experience a momentary lapse of memory, know a 'senior moment', or suffer from Alzheimer's disease. I make this point simply to note that when God says in Jeremiah 31:34 that he will not remember our sins he means that he will not remember our sins *against us*, but he will never forget that we are redeemed sinners. All this is what we intend when we attribute *omniscience* to him. And he has always been, is now, and ever shall be everlastingly omniscience.

Let's take all this one step farther. Since God's knowledge is coextensive with all that is, this means that all created things, falling as they do within the compass of his eternal purpose and creative and providential activity, are what they are by virtue of their place in his prior eternal purpose, his wise determining counsel, and his creative and providential arrangement of things. Every fact in the universe has meaning (may I say an interpretation?), then, by virtue of its place in God's purpose and governance. There is no such thing as a brute, uninterpreted datum anywhere in the entire universe scattered there by an impersonal cosmic 'litterbug' that awaits man's coming to it and, by his finite wisdom and knowledge, placing a meaning on it for the very first time. *Every* datum of whatever kind is already a God-interpreted datum that has meaning. *Every* fact is a 'theistic' fact; there is not one single 'non-theistic' fact anywhere in the universe.[2] Therefore, man's knowledge of things will necessarily always be 'receptively reconstructive' and never 'creatively constructive', to employ Cornelius Van Til's terminology. From this it follows that if a man ever truly learns a fact to any degree his knowledge of that fact must and will coincide univocally with God's prior interpretation of that fact. And God has said something in his Word about everything in the Universe, if nothing more than that it is a *created* datum. This means that the atheistic scientist who denies the doctrine of creation in favor of evolution does not know the most basic truth about anything – where and how it got here. That portion of his knowledge that God has chosen to reveal in Holy Scripture is then the criterion of validation for all human predication. It is only in God's light that we can see light (Ps. 36:9).

A few early church fathers questioned whether God concerns himself with such earthly trivia as the number of gnats that are born or die every second or the number of fleas that are on earth.[3] But the Holy Scriptures affirm that God has just that kind of knowledge. He not only determines the number of the stars and calls them each by name (Ps. 147:4), but he also knows when the sparrow falls (Luke 12:6) and he determines the number of hairs on our heads (Matt. 10:29-30) – as well as the number of fleas on earth at any given moment. To all this we can only say with the psalmist: 'Such knowledge

---

[2]There are, of course, *anti*-theistic and *anti*-Christian facts.

[3]Jerome, *Commentary on Habakkuk*, on 1:13, 14. See also Thomas Aquinas, *Summa theologicale*, I, Q. 23, Art. 7.

is too wonderful for me; it is too high, I cannot attain to it' (Ps. 139:6).

The Open Theist's Objection

Now this representation of God's knowledge as being absolutely and eternally comprehensive – an infallible, exhaustive knowledge encompassing the future as well as the past and the present – is, however, quite troublesome to some thinkers. They quite correctly observe that if God infallibly knows all things, then he must infallibly know the future as well. And if he infallibly knows the future, then he infallibly knows all the future acts of men. And if he infallibly knows all the future acts of men, then their acts are *certain* to occur, and that leaves no room for them to choose or to act as they will. Thus the libertarian 'freedom of indifference' that Arminians in general are so zealous to affirm and defend would all but disappear. Accordingly, they conclude that God's omniscience is incompatible with human freedom unless the former is modified to allow room for the latter. Accordingly, they declare that God limits his knowledge so that he does not know what men will do until they do it. But, of course, a God with limited knowledge is no longer omniscient and would need to enroll along with his rational creatures in Epistemology 101.

Do I need to tell you that the Bible does not endorse this man-centered adjustment? The Bible teaches that God infallibly knows the future because he decreed the future. And God himself declared that a major distinction between himself and all the false gods of this world is his infallible ability to predict the future and to bring that future to pass precisely as he declared it would be over against the inability of all the false gods either to predict the future or to bring it to pass. Isaiah teaches this in the following verses:

Isaiah 41:22-23, 25-27: 'Bring in your idols to tell ... what is going to happen ... I was the first to tell Zion, 'Look, here they are."

Isaiah 42:8-9: 'I am the LORD ... new things I declare; before they spring into being, I announce them to you.'

Isaiah 43:11-12: 'I have proclaimed ... I, and not some foreign god among you.'

Isaiah 44:7-8: 'Let [your idol] declare ... what is yet to come – yes, let him foretell what will come.'

Isaiah 45:18-21: 'For this is what the LORD says ... 'Who foretold this long ago, who declared it from the distant past? Was it not I, the LORD?"

Isaiah 46:10-11: 'I make known the end from the beginning, from ancient times, what is still to come.... What I have said, that will I bring about; what I have planned, that will I do.'

Isaiah 48:3-7: 'I foretold the former things long ago, my mouth announced them and I made them known; then suddenly I acted, and they came to pass.... I told you these things long ago; before they happened I announced them to you so that you could not say, "My idols did them, my wooden image and metal god ordained them."'

I can only mention one additional passage – I do not have time to discuss it – namely, Isaiah 44:24-28. But every student at this seminary before he or she graduates should either be required to read carefully and to digest thoroughly O. T. Allis's magnificent analysis of Isaiah's 'hymn of transcendence' that may be found in his book, *The Unity of Isaiah*,[4] or read and

---

[4]O. T. Allis, *The Unity of Isaiah* (Philadelphia: Presbyterian & Reformed, 1950), 62-80. It originally appeared in the volume, *Biblical and Theological Studies*, marking the centennial commemoration in 1912 of Princeton Theological Seminary.

analyze it on his own. Allis' analysis of this carefully composed hymn demonstrates beyond controversy that God through Isaiah, son of Amoz, specifically predicted in detail around the mid-8th century BC the Babylonian Exile in the early 6th century BC and the rebuilding of the city of Jerusalem after the Exile under Cyrus's decree in the late 6th and early 5th centuries BC, thereby binding the entire book of Isaiah together under the authorship of Isaiah, son of Amoz.

But in spite of God's explicit statements that he knows the future and that he alone can infallibly predict the future and bring whatever he predicts to pass, the authors of the book entitled *The Openness of God* [5] contend that the God of the Bible restricted himself at creation with respect to his omniscience and sovereignty, viewed in terms of domination and control, and therefore is ignorant of the future free acts of moral agents and can be taken by surprise. Clark Pinnock, for instance, argues that the God of Scripture also freely limited his power for the sake of man's unabridged human freedom. He views God's sovereignty as open and flexible, a sovereignty of 'infinite resourcefulness in the subtle use of power' rather than a sovereignty that 'dominates, manipulates, coerces, and tyrannizes' people. What a mean-spirited, inflammatory, not to mention fallacious, list of pejorative verbs to describe the system of his Calvinistic opponents!

According to Pinnock God's knowledge does not include an exhaustive knowledge of the future, for if it did 'the future would be fixed and determined' and human freedom would be an illusion. He contends that 'more power and wisdom are required for God to bring his will to pass in a world that he does not control than in one that he did control'. [6] He states:

---

[5]Clark Pinnock, Richard Rice, John Sanders, William Hasker, David Basinger, *The Openness of God* (Downers Grove, Illinois: InterVarsity, 1994).

[6]Pinnock, *The Openness of God*, 124.

> [In the Bible] God is delighted by something that happened or made angry by it; sometimes he relates to such events by repenting or changing his mind. So we [the authors of *Openness*] think that God is monitoring everything that happens and that he knows the future in great detail [except the future acts of people – RLR], but that surprises happen in history and *God's own knowledge takes account of them when they happen rather than before.* We see the future as not totally settled, and ... our assurance comes not from believing that God knows everything exhaustively ... but from believing he has the wisdom to handle any surprises that arise.... [He] voluntarily limits his own power so that the creature is able to decide things....[7]

Pinnock's depiction of God's knowledge of the future, in light of the hundreds of predictions that God makes about future events, and specifically about his Messiah, quite frankly places God within the ranks of the idols of this world and makes him no better than a soothsayer or a fortune-teller when he predicts the future, and it renders his prophecies, at best, wishful thinking. But for the God of the Bible nothing relating to the future is uncertain; there is no future event that is only a possibility until actualized by the will of man.

What these authors apparently *fail to realize* is that absolutely arbitrary future actions of people do not and cannot even exist because they do not exist in God's mind as an aspect of the universe whose every event he predetermined, creatively caused, and providentially preserves and governs. And what these authors apparently *fail to appreciate* is that were one square inch of this entire universe not under God's sovereign governance, indeed, were one infinitesimal atom not his to do with as he pleased, then that square inch, that

---

[7]Pinnock, 'Does God Relate?' *Academic Alert* (IVP's book bulletin, 3, no. 4).

infinitesimal atom, sovereign within themselves, would have the right to erect a sign that reads: 'Keep Out!' and God would cease to be the sovereign God, his universal kingdom would be undone, and he would have to share his glory with another. And the construction of these 'Openness' authors allows billions upon billions of sovereign human 'square inches' to flourish, virtually all of them denying by their self-acclaimed sovereignty God's sovereignty over them. But can we really imagine the sovereign Lord God of Hosts having to wait for those human 'square inches' to act before he knows what they will do or, having learned of their purposes, to apply to them for permission to redirect their aims? To deny to God comprehensive knowledge of the future and his sovereignty over mankind in order to preserve for mankind an alleged libertarian 'freedom of indifference' is, in my opinion, a radical false step that I hope none of us here will ever be willing to take, for I do not believe that 'openness theology' should be viewed, as Pinnock would urge, as a viable alternative to the classical doctrine of God's omniscience. Rather, it is a 'free will heresy' and God's people must be warned about it.[8]

Other Arminians, while they acknowledge that God infallibly knows the future with certainty, nevertheless contend that 'future certainty is not future necessity' and that mankind has the built-in ability *independently* and *freely* to create events. They thereby seek to save for mankind the 'freedom of indifference' by employing the semantic distinction between certainty and necessity. But their semantic exercise only props up their 'house of cards' and fails to convince logical minds. To see this

---

[8]I would recommend that pastors who want to read more about 'open theism' and how to respond to it should read Roger R. Nicole's review of *The Openness of God. A Biblical Challenge to the Traditional Understanding of God* in his *Standing Forth: Collected Writings of Roger Nicole* (Ross-shire, Scotland: Mentor/ Christian Focus, 2002), 397-401, and John M. Frame's *No Other God: A Response to Open Theism* (Phillipsburg, NJ: Presbyterian and Reformed, 2001), 191-203.

consider the following illustration of an observer on a high cliff:

> On the road below, to the observer's left, a car is being driven west. To the observer's right a car is coming south. He can see and know that there will be a collision at the intersection immediately beneath him. But his foreknowledge, so the argument runs, does not cause [that is, make necessary] the accident. Similarly, God is supposed to know the future without causing it.
>
> The similarity, however, is deceptive on several points. A human observer cannot really know that a collision will occur. Though it is unlikely, it is possible for both cars to have blowouts before reaching the intersection and swerve apart. It is also possible that the observer has misjudged the speeds, in which case one car could slow down and the other accelerate, so that they would not collide. The human observer, therefore, does not have infallible foreknowledge.
>
> No such mistakes can be assumed for God. The human observer may make a probable guess that the accident will occur, and this guess does not make the accident unavoidable; but if God knows, there is no possibility of avoiding the accident. A hundred years before the drivers were born, there was no possibility that either of them could have chosen to stay home that day, to have driven a different route, to have driven a different time, to have driven a different speed. They could not have chosen otherwise than as they did. This means either that they had no free will or that God did not know.
>
> Suppose it be granted, just for the moment, that divine foreknowledge, like human guesses, does not cause the foreknown event. Even so, if there is foreknowledge, in contrast with fallible guesses, free will is impossible. If man has free will, and things can be different, God cannot be omniscient. Some Arminians have admitted this and have denied omniscience [the open theists], but this puts them obviously at odds with Biblical Christianity. There is also another difficulty. If the

Arminian ... wishes to retain divine omniscience and at the same time assert that foreknowledge has no causal efficacy, he is put to it to explain how the collision was made certain a hundred years, an eternity, before the drivers were born. If God did not arrange the universe this way, who did?

If God did not arrange it this way, then there must be an independent factor in the universe. And if there is such, one consequence and perhaps two follow. First, the doctrine of creation must be abandoned.... Independent forces cannot be created forces, and created forces cannot be independent. Then, second, if the universe is not God's creation, his knowledge of it – past and future – cannot depend on what he intends to do, but on his observation of how it works. In such a case, how could we be sure that God's observations are accurate? How could we be sure that these independent forces will not later show an unsuspected twist that will falsify God's predictions? And finally, on this view God knowledge would be empirical, rather than an integral part of his essence, and thus he would be a dependent knower. These objections are insurmountable. We can consistently believe in creation, omnipotence, omniscience, and the divine decree. But we cannot retain sanity and combine any of these with free will.[9]

So much for Arminianism's belief in humankind's 'significant free will' that it declares is 'a key ingredient in the Arminian system and a necessary presupposition of the Arminian view of predestination'. Since humankind's 'significant free will' in the libertarian sense does not exist and cannot be justified in this particular theistic world in which the Bible places us, it is patently plain that its view of predestination is necessarily false.[10]

---

[9]Gordon H. Clark, *God and Evil* (Unicoi, TN: Trinity Foundation, 2004), 25-6; see also Jonathan Edwards, *Miscellaneous Observations* (1811 edition), Part II, chapter 3 (Volume VIII, 384).

[10]Interested readers may consult my *A New Systematic Theology of the Christian Faith*, 2nd edition (Nashville, TN: Thomas Nelson, 2001), chapter 10, for a full discussion of Arminian free-willism.

Well, once again this is enough pure theology. Let us now apply the doctrine of God's eternal and unchangeable omniscience for our spiritual benefit. I will make three applications and be done, the first having to do with us, the second with the church, and the third with Christ.

Application

My first application is this: Awareness of God's omniscience should *comfort and encourage believers*. The Scriptures inform us that no matter how bleak things appear to be in this world our wise God is in control and that all his acts are carried out in perfect wisdom to accomplish his wise and holy ends. The Scriptures also inform us that in our times of weariness and weakness, of discouragement and despair, the all-knowing God knows about our trials and that he 'works for the good of those who love him, who have been called according to his purpose' (Rom. 8:28). When we stumble and fall, 'he knows how we are formed; he remembers that we are dust' (Ps. 103:14). And he is concerned and will act to address our problem.

Awareness of his omniscience should also *restrain believers* from sin. Adam could not hide from God in Eden, Achan could not hide his theft of the banned booty from Jericho, and David could not cover up his adultery and murder. And neither can we hide our sin. God says to us, indeed, to all mankind, as well: 'Be sure *your* sin will find *you* out' (Num. 32:23). So don't sin! Avoid places of temptation; close to its evil ways your 'ear gate' and your 'eye gate' as you walk through this Vanity Fair world.

Awareness of God's omniscience also should *fill believers with amazement* and *awe*. The wisest mortal does not even know what the next minute will bring forth but all futurity down to the minutest detail is open to God's omniscient gaze.

Finally, awareness of God's omniscience should also *fill believers with worship, adoration, and praise* when they recall that God already knew their every lapse, their every sin, their every backsliding before the foundation of the world; yet, in spite of them all, he set his great heart of love upon them, and having loved them, gave his Son for them, and will love them to the end of the world, through the Final Judgment, and throughout all the ages of eternity to follow.

My second point of application is drawn from Paul's statement that God 'created all things in order that the "many-faceted" or "manifold" wisdom of God [*hē polupoikilos sophia tou theou*] might now be made known ... to the rulers and authorities in the heavenly places' (Eph. 3:9-10).

Here Paul informs us of the ultimate reason, insofar as the angelic order is concerned, for God's creation of the world, namely, that he might show to them his 'many-faceted wisdom'. God never says *anywhere* else – *polypoikilos*, is a *hapax legomenon* (a 'once spoken' word) – that by *anything* else the angels see such a display. And how does he display his 'many-faceted' or 'manifold wisdom' to them? Did he display it when he spoke suns and moons and stars into existence? Not as far as we are informed. Did he manifest it when he created this earth and in particular man, his image? Not as far as the Bible tells us. Did he display it by his general works of providence? Not as far as Scripture enlightens us. Then how does he display to the angelic world his 'many-faceted' or 'manifold wisdom'? Paul replies, *by the church of Jesus Christ, the redeemed community of God!* The grand object of the angels' attention today is the church because God's 'manifold wisdom' shines forth in and by it alone with undiminished luster. Into *its* things the angels long to look (1 Pet. 1:12). They observe our decorum in our worship services (1 Cor. 11:10). The church's very entryway – the gospel – is a display of the *wisdom* of God (1 Cor. 1:24), for therein is the *righteousness* of God revealed to faith (Rom. 1:16), and if by faith, then it is by the *grace* of God (Rom. 4:16).

The angels saw God's mighty power when he spoke the entire universe into existence. They saw the display of his awesome justice when he cast Satan out of heaven. But it is only in God's 'so great salvation' and the church he created by it, beginning with Genesis 3:15 onward, that they see by virtue of his 'manifold wisdom' particularly his grace, his love, his mercy, his pity, his kindness, his longsuffering, his gentleness displayed to the sinful sons and daughters of Adam. The church truly amazes them, and it ought to amaze us as well!

Does this give you some estimate of the importance and worth of the church? It should, for there are more 'sides' of the wisdom of God on display in the church, Paul declares, than in the entire creation throughout its length and breadth. There are more 'aspects' of the wisdom of God to behold in his saving of souls and 'fitly framing them together' into the church of Jesus Christ than in all the splendors of the natural universe. When the angels behold the ruin that sin brought upon us removed through the death and resurrection of our Savior Lord, they stand in utter amazement at God's 'manifold wisdom'. Even the poorest, lowliest, least gifted member of the church – now think for a moment: of the Christians you know, who in your estimation would you judge him or her to be? I hope at least some of you thought of yourselves! – well, even that person – the poorest, lowliest, least gifted Christian – exhibits to the angelic host of heaven God's 'manifold wisdom', and we should not despise that one but rather hold him in high esteem, for the angels surely do! This suggests that the most significant work God is doing in the world today is not the work of the United States of America or that of the United Nations – these are but instrumentalities in his plan to give to his Son his bride. Rather, it is the saving of souls and the building of Christ's church, and you men and women should humbly thank God that he has counted you worthy to serve him in its ministrations. Because I don't have time to develop this idea further here, I must simply refer you to my *Systematic Theology* where I develop it more fully in chapters ten and thirteen.

My third and final point of application has to do with God's infinite knowledge *vis à vis* Christ's identity. Is Jesus Christ really God the Son, the Second Person of the Holy Trinity? If you have been carefully listening to this address, I can believe that more than once your spirit has uttered: '[God's] knowledge is too wonderful for me; it is too high, I cannot attain to it' (Ps 139:6). For what mortal could or would even dare to claim equality with God in knowledge? Well, one mortal did – Jesus Christ! In Matthew 11:25-27 (and, by the way, Luke 10:21-22 is a close parallel, and appearing then as this saying does in both Matthew and Luke, according to the critic's own canons of textual criticism, insures that it came from the alleged but questionable early 'Q' source) Jesus said at the very moment that entire cities, indeed, his generation, were rejecting him:

> I praise you, Father, Lord of heaven and earth, because you have hidden these things [about me] from the wise and learned, and revealed them to little children. Yes, Father, for this was your good pleasure.... No one knows the Son except the Father, and no one knows the Father except the Son and those to whom the Son chooses to reveal him.

By these assertions (and you may want to turn in your Bibles at this time to Matthew 11:25-27) – assertions that Benjamin B. Warfield declared contain 'in some respects the most remarkable [utterances] in the whole compass of the four Gospels'[11] and that Geerhardus Vos judged to be 'by far the most important seat of the testimony which Jesus bears to his sonship' as well as being 'the culminating point of our Lord's self-disclosure

---

[11]Benjamin B. Warfield, *The Lord of Glory* (Reprint of 1907 edition; Grand Rapids: Baker, 1974), 82-3; see also 118-19.

in the Synoptics'[12] – by these assertions, I say, we are brought face to face with some of the most wonderful words Jesus ever spoke and several of the greatest claims he ever made.

Follow my exposition of the passage and discover for yourself that Matthew 11:25-27 (as well as its parallel in Luke 10:21-22) confronts us with some remarkable utterances of Jesus. We will focus on what I am calling 'the three great parallels' that Jesus draws between God as 'the Father' and himself as 'the loved Son' of Matthew 3:17. The *unique* and *intimate* nature of the Father–Son relationship Jesus asserts here of himself – higher than which it is impossible to conceptualize unless it be in certain of his utterances found in the Fourth Gospel such as 'I and the Father are one' (10:30) – comes to expression precisely in these parallels.

The first parallel that he draws is the *exclusive, mutual knowledge that God the Father and he the Son each has of the other.* Jesus declares in 11:27: 'No one knows the Son except the Father, and no one knows the Father except the Son.' The first thing I would note here is Jesus' dual employment of the same Greek verb (*epiginōskei*) to describe the Father's knowledge of him and his knowledge of the Father, which verb with its attached preposition *epi*, means, I would suggest, 'to know exactly, completely, through and through,'[13] implying in Jesus' case that the depths of the Father's Being, incomprehensibly infinite and as such inscrutable to the finite intelligence, his knowledge alone is competent to plumb. And the second thing I would note is Jesus' emphasis upon the *exclusiveness* of this mutual knowledge reflected by his twice-used

---

[12]Geerhardus Vos, *The Self-Disclosure of Jesus* (Reprint of 1926 edition; Phillipsburg, N.J.: Presbyterian and Reformed, 1978), 143.

[13]Bauer, Arndt, Gingrich, Danker, ἐπιγινώσκω, *A Greek-English Lexicon of the New Testament and other Early Christian Literature* (Second edition; Chicago: University Press, 1979), 291, a.

[14]The exclusiveness of Jesus' knowledge is not invalidated by his following remark, 'and to whomever the Son wills to reveal him,'

phrase, 'no one knows *except*' (*ei mē*).[14] Only a moment's reflection will show that the nature of this exclusive knowledge which Jesus claims to have lifts him above the sphere of the ordinary mortal and places him 'in a position, not of equality merely, but of absolute reciprocity and interpenetration of knowledge with the Father'.[15] Geerhardus Vos astutely observes:

> That essential rather than acquired knowledge is meant follows ... from the correlation of the [parallel] clauses: the knowledge God has of Jesus cannot be acquired knowledge [it must, from the fact that it is God's knowledge, be direct, intuited, and immediate – in a word, divine – knowledge, grounded in the fact that the Knower is divine[16]]; consequently the knowledge Jesus has of God cannot be acquired knowledge either [it too must be direct, intuited, and immediate – in a word, divine – knowledge], for these two are placed entirely on a line. In other words, if the one is different from human knowledge, then the other must be so likewise.[17]

The only conclusions that this correlation of the two clauses justly warrants are, first, that God possesses his exclusive and penetrating knowledge of the Son because he is God, the Father of the Son, and, second, that Jesus possesses his exclusive and penetrating knowledge of the Father because he is God, the Son of the Father.

The second parallel, which rests upon the first, comes to focus in Jesus' assertion of *the mutual necessity of God the Father and of him the Son each to reveal the other if men are ever to have an acquired*

---

since the very point of his statement is that other men must acquire their saving knowledge of the Father *from him* if they are to know him at all since he is the only one who knows him.

[15]Benjamin B. Warfield, 'The Person of Christ According to the New Testament' in *The Person and Work of Christ* (Philadelphia: Presbyterian and Reformed, 1950), 65.

[16]See George Eldon Ladd, *A Theology of the New Testament* (Grand Rapids: Eerdmans, 1974), 166.

[17]Vos, *The Self-Disclosure of Jesus*, 149.

saving knowledge of them. This parallel is highlighted
by Jesus' declaration in Matthew 11:25 that the Father
had hidden (*ekrypsas*) from the wise the mysteries of
the Kingdom that were *centered in him the Son* and had
revealed (*apekalypsas*) them to 'babes' (such as Peter
to whom, you will recall, Jesus said in Matthew 16:17:
'...flesh and blood has not revealed this to you, but my
Father who is in heaven') and his statement in 11:27
that 'no one knows the Father except the Son and those
to whom the Son chooses to *reveal* [*apokalupsai*] him.'
I call your attention again to Jesus' dual employment
of the same Greek verb (*apokalyptō*) to describe the
activities of the two: The Father must *reveal* the Son;
the Son must *reveal* the Father.

The third parallel Jesus draws is that of the *mutual
absolute sovereignty God the Father and the Son each
exercises in dispensing his knowledge of the other.* The
Father's sovereignty in this regard is displayed in Jesus'
words in 11:26: '...for this was your *good pleasure*
[*eudokia*]'; the Son's sovereignty is exhibited in his
words in 11:27: 'to whomever the Son *wills* [*boulētai*] to
reveal him.' A higher expression of parity between the
Father and the Son with respect to the possession of
the divine attribute of sovereignty in the dispensing of
saving knowledge is inconceivable. Jesus teaches here
by implication that no sinful creature has a right to such
revelation. If the creature ever learns about the Son it
is because the Father has sovereignly determined in his
grace to reveal him. If the creature ever learns about the
Father it is because the Son has sovereignly determined
in his grace to reveal him!

Warfield is surely justified when he summarizes
Jesus' amazing utterances in this pericope with these
words:

> ...in it our Lord asserts for Himself a relation of practical
> equality with the Father.... As the Father only can know
> the Son, so the Son only can know the Father: and
> others may know the Father only as He is revealed by

the Son. That is, not merely is the Son the exclusive revealer of God, but the mutual knowledge of Father and Son is put on what seems very much a par. The Son can be known only by the Father in all that He is, as if His being were infinite and as such inscrutable to the finite intelligence; and His knowledge alone – again as if He were infinite in His attributes – is competent to compass the depths of the Father's infinite being. He who holds this relation to the Father cannot conceivably be a creature.[18]

Can you understand better now why Jesus then issued the invitation: 'Come to me, all you who are weary and burdened, and I will give you rest'? He alone is the Revealer of the Father! He alone is the Father's 'Exegete' (John 1:18)! Jesus' invitation here provides a fourth and *formal* New Testament parallel to Yahweh's Old Testament invitation in Isaiah 45:22, as is clear if one places the two invitations in their several parts beside each other as follows:

God states in Isaiah 45:22: 'Turn to me, all the ends of the earth, and I will save you.'

Jesus states in Matthew 11:28: 'Come to me, all you who are weary and burdened, and I will give you rest.'

Here Jesus places himself centrally in and at the forefront of this invitation as the great healer of all of mankind's spiritual, mental and emotional problems. His invitation is *universal* in its all-encompassing comprehensiveness: '*all* you who are weary and burdened.' That includes everyone here. And his invitation is *unqualified* in its promise to grant the blessing of rest to all who come to him ('and *I will* give you rest'). It contains no qualifying clauses. Such an invitation would be nothing less than grossly audacious – indeed, it would be indicative of

---

[18]Warfield, *The Lord of Glory*, 82-3; see also 118-19.

delusions of grandeur – were it to come from the lips of any other person. No pastor, however great his gifts, abilities, and fame, has ever dared to issue such an invitation. Nor would it ever enter his mind to do so. But were he to do so, the entire world would scoff at him and would have the right to ask him, 'How do you have the temerity to say such a thing?' And if he continued to issue such an invitation, the world would have the right to judge him to be insane. And yet millions and millions of Christians through the ages have testified that such an invitation is perfectly proper and the very model of sanity on the lips of Jesus, for they have discovered, in light of the fact that he is God incarnate, that he can keep and has indeed kept this promise and they have found rest for their souls through faith in him.

So now I must ask you: Have *you*, tired and weary one, heeded his invitation and have you come – I mean, really come in trustful repose – to Jesus Christ for your rest? Have you come humbly, not as his equal or as his teacher, but as one who is at the end of himself in order to become his disciple? Have you taken his yoke upon you and begun to sit at his feet as his disciple and to learn about his Father, and are you learning from him daily about his Father? Only as you do so will you 'find rest for your souls'.

Why do you delay? You have no need to hold back or to fear *this* divine Teacher, for *this* Teacher is gentle and humble in heart, his yoke is easy, and the burden of discipleship that he places upon you is *infinitely* lighter than the burden of sin you presently bear. So respond now to his invitation. Come to him, I implore you, and find

> that rest that can be found nowhere else,
> that rest that can be found only in him,
> that rest that alone can deliver you *from* the guilt and power of sin and hell,
> that rest that alone can save you *for* a life of fruitfulness and heaven.

Come to him now, I beg you, tired and weary one, and trust his teaching to meet your every need.

Let us pray:
Our Father and our God – the only wise God – to whom belongs all praise and glory, through Jesus Christ, forever: I stand in awe of your creative wisdom when I view the pictures of this universe that are being sent back to earth in our day from the Hubble space telescope. And surely there is reason for such awe because the universe does display your eternal wisdom. But this morning, my Father, I'm overcome by the display of your manifold wisdom revealed to the angelic hosts in the gospel of Jesus Christ and his church. May sinful mortals also stand with the angel bands and sing of your 'amazing grace'? I trust so, for indeed,

> I stand amazed in the presence of Jesus the Nazarene,
> and wonder how he could love me, a sinner condemned, unclean.
> O how marvelous, O how wonderful, and my song shall ever be,
> O how marvelous, O how wonderful, is my Savior's love for me.

And in light of Paul's declaration that your manifold wisdom is on display nowhere else than in the church of Jesus Christ, what more can we mortals say?

> 'Tis mystery all! Th'Immortal dies:
> who can explore his strange design?
> In vain the first-born seraph tries
> to sound the depths of love divine.
> 'Tis mercy all! Let earth adore,
> Let angel minds inquire no more.
> Amazing love! How can it be
> that thou, my God, shouldst die for me?

In Christ's redeeming name, our God, we bring our praise and adoration as beneficiaries of your 'so great salvation' to you. And should someone here not yet know the sweetness of your salvation, move him to close with you through Christ this very hour. Amen.

Sixth Address

'Infinite, Eternal, and Unchangeable in His Power'

Then Moses and the Israelites sang this song to the Lord:

'I will sing to the Lord, for he is highly exalted. The horse and its rider he has hurled into the sea. The Lord is my strength and my song; he has become my salvation. He is my God, and I will praise him, my father's God, and I will exalt him. The Lord is a warrior; the Lord is his name. Pharaoh's chariots and his army he has hurled into the sea. The best of Pharaoh's officers are drowned in the Red Sea. The deep waters have covered them; they sank to the depths like a stone.

'Your right hand, O Lord, was majestic in power. Your right hand, O Lord, shattered the enemy. In the greatness of your majesty you threw down those who opposed you. You unleashed your burning anger; it consumed them like stubble. By the blast of your nostril the waters piled up. The surging waters stood firm like a wall; the deep waters congealed in the heart of the sea.

'The enemy boasted, "I will pursue, I will overtake them. I will divide the spoils; I will gorge myself on them. I will draw my sword and my hand will destroy them." But you blew with your breath, and the sea covered them. They sank like lead in the mighty waters.

'Who among the gods is like you, O LORD? Who is like you – majestic in holiness, awesome in glory, working wonders? You stretched out your right hand and the earth swallowed them.

'In your unfailing love you will lead the people you have redeemed. In your strength you will guide them to your holy dwelling. The nations will hear and tremble; anguish will grip the people of Philistia. The chiefs of Edom will be terrified, the leaders of Moab will be seized with trembling, the people of Canaan will melt away; terror and dread will fall upon them. By the power of your arm they will be as still as a stone – until your people pass by, O LORD, until the people you bought pass by. You will bring them in and plant them on the mountain of your inheritance – the place, O LORD, you made for your dwelling, the sanctuary, O Lord, your hands established. The LORD will reign for ever and ever' (Exod. 15:1-18)

Introduction

Good morning, beloved brothers and sisters in Christ: Grace to you and peace from God our Father and the Lord Jesus Christ. I've been praying that through these chapel addresses the God of our Lord Jesus Christ may give you the Spirit of wisdom so that you may know the triune God of your salvation more fully and more profoundly. For it is only the God whom you know that you preachers can or will preach from your pulpits and teach from your lecterns someday. And if your God is 'small' your preaching will not expect much of him or of your congregations. Conversely, if your God is great – the living, infinite, tri-personal God of Scripture – then your preaching will exhibit that fact and both your own life and the lives of your people will reflect his majesty and greatness. That is to say, every aspiring preacher here will either be a 'little-God-er' or a 'big God-er'. And we faculty members are earnestly desirous that you all will be the latter – 'big God-ers.'

Now it doesn't take much daring on my part to say that never has the need been greater for Spirit-animated preachers who can stand in pulpits across the world and with power and in proportion proclaim and 'rightly handle' for their congregations the attributes of God. A dearth of biblical preaching exists today on this subject, so we should not be surprised at the great theological illiteracy that abounds in this country and around the world regarding what the one living and true God is really like. Most people, if they profess to believe in God at all, regard him as an indulgent, grandfatherly 'man upstairs' who, while he himself has no relish for folly, leniently winks at their 'youthful indiscretions' and who always has their best interests at heart. He doesn't ask much of them and they don't ask much of him other than just speedily to be there with help if and when they need him for something. At all other times he is free to do as he pleases as long as he lets them do their own thing.

I believe this series of addresses has already shown how seriously flawed is such a perception of God; and to put it plainly, there is one and only one remedy for such broad-based theological illiteracy, and that is to train a generation of men who, to paraphrase our *Larger Catechism*, Question 159, will preach sound biblical doctrine about the one living and true God in the following ways:

first, *diligently*, in season and out of season, that is to say, when they feel like doing it and when they do not feel like doing it; when their congregations want to hear sound doctrine about God and when they do not want to hear sound doctrine about him;

second, *plainly*, not in the enticing words of man's wisdom, but in demonstration of the Spirit and of power;

third, *faithfully*, making known the whole counsel of the triune God who, as we have been affirming, is infinite, eternal, and unchangeable in his being, wisdom, power, holiness, justice, goodness, and truth;

fourth, *wisely*, applying themselves to the necessities and capacities of their hearers, being always as wise as serpents and as harmless as doves toward them;

fifth, *zealously*, with fervent love for God and for the salvation of the souls of their people from sin and hell and for Christ's service and heaven; and

sixth and finally, *sincerely*, aiming at God's glory and their people's conversion, edification, and final salvation.

Before we begin today's address on God's infinite, eternal, and unchangeable power, let us pray for his blessing upon your faithful attendance upon what I am about to say:

Prayer:
Almighty God, our heavenly Father, and Jesus Christ, our Lord and equally mighty Savior, drawn once again to this assembly today both by your blessed Holy Spirit who is eternally and co-equally God with you, the Father and the Son, and by your triune mercies, enable us through our attendance upon your Word

> to know you more perfectly,
> to adore you more fully, and
> to serve you more single-mindedly.

Grant to me the ability to proclaim the truth, and only the truth, about your sovereign power, and grant your Spirit's anointing upon this assembly of faculty, students, and friends that they may truly hear my words with that special set of ears that Jesus intended when he said: 'Let him who has ears to hear, let him hear.' May they heed my words in this hour as Heaven's message to them. Prevent them from trivializing my thoughts into simple entertainment. Give to us what you know we need. Make my words about your power powerful 'armies' and this chapel hour full of blessing, indeed, a harvest time yielding high and eternal good to each of us.

All these things I ask for our souls' health and for the glory and cause of Jesus Christ our Lord. Amen.

* * *

According to Holy Scripture the one living and true God is all-powerful or, to use the common Latinized term for it, he is *omnipotent*, infinitely, eternally and unchangeably so. This means that his power can be neither increased since it is already infinite nor diminished since it is eternally unchangeable. This also means that 'God is able to do whatever he wills in the way in which he wills it'.[1] That he is not subject to another's dominion but is rather the sovereign King and Lord of the entire Universe that he created is a legitimate inference from his attribute of omnipotence. Scripture passages could fill pages to this effect but the following fourteen passages will suffice to make my point:

Texts

Genesis 17:1: God revealed himself to Abraham by his name *'ēl shaddai*, translated 'God Almighty' because in the contexts in which it occurs in the Pentateuch (Gen. 17:1; 28:3; 35:11; 43:14; 48:3; 49:25; Exod. 6:3) God subjects 'nature' to his wise and gracious 'supernature' purposes and compels it to advance his predetermined ends.

Genesis 18:14: The Lord himself asks: *'Is anything too hard for the LORD [hᵃyippālē' mēyhwh dābhār*, lit., 'Is [such] a thing [as enabling barren Sarah to have a child] too wonderful for the LORD?':* a rhetorical

---

[1]Gordon R. Lewis, 'God, Attributes of' in *Evangelical Dictionary of Theology*, edited by Walter A. Elwell (Grand Rapids: Baker, 1984), 457-8.

question that, from its context, expects a negative response.

Exodus 15:6-11: After the exodus Moses sang of God's deliverance of Israel from Egypt by his awesome might and power: 'Your right hand, O LORD, was majestic in power, your right hand, O LORD, scattered the enemy. In the greatness of your majesty you threw down those who opposed you. You unleashed your burning anger; it consumed them like stubble. By the blast of your nostrils the waters piled up. The surging water stood firm like a wall; the deep waters congealed in the heart of the sea. The enemy boasted.... But you blew with your breath, and the sea covered them. They sank like lead in the mighty waters. Who among the gods is like you, O LORD? Who is like you – majestic in holiness, awesome in glory [power], *working wonders* [*'ôseh phele'*]?'

Psalm 18:13-15: 'The LORD thundered from heaven; the voice of the Most High resounded. He shot his arrows and scattered the enemies, great bolts of lightning and routed them. The valleys of the sea were exposed and the foundations of the earth laid bare at your rebuke, O LORD, at the blast of breath from your nostrils.

Psalm 89:8-13: 'O LORD God of Hosts, who is like you? You are mighty, O LORD, and your faithfulness surrounds you. You rule over the surging sea; when its waves mount up, you still them. You crushed Rahab [Egypt]...; with your strong arm you scattered your enemies. The heavens are yours, and yours also is the earth; you founded the world and all that is in it. You created the north and the south.... Your arm is endued with power; your hand is strong, your right hand exalted.'

Job 38:4-6: 'Where were you,' God asks Job, 'when I laid the earth's foundation? Tell me if you understand. Who marked off its dimensions? ...Who stretched a measuring line across it? On what were its footings set, or who laid its cornerstone? [Did not I, the Lord?']

Isaiah 7:11: To hypocritical Ahaz God said: 'Ask the LORD your God for a sign, whether in the deepest depths or in the highest heights [that is, 'Ask me anything at all, and I will do it].' It is clear that God was thinking 'miracle' when he extended this open-ended invitation to Ahaz.

Isaiah 40:12, 15, 17-18, 22-23, 25-26, 28-31: 'Who has measured the waters in the hollow of his hand, or with the breadth of his hand marked off the heavens? Who has held the dust of the earth in a basket, or weighed the mountains on the scales and the hills in a balance? *...Surely the nations are like a drop in a bucket; they are regarded as dust on the scales; he weighs the islands as though they were fine dust. ...Before him all the nations are as nothing; they are regarded by him as worthless and less than nothing.* To whom then will you compare God? ...He sits enthroned above the circle of the earth, and *its people are like grasshoppers.* He stretches out the heavens like a canopy, and spreads them out like a tent to live in. He brings princes to naught and reduces the rulers of this world to nothing.... 'To whom will you compare me? Or who is my equal?' says the Holy One. Lift your eyes and look to the heavens: Who created all these? He who brings out the starry host one by one, and calls them each by name. Because of his *great power* [*rōbh 'ônîm*] and *mighty strength* [*'ammîts*] not one of them is missing.... Do you not know? Have you not heard? The LORD is the everlasting God, the Creator of the ends of the earth. He will not grow tired or weary.... He gives strength to the weary and increases the power of the weak. Even youths grow tired and weary, and young men stumble and fall; but those who hope in the LORD will renew their strength. They will soar on wings like eagles; they will run and not grow weary, they will walk and not be faint.'

Jeremiah 32:17, 26-27: Jeremiah prayed: 'Ah, Sovereign
LORD, you have made the heavens and the earth by
your great power and outstretched arm. *Nothing is too
wonderful for you [lô' yippālē' mimmᵉkā kôl dābār]'*....
Then the word of the LORD came to Jeremiah: 'I am
the LORD, the God of all mankind. *Is anything too
wonderful for me [hᵃmimmennî yippālē' kōl dābhār]?'*
– this last question being again rhetorical, expecting
a negative response.

Daniel 4:34-35: '[God's] dominion is an eternal
dominion.... All the peoples of the earth are regarded
as nothing. He does as he pleases with the powers
of heaven and the peoples of the earth. No one can
hold back his hand or say to him: "What have you
done?"'

Matthew 3:9: John the Baptist declared: 'God is able
from these stones to raise up children to Abraham.'

Matthew 19:26: Jesus himself says: 'With God all things
are possible [*para de theō panta dunata*].'

Luke 1:34, 37: To Mary's question: 'How will this
[conception come about] since I am a virgin?'
Gabriel replied: '*Nothing is impossible with God [ouk
adunatēsei para tou theou pan rhēma]*.'

Ephesians 1:19-20: Paul speaks here of God's
'*incomparably great power [to hyperballon megethos
tēs dynameōs]* ... according to *the working of his
mighty strength [tēn energeian tou kratous tēs ischuos
autou]*, which he exerted in Christ when he raised
him from the dead.'

Revelation 19:6: John summarizes the entire teaching
of Scripture on this topic by declaring that '*the Lord
God omnipotent reigns [ebasileusen kurios ho theos ho
pantokratōr]*,' *ho pantokratōr* ('omnipotent'), being the
New Testament counterpart of the two Old Testament
titles of God, *'ēl shaddai* ('God Almighty'), and *yhwh
tsᵉbhā'ôth* ('Lord, [God] of Hosts').

The doctrine

These verses and passages teach what the totality of Scripture consistently and repeatedly declares – that God's works of creation, general and special providence, redemption, and the consummation of all things are all effects of his mighty power. Charles Haddon Spurgeon writes:

> God's power is like Himself, self-existent, self-sustained. The mightiest of men cannot add so much as a shadow of increased power to the Omnipotent One. He sits on no buttressed throne and leans on no assisting arm. His court is not maintained by His courtiers, nor does it borrow its splendor from His creatures. He is Himself the great central source and Originator of all power.[2]

And before Spurgeon, Stephen Charnock declared that God's power is such that 'he can do whatsoever he pleases without difficulty, without resistance; it cannot be checked, restrained, [or] frustrated'[3] by the creature. If this were not so, how vain would be his eternal counsels, how empty would be his promises, how 'scarecrowish' would be his threatenings! But 'power belongs to God' (Ps. 62:11), and we may be certain that, though he uses his power judiciously – which is just to say that his power is ever a controlled and never a 'wild' power operating without direction or purpose – he can and does use it according to his good pleasure to accomplish whatever he pleases.

Let's develop our doctrine a little more for the sake of precision: just two points here: My first point – now listen carefully – is this: *it is inherently impossible for the infinitely powerful God ever to employ all of his power.* To say that he can immediately places a limitation upon it.

---

[2] Cited by Arthur W. Pink, *The Attributes of God* (Reprint; Grand Rapids: Baker, 1975), 47.

[3] Stephen Charnock, *The Existence and Attributes of God* (Reprint; Grand Rapids: Baker, 1996), 2:14.

The fact of the matter is that to nothing in the Universe or to the Universe itself can I direct your attention as the visible result or the display of the full exercise of his *omni*potence, that is, *all* of his power. Granted, this Universe, from mankind's perspective, is titanically immense and awesomely glorious. To give you some sense of its immensity, let's reconfigure our Universe for a moment: Imagine our sun[4] – a medium-sized star[5] in the Milky Way galaxy that is comprised of billion of stars, star clusters, nebulae, and globular clusters – the size of a ping-pong ball. Planet earth would then be the size of a speck of dust one/one hundredth of an inch across orbiting that ball ten feet away. Pluto, our sun's most distant known 'demated' planet (Sedna, a recently-discovered planet-like body three times as far from the Sun as Pluto, excepted), would be a smaller speck within the sun's gravitational pull, orbiting that ping-pong ball one hundred and twenty yards away. The next nearest star to us in our galaxy after the sun, Alpha Centauri, being in actual miles some four and a half light years distant[6] or around twenty-seven trillion miles away, would be in our imagined Universe roughly five hundred miles away! Andromeda, our sister galaxy with an estimated hundred billion stars – one of nearly

---

[4]For this illustration I have embellished the suggestion made by Kenneth D. Boa and Robert M. Bowman, Jr., *20 Compelling Evidences That God Exists* (Tulsa, OK: RiverOak, 2002), 68.

[5]Our sun may be a medium-sized star but it is hardly an ordinary star, that is, one of the so-called 'red dwarfs' that make up eighty percent of the stars in the Milky Way galaxy or the 'G dwarfs' that comprise another ten percent, both groups being far less massive than our sun. Rather, it is among the ten percent most massive stars in our galaxy known as 'yellow dwarfs,' the G2 Spectral Type, with just the right mass, the right light, the right composition, the right stability, the right distance from the earth, the right orbit in the right galaxy to nurture living organisms on this particular circling planet – a rare star indeed!

[6]A light year, the distance that light traveling 186,000+ miles a second travels in a year, is slightly less than six trillion miles, 5,865,696,000,000+ miles to be more precise.

one trillion other observed galaxies of different sizes and shapes – being in actual miles three million light years distant or around eighteen million trillion miles away, would be in our model Universe three hundred and fifty million miles away from our ping-pong-ball sun. Do we need to say any more? Clearly, from our point of view – and this is gross understatement – ours is an immense Universe. But even so, this entire Universe with all its grandeur is the display of only a portion of God's power and an infinitesimal portion at that, for the plenitude of his power is measureless. There is no reason to assume that he could not have made a trillion more galaxies or a trillion more varieties of flora and fauna had he willed to do so. In fact, he was not 'exercised' in the slightest or to any degree by his creative activity. He merely 'spoke and [this Universe] came to be; he commanded, and it stood firm' (Ps. 33:9).

How does Job describe in Job 26:5-14 what for us is this vast Universe with all of its intricate details and inter-related workings – and even then, it still comes infinitely short of the reality? The cosmos with all that it contains, Job strikingly declares, reflects but the 'outer fringe' [*qᵉtsôth*] of his power, just a 'faint whisper' [*shēmets*] of his might. But of God's infinite power – well, Job says: 'Who ... can understand *the thunder of his power* [*ra'am gᵉbhûrōthāw*]?' Habakkuk also strikingly states that when God shook the earth, scattered the ancient mountains, split the earth with rivers, and caused the sun and the moon to stand still with 'rays from his hand', 'even there, his power *was hidden* [*wᵉshām hebhyôn 'uzzāh*]' (Hab. 3:4). O. Palmer Robertson comments: 'Rays of unapproachable glory stream from his [creative and chastening] hand; what then must be the nature of this power and glory hidden in his clenched fist!'[7] In other words, so inconceivably immense is the power of God,

---

[7]O. Palmer Robertson, *The Books of Nahum, Habakkuk, and Zephaniah* (NICOT; Grand Rapids: Eerdmans, 1990), 225.

declares Habakkuk, that the power he creatively displays in the natural Universe and providentially exhibits in the history of this Universe actually *conceals* far more of his infinite power than it reveals. Stephen Charnock rightly stated in this regard:

> When I have spoken of Divine power all that I can, when you have thought all that you can think of it, your souls will prompt you to conceive something more beyond what I have spoken and you have thought ... there is infinitely more power lodged in His nature [that is] not expressed in the world.[8]

In sum, this Universe *constitutes more a hiding of his power than a revelation of it!* God has the power to do infinitely beyond what he has revealed to date by all his works. This entire Universe, for all its spectacular grandeur in *our* eyes, is only a pale reflection, a dim shadow, a faint whisper of the thunderous infinitude of his power, indeed, a 'hiding' of the immeasurable immensity of the power and might of his hand! God's power is simply incomprehensible to us, as we might well expect it to be, given the fact of God's infinitude. Professor Huxley's words are quite apropos here: 'We must sit down before [these] facts *as little children.*'

The Scriptures intend then when they ascribe omnipotence to God that he has the power to do whatever it takes power to do. He has the power to do even that which he does not will to do, and the only reason he does not exercise his power in such arenas is that he does not will to do so. But whatever he wills to do, which is not determined by any limitation upon his power but only by his own nature and his wise, just and holy purpose, he has the power to do. And while God does not will to do all that he has the power to do, he *can* do and *does* do *all his holy will!* As John

---

[8]Stephen Charnock, *Discourses on the Existence and Attributes of God*, 2:9-10.

Frame states: 'God's power always accomplishes his purpose. God does not intend to bring about everything he values, but he never fails to bring about what he intends.'[9] God has the power, for example, to rid the world of all its evil at this very moment, but for wise and holy reasons, eternally determined before the creation of the world, among these reasons being his design to gather to himself his elect throughout the ages, he does not will to do so yet.[10]

My second point of development is this: when we speak of God's omnipotence and say that God has the power to do anything he wants, we must make clear to our congregations when we say this that we do not mean that God can do *anything*: He can do neither the logically irrational nor that which is ontologically or ethically contrary to his nature. I will explain what I mean here by two sub-points: First, God cannot do the logically irrational, that is, the self-contradictory, nor would he even try to do so because he is rational and contradictions are eternal disruptions of his rationality. He cannot make or think that two and two are five; he cannot make four-cornered triangles or square circles; he cannot make a stone too heavy for him to lift; he cannot create adjacent mountains with no valley between them. These are 'pseudo-tasks' (Mavrodes), 'imaginary inventions' (Bray), totally unrelated to power, that cannot exist in reality, and all one has to do in order to verify to himself that what I have just said is true is to ask himself: 'How much *power* would it take to make a wrong answer in

---

[9]John M. Frame, *No Other God: A Response to Open Theism* (Phillipsburg, NJ: Presbyterian and Reformed, 2001), 113.

[10]This 'yet' is the Christian's answer to the unbeliever's framing of the problem of evil. God, he says, cannot be both all good and all powerful because of the presence of evil in the world, for if he were all good he would rid the world of evil but since he does not do so he must not be omnipotent; if he were omnipotent he could rid the world of evil but since he does not do so he must not be all good. The Christian simply replies that God is all good and hates evil and has the power to rid the world of it but he will do so when he sees fit.

arithmetical calculation, without changing anything, the correct answer?' to realize that such pseudo-tasks belong to the domain of logic (and are condemned by it) and not to the domain of power at all.

Second, God cannot do that which is ontologically or ethically contrary to his nature. He

♦ cannot cease to exist or cease to be God; and he
♦ cannot divest himself of any of his attributes, which would be tantamount to his ceasing to be God. And, as we just argued, he
♦ cannot exercise all of his power since it has no limits. Nor can he
♦ change (Num. 23:19; 1 Sam. 15:29; Mal. 3:6), or
♦ disown himself (2 Tim. 2:13: *arnēsasthai heauton ou dunatai*), or
♦ lie (Titus 1:2: *apseudēs*; Heb. 6:17-18: *adunaton pseusasthai*), or
♦ break a promise (2 Cor. 1:20), or
♦ ignore sin (Hab. 1:13; *lô' thûkal*, lit. 'you cannot'), or
♦ be tempted to sin (Jas. 1:13: *apeirastos estin kakōn*), or
♦ allow his grace to override his justice; if he would be the justifier of sinful men in his grace, he must still be just and uphold his law and have a valid ground for such justification (Rom. 3:25-26), which ground, of course, is the work of Christ.

Such divine 'cannots', far from detracting from God's glory 'are his glory, and for us to refrain from reckoning with such 'impossibilities' [for God] would be to deny his glory and his perfection.'[11]

This then is what we mean when we say that God is 'infinite, eternal, and unchangeable in his power'.

---

[11]John Murray, *Redemption – Accomplished and Applied* (Grand Rapids: Eerdmans, 1955), 13.

And I think you will agree with me when I say that our Reformed doctrine of God's omnipotence is truly mind-expanding and awe-inspiring. Let's apply this doctrine now to our lives.

Application

I have only two major points of application, each with its sub-points: The first has to do with God's sovereignty. We cannot speak of God's omnipotence without speaking of the *exercise* of that almighty power over his creation and all things in it, including mankind. This absolute exercise of power we speak of as his *sovereignty*, and his almighty power is the guarantor of his sovereignty. His sovereignty is his absolute rule over the creation, backed by his omnipotent arm. His is the transcendent invincible supremacy in decrees, in predestination, in actual government of nature, human life and the world's societies, and in final consummation. And because God's wisdom and power are infinite and unchangeable, we have every right to declare that God, who moves ceaselessly and effortlessly to accomplish his purposes, is *absolutely* sovereign over his Universe. Never is his decretive will thwarted by anyone or anything; never is his wise design frustrated; never is his eternal purpose checkmated; never does any man veto God's eternal plan for him. All things and all creatures serve and shall ever continue to serve his holy will. Even angelic and human sin and evil have their instrumental roles to play in his sovereign plan so that when he creates the whirlwind it is because he proposes to ride upon the storm.[12] The Apostle Paul declares that God works *all* things in conformity with the counsel of his will (Eph. 1:11), causes *all* things to work together for good for those

---

[12]For fuller discussion and defense of this assertion, see Gordon H. Clark, *God and Evil: The Problem Solved* (Unicoi, TN: Trinity Foundation, 2004), and my *A New Systematic Theology of the Christian Faith* (Second edition; Nashville, TN: Thomas Nelson, 2002), chapter 10: 'The Eternal Decree of God.'

who love him (Rom. 8:28), and is bringing *all* things in heaven and on earth together under the headship of Christ (Eph. 1:10). Our *Catechism*, Question 7, declares: 'The decrees of God are, his eternal purpose, according to the counsel of his will, whereby, for his own glory he hath foreordained *whatsoever* comes to pass,' and in Question 11 it defines God's works of providence as 'his most holy, wise, and *powerful* preserving and governing *all* his creatures, and *all* their actions.' And both Testaments are filled with illustrations and didactic statements concerning God's sovereign providential governance of all his creatures and all their actions. The following are but a tiny sampling of passages that might be cited:

♦ All of the main characters of Genesis – Noah, Abraham, Isaac, Jacob, and Joseph – God *chose* in his sovereignty to their positions of covenant blessing.

♦ Joseph declared that the wicked treatment he had received at the hands of his brothers had been an essential element of God's sovereign plan to save Jacob's family during the time of famine (Gen. 45:7; 50:20).

♦ Job affirmed God's sovereignty over all men and all of life in Job 12:10-24:

In [God's] hand is the life of every creature
and the breath of all mankind....
To God belong wisdom and power;
counsel and understanding are his.
What he tears down cannot be rebuilt;
the man he imprisons cannot be released.
If he holds back the waters,
there is drought;
if he lets them loose,
they devastate the land.
To him belong strength and victory;

both deceived and deceiver are his.
He leads counselors away stripped
and makes fools of judges.
He takes off the shackles put on by kings
and ties a loincloth around their waist....
He silences the lips of trusted advisors
and takes away the discernment of elders.
He pours contempt on nobles
and disarms the mighty....
He makes nations great, and destroys them;
he enlarges nations, and disperses them.
He deprives the leaders of the earth of their
    reason;
he sends them wandering through a trackless
    waste.

♦ God declared that it is he who makes man 'dumb or deaf, or seeing or blind' (Exod. 4:11), and that he would harden Pharaoh's heart throughout the course of the ten plagues precisely in order to 'multiply' his signs so that he might place his sovereign power in the boldest possible relief (Exod. 10:1; 11:9).

♦ On the eve of Israel's conquest of Canaan Moses informed Israel that God had sovereignly chosen them, not because of their greatness or their righteousness, but simply because he loved them (Deut. 7:6-8; 9:4-6).

♦ With regard to God's sovereign election, the psalmist declares: 'Blessed is the man you choose and cause to approach your courts' (Ps. 65:4).

♦ The psalmist exclaims: 'Our God is in the heavens; he does whatever he pleases' (Ps. 115:3).

♦ Again the psalmist declares: 'The LORD does whatever pleases him, in the heavens and on the earth, in the seas and all their depths' (Ps. 135:6).

161

♦ The wise man of Proverbs 16 acclaimed God's sovereign rule over men when he declared: 'To man belong the plans of the heart, but from the LORD comes the reply of the tongue' (v. 1); again, 'The LORD has made everything for himself, even the wicked for the day of evil' (v. 4); yet again, 'In his heart a man plans his course, but the LORD determines his steps' (v. 9); and still yet again, 'The lot is cast into the lap, but its every decision is from the LORD' (v. 33). This is just to say that 'man may propose his things, but it is God who disposes all things.'

♦ The wise man of Proverbs continues in the same vein: 'Many are the plans in a man's heart, but it is the LORD's purpose that prevails' (Prov. 19:21); again, 'The king's heart is in the hand of the LORD; he directs it like a watercourse wherever he pleases' (Prov. 21:1); and yet again, 'There is no wisdom, no insight, no plan that can succeed against the LORD' (Prov, 21:30).

♦ God says in Isaiah 14:24, 27: 'Surely, as I have planned, so it will be, and as I have purposed so it will stand.... For the LORD Almighty has purposed, and who can thwart him?'

♦ In Isaiah 46:10-11 he again declares his sovereignty: 'I make known the end from the beginning, from ancient times, what is still to come. I say: My purpose will stand, and I will do as I please.'

---

[13]Some authorities have opined that the Asian tsunami of December 26, 2004 is the worst natural disaster that has ever occurred in recorded human history. Hardly! The flood of Genesis 6–8 destroyed all mankind except for eight people. But even that event will not be the greatest natural disaster, for this present earth and all its works will in the eschatological Day of the Lord 'be burned up' and 'the elements will melt with fire' (2 Pet. 3:10, 12). God was and will be behind all these events as he works out his kingly will and puts all of his enemies under his Son's feet (1 Cor. 15:25-27)!

♦ Amos queried: 'When disaster[13] comes to a city, has not the LORD caused it' (Amos 3:6).

♦ Daniel 4:31-32, 34-35 declares: '...the Most High is sovereign over the kingdoms of men and gives them to anyone he wishes.... His dominion is an eternal dominion; his kingdom endures from generation to generation. All the peoples of the earth are regarded as nothing. He does as he pleases with the powers of heaven and the peoples of the earth. No one can hold back his hand or say to him: "What have you done?"'

♦ Jesus taught in John 6:44, 45, 65: 'No one can come to me unless the Father ... draws him,' no one can come to me unless the Father teaches him to come, and 'no one can come to me unless the Father has enabled him.'

♦ Jesus also taught in John 15:16: 'You did not choose me, but I chose you...'; and to Pilate he declared in John 19:11: 'You could have no authority against me, except it were given you from above.'

♦ Peter declared that the treatment and death by crucifixion inflicted on the Son of God by the wicked hands of men were in accordance with 'the predetermined plan and foreknowledge of God' (Acts 2:23). (Here is one of the clearest biblical assertions to the effect that God decreed evil.)

♦ The entire early church in Jerusalem affirmed God's sovereignty over all of life, and specifically over Herod, Pilate, the Roman soldiers, and the Jewish religious leadership when it declared that all that been done to Jesus was 'what [God's] power and will had decided beforehand should happen' (Acts 4:28).

♦ In the following passages Paul teaches that it is 'by God's doing [not ours] that we are in Christ Jesus' (1 Cor. 1:30):

Romans 8:29: '...those God foreknew he also predestined to be conformed to the likeness of his Son.'

Romans 9:15-18: 'For [God] says to Moses: "I will have mercy on whom I will have mercy, and I will have compassion on whom I will have compassion." [Salvation] does not, therefore, depend on man's willing or trying, but on God's mercy.... Therefore, God has mercy on whom he wants to have mercy, and he hardens whom he wants to harden.'

Ephesians 1:4-5, 11: '[God] chose us in [Christ] before the creation of the world.... In love he predestined us to be adopted as his sons through Jesus Christ, in accordance with his pleasure and will....In [Christ] we were also chosen, having been predestined according to the plan of him who works everything in conformity with the purpose of his will.'

Titus 3:5: '[God] saved us, not because of righteous things we had done, but because of his mercy.'

2 Timothy 1:9: '[God] saved us and called us with a holy calling, not because of anything we have done, but because of his own purpose and grace that was given us in Christ Jesus from all eternity.'

♦ Finally, Paul declares in summary: 'For from him and through him and to him are *all* things' (Rom. 11:36).

These are just a few of the scriptural affirmations that compelled John Calvin to write: 'God's will is, and rightly ought to be, the cause of all things that are.'[14] They also make clear how gravely in error is the Arminian system

---

[14]John Calvin, *Institutes*, 3.23.2.

when it rejects the Calvinistic view of predestination that teaches that God's sovereign decree determines all human actions and destinies and substitutes for it on God's part a *laissez-faire* posture toward man's choices and actions and on man's part the complete libertarian freedom to choose any one of two or more incompatible courses of action with equal ease. And they also underscore the simple fact that *the triune God is not only mankind's but also the Christian's sovereign king*. We, therefore, as his redeemed subjects, should submit to him, make his Word the lamp for our feet and the light for our pathway, and obey every normative precept of his law.

My second point of application is this: the New Testament relates God's power specifically to his works of redemption and consummation. In connection with the former work, that of redemption, we are informed that

♦ It was the power of the Spirit that created the human nature of our Lord: To Mary the angel declared: '...the power [that is, the Holy Spirit] of the Most High shall overshadow you' (Luke 1:35).

♦ It was God's power that raised Christ from the dead and enthroned him in the heavenly realms as the king and head of his church.[15] Paul writes

---

[15]The sovereignty of God, particularly as it comes to expression on earth in the Lordship of Christ (Matt. 11:27; 28:18; John 17:2; Rev. 2:27), is the hammer that has smashed all earthly tyrannies and established workable democracies in accordance with the rule of law. In our time Western democracies, having been originally blessed by being established on the sovereignty of God expressed in the Lordship of Christ, are trying to 'nation-build' and establish democracies elsewhere in the world, particularly in the Middle East, on other bases such as human rights, human dignity, and economic and social equality, forgetting that it is only on the basis of the sovereignty of God that any of these other bases are true. Which is just to say, *only on the basis of Christian theocracy can one*

here: '[Jesus] on [his] divine side was *powerfully* declared to be the Son of God by the resurrection from the dead' (Rom. 1:4; 6:4) when the Father by his 'incomparably great power' and 'mighty strength' (Eph. 1:19-20) raised him from the dead and exalted him to what Mark 14:62 reports as the right hand of 'the Power [*tēs dunameōs*]' – a striking synonym for God the Father.

♦ It is God's power that is also exhibited in the good news of the gospel, for 'the gospel is *the power of God* for the salvation of all who believe, first for the Jew, then for the Gentile. For in the gospel is God's righteousness revealed, a righteousness that is by faith from first to last' (Rom. 1:16-17). Moreover, Paul declares that the proclamation of the crucified Christ is not only the wisdom of God; it is also 'the *power of God*' (1 Cor. 1:24), which affirmations lead me to remind you aspiring preachers as I did in my last address that preaching devoid of the cross not only will be morally platitudinous and vacuous at best, lacking the wisdom of God, but also will be spiritually infirm and invalid, lacking the power of God to transform lives. Such preaching will never change lives except for the worse for, as I said earlier, it will foster either self-righteousness in those who think they are good or despair in those who know themselves to be incapable of reversing their irremediable corruption by themselves.

♦ It is God's power that quickens and raises the sinner from spiritual death and exalts him to heaven by the same power that raised Jesus from the dead (Eph. 1:19; 2:1-4).

---

have a workable democracy, and only on the basis of the Kingship of Christ will men live and die for democracy. Every effort to establish democracies on any other basis than the Kingship of Christ is doomed ultimately to failure.

♦ It is God's power that enables the Christian to walk daily in the Way as he should: 'I will all the more gladly boast of my weaknesses, that the power of Christ may rest upon me ... for when I am weak, then I am strong' (2 Cor. 12:9-10).

♦ It is God's power that shields and preserves the saints: '...through faith,' Peter writes, '[you] are shielded by God's power until the coming of the salvation that is ready to be revealed in the last time' (1 Pet. 1:5).

♦ Finally, it will be God's power that will someday raise believers from physical death and transform them: '[The glorified Christ], by the power that enables him to bring everything under his control, will transform our lowly bodies so that they will be like his glorious body' (Phil. 3:21).

In connection with the Consummation, God by his power, just as he destroyed the antediluvian world by the Flood, will someday destroy this present world by fire: 'The heavens will disappear with a roar; the elements will be destroyed by fire, and the earth and everything in it will be laid bare' (2 Pet. 3:10). At that time God will remove the wicked from the earth (Ps. 104:35) and will cast them, death, hades, and Satan into the lake of fire (Rev. 20:10, 14). He will restore the cosmos in the sense that only righteousness will dwell within it. And with our new glorified bodies there will be 'no more death or mourning or crying or pain, for the old order of things will have passed away' (Rev. 21:4). But, as Donald Macleod quite properly reminds us – and his reminder is sorely needed in this day when the *Left Behind* series is sweeping across the evangelical church and by its eschatological teaching is raising false hopes that Jesus is coming soon and that Christians before he comes will be raptured out of the world and not face tribulation –

Our confidence that this is the pattern of our future *rests solely on the promise of God* (2 Pet. 3:13). *There are no evidences in the world around us that such a consummation is either imminent or inevitable.* Nor do we know of any force within the Universe capable of effecting it. What we do know is that the God who made this world and who at present sustains it has declared His intention to transform it, and although our minds may stagger at the magnitude of the undertaking, yet, in the face of his almightiness, such hesitation is absurd. Here, too, what He has promised, He is able also to perform (Rom. 4:21).[16]

What should all this mean for us? First, if all this is so and God's sovereign power is so great, and I trust that you believe that it is, then *to all of his enemies*, and perhaps one is sitting here before me, I would first say, 'Do you really think you can resist God? Yield to him. Cease your hopeless war against him. Capitulate! Surrender at once. Count the cost before you continue to brave it out against him. You are as wax before the flame! Why, he could go through a mighty host of people such as you as fire burns up stubble. "Kiss the Son, [and do it now,] lest he be angry and you perish from the way when his wrath [against you] is kindled but a little"' (Ps. 2:12).

Second, if all this is so and God's sovereign power is so great, and I trust that you believe that it is, then *to his enemy who would desire to make peace with him,* I would say: 'Then trust him to save you. Do not doubt for a second that he is able to lift *you* from the depths of your sin and away from the flames of perdition and to transform your depraved heart. The *powers of his grace* God has treasured up in his Son, Jesus Christ, and when you place your trust in him, he will forgive you of all your sins and iniquities and carry them away to the land of forgetfulness where not even he will ever

---

[16]Donald Macleod, *Behold Your God*, 53.

remember them against you again forever. "As far as the east is from the west so far will he remove your transgressions from you" (Ps. 103:12). So "trust in the LORD forever, for in the LORD is everlasting strength" (Isa. 26:4).'

Third, if all this is so and God's sovereign power is so great, and I trust that you believe that it is, then *to you his sons and daughters* I would say: 'Since God is so strong, never dare to distrust him. Is his arm so short that he cannot deliver you from all your troubles, all your sorrows, all your grief, and all your needs? He who keeps the planets hurtling along in their orbits, he who maintains Orion and the Pleiades, does he not possess the power to provide you with your daily food and clothing? Surely he does, so bring your burdens and needs to him, pour them out like water before him, and they shall pass away and you will yet sing: "'The LORD is my strength and my song. He also has become my salvation" (Ps. 118:14).'

Fourth, if all this is so and God's sovereign power is so great, and I trust that you believe that it is, then *to you his sons and daughters* I would also say: 'Since God is so strong, then shake off all fear of men. They are but grass and will wither within the hour. Why should you tremble at the tyrant's frown or cower before the enemies of Christ? Don't let the faces of proud men confound you. Trust in the Lord and fear not, because "if God is for us, who can be against us" (Rom. 8:31), and "because the one who is in you is greater than he who is in the world" (1 John 4:4).'

Fifth, if all this is so and God's sovereign power is so great, and I trust that you believe that it is, I would say *to you his sons and daughters* yet again: 'Since God is so strong, commit your future to him. Do not be afraid of tomorrow, for the sovereign Lord lives! The mighty God of Jacob is your refuge. He is the God of all your tomorrows as well as your God today. Whatever you are facing, in patience and quietness wait for him;

rest in him and be at peace. Stand still, and see the salvation of your God who will manifest the greatness of his power and reveal the might of his right arm in your behalf. "Be anxious for nothing, but in everything, by prayer and petition, with thanksgiving, present your requests to God. And the peace of God that transcends all human understanding will guard your hearts and your minds in Christ Jesus" (Phil. 4:6-7), for he "is able to do immeasurably more than all we ask or imagine" (Eph. 3:20).'

Sixth, if all this is so and God's sovereign power is so great, and I trust that you believe that it is, then I would say in particular today *to you his sons and daughters whom he has called to serve him in his church*: 'Since *he* is so strong, then you need not rely on *your* strength. Nor do you need to pine over your weaknesses for they are the platforms for the exhibition of his power. Did he not say to Paul: "My grace is sufficient for you, for my power is made perfect in [your] weaknesses" (2 Cor. 12:9)? Are you a "one-talent" Christian? God is not limited by your limitations; he can make your one talent as fruitful as another man's ten. Are you as weak as water? Then rejoice today, and glory in your infirmity, because now the power of God shall rest upon you. Don't think about what *you* are able to do – that will be little enough however much it is – but consider what *he* can do with and through you. Has he not told us in 1 Corinthians 1:27-29 that he purposely "chose the *foolish* things of the world to shame the wise ... the *weak* things of the world to shame the strong ... the *lowly* things of the world and the *despised* things – and the things *that are not* – to nullify the things that are, so that no one may boast before him"? He can lift up the fallen hand, he can strengthen the weakened knee, he can fan once again into a bright and burning flame the smoking flax. And today he says to you:

Do not be afraid, O *worm* Jacob, O *little* Israel, for *I myself will help you.*... You will thresh the mountains and crush them, and reduce the hills to chaff.... And you will rejoice in the Lord, and glory in the Holy One of Israel (Isa. 41:15-16).

Let us pray:
Almighty God, our heavenly Father, you are indeed our 'strength and our song; you have become our salvation.' You are exalted above this earth and all mankind, and mighty and exalted is your right hand.

Glorify yourself today in our lives; manifest the incomparable greatness of your power in us – even that power of your mighty strength that you exerted when you raised Christ from the dead – for you have a mighty arm; you are strong in battle.

Bless us, O Lord, with the truth of your sovereignty over us and show us your might that is available to us.

All this we pray in the mighty name of Christ, our glorious Savior. Amen.

Introduction

Good morning once again, esteemed faculty, beloved seminarians, and friends of the seminary, brothers and sisters all in Jesus Christ. I sincerely hope and pray that through these chapel addresses all of us are growing in our love for the great God of Scripture. You students

SEVENTH ADDRESS

'INFINITE, ETERNAL, AND UNCHANGEABLE IN HIS HOLINESS'

In the year that King Uzziah died, I saw the Lord seated on a throne, high and exalted, and the train of his robe filled the temple. Above him were seraphs, each with six wings: With two wings they covered their faces, with two they covered their feet, and with two they were flying. And they were calling to one another: 'Holy, holy, holy is the LORD Almighty; the whole earth is full of his glory.' At the sound of their voices the doorposts and thresholds shook and the temple was filled with smoke.

'Woe to me!' I cried. 'I am ruined! For I am a man of unclean lips, and I live among a people of unclean lips, and my eyes have seen the King, the LORD Almighty.'

Then one of the seraphs flew to me with a live coal in his hand, which he had taken with tongs from the altar. With it he touched my mouth and said, 'See, this has touched your lips; your guilt is taken away and your sin atoned for' (Isa. 6:1-7).

Introduction

Good morning once again, esteemed faculty, beloved seminarians, and friends of the seminary – brothers and sisters all in Jesus Christ. I sincerely hope and pray that through these chapel addresses all of us are growing in our love for the great God of Scripture. You students who have had me as your teacher have heard me ask many times: 'What is the value of all your learning about God, if after all of your study about him you don't love and revere him more as a result?' Such learning will result only in a cold, dead orthodoxy with no animation of the Spirit about it, and a cold wind will blow across all your ministerial efforts as a result. And before a watching world such orthodoxy is ugly and repulsive. Francis Schaeffer often reminded those of us who had the privilege of knowing him and sharing classroom responsibilities with him at Covenant Theological Seminary that there are two essential orthodoxies in the Christian life – the orthodoxy of doctrine and the orthodoxy of practice – and either one, absent the other, is powerless in taking our world captive for Christ. So as we move through these chapel addresses on God's attributes, I would urge you to spend time with your Lord – and no one knows better than I how difficult it is to develop the habit of spending time with him – that you may grow in your love and reverence for him. Let us pray even now that what we learn about him in these addresses will result in greater love and reverence for him.

Prayer:
Our great and gracious God: New every morning are your mercies to us. Great is your faithfulness!

We know that you have loved us everlastingly with your 'four-dimensional' love – O how wide, how long, how high, how deep is your love that surpasses human knowledge! – and we know and confess with shamefacedness that never have we responded to your love with the degree of love that such love as yours deserves. Our love for you is so insipid, so frail, so giddy, so wavering, so faithless, so filled with imperfections, that we must repent of our love for you and cry, 'I love; help thou my unlove.'

We look forward to that day when, finally glorified, we will respond to your love with an unsinning love of our own, but until that rapturous day, because we know that your inspired Apostle declared that 'if anyone does not love the Lord – a curse be upon him,' we urgently cry to you to increase our love for Christ and never to allow us to outlive our love for him. We confess that love for him is not native to our breasts. So do a work in our hearts today, and may we fall in love with Christ afresh today.

As we turn now to your Word may your Spirit instruct us not only about you, the triune God, but also about ourselves and our great need of you. And may we find in your Word's blessed instruction our solid ground and our solace for the evil days that lie ahead, days when other men's hearts regretfully will fail them for fear.

This I pray in Jesus' most holy but infinitely gracious name, Amen.

* * *

Ladies and gentlemen, we turn now to the *Shorter Catechism*'s next affirmation about God. Our God – infinite, eternal, and unchangeable in his Being, wisdom, and power – the *Catechism* now informs us, is also holy – *infinitely, eternally, and unchangeably* holy! In addition to the thirty-one 'divided kingdom' texts (primarily Isaianic) in which God is called the 'Holy One of Israel [*q^edhôsh Yisrā'ēl*],'[1] the following verses, among many others that could be cited, set forth the biblical witness to God's attribute of holiness.

Texts

Exodus 15:11: 'Who among the gods is like you, O LORD? Who is like you – *majestic* [or 'glorious'] *in holiness* [*ne'dhār baqqōdhesh*], awesome in glory, working wonders?'

---

[1] See 2 Kings 19:22; Pss. 71:22: 78:41; 89:18 [MT 89:19]; Isa. 1:4; 5:19, 24; 10:20; 12:6; 17:7; 29:19; 30:11, 12, 15; 31:1; 37:23; 41:14, 16, 20; 43:3, 14; 45:11; 47:4; 48:7; 49:7; 54:5; 55:5; 60:9, 14; Jer 50:29; 51:5.

1 Samuel 2:2: *'There is no one holy like the* LORD *['ên qādhôsh kayhwh]*; there is no one besides you; there is no Rock like our God.'

Psalm 22:3: '...you are enthroned as the holy One.'

Psalm 99:3, 5, 9: '[The LORD] is holy ... he is holy.... Exalt the LORD our God and worship at his holy mountain, for the LORD our God is holy.'

Isaiah 6:3: 'And [the seraphs that flew around his throne] were calling to one another: "Holy, holy, holy [qādhôsh qādhôsh qādhôsh] is the LORD of hosts."'

Isaiah 8:13: 'The LORD Almighty is the one you are to regard as holy; he is the one you are to fear, he is the one you are to dread.'

Isaiah 57:15: 'For this is what the high and lofty One says [the same two words, 'high' and 'lofty' also appear in Isaiah 6:1 as 'high and exalted'] – he who lives forever, *whose name is holy [qādhôsh sh^emô]* 'I live in a high and holy place, but also with him who is contrite and lowly in spirit."

Hosea 11:9: 'I am God and not man – the Holy One among you.'

Revelation 4:8: 'Each of the four living creatures had six wings and was covered with eyes all around, even under his wings. Day and night they never stop saying: "Holy, holy, holy [*Hagios hagios hagios*] is the Lord God Almighty."'

Revelation 15:4: 'Who will not fear you, O Lord, and bring glory to your name? For you *alone [monos]* are holy.'

The Doctrine
The Scriptures are quite clear: our God alone is all-holy – infinitely, eternally, and unchangeably so! But what does this mean to minds that find it impossible to grasp even the simplest truths about God without divine aid

and, more importantly, to *sin-ravaged* minds that know nothing about the nature of true holiness as such? What is the Bible saying when it says that God is holy? The Hebrew verb *qādhash* and the Greek verb *hagiazō* that are employed to express this idea about God in the Old and New Testaments respectively both have the basic meaning of 'withdrawal' or 'separateness'. And a careful exegesis of the occurrences of these words will show that, when used of God, they both intend two ideas. In the first instance, the 'withdrawal' or 'separateness' of his holiness intends God's majestic transcendence, his intrinsic 'unapproachableness', as the Deity who dwells in unapproachable light *vis à vis* the finite creature. One sees this transcendent dimension of God's holiness reflected in one significant detail of Isaiah's vision of God in Isaiah 6:1-3. The prophet writes:

> In the year that King Uzziah died, I saw the Lord seated upon a throne, high and exalted, and the train of his robe filled the temple. Above him were seraphs, each with six wings: With two wings they covered their faces, with two they covered their feet, and with two they were flying. And they were calling to one another: 'Holy, holy, holy is the LORD of [angelic] Hosts; the whole earth is full of his glory.'

The Apostle John, who tells us in John 12:40-41 that it was upon the preincarnate Second Person of the Godhead in all of his glory that Isaiah was gazing, had a similar vision in Revelation 4:6-8 and he gives us additional information about these seraphs and their antiphonal singing:

> In the center, around the throne, were four living creatures, and they were covered with eyes, in front and in back. The first living creature was like a lion, the second was like an ox, the third had a face like a man, the fourth was like a flying eagle. Each of the four living creatures had six wings and was covered with eyes all

around, even under his wings. *Day and night they never stop saying: 'Holy, holy, holy is the Lord God Almighty, who was, and is, and is to come.'*

Now when Isaiah saw this awesome scene and heard these four creatures singing of God's holiness, he was immediately struck with both his creatureliness and his moral impurity. But what is often overlooked – and here is the detail to which I referred earlier – is that the four seraphs, themselves all *sinless* creatures, still feel it necessary in the presence of the Second Person of the Godhead continually to cover themselves all over by their wings. Clearly, *for them* his 'holiness' was his 'withdrawnness' or 'separateness' due simply to his divine transcendence or 'unapproachableness' over against their creatureliness, albeit absolutely *sinless* creatureliness.

It is also most likely that it is God's transcendent majesty that is being celebrated in the following contexts, as evidenced by the sustained emphasis upon his *uniqueness* among both the gods of this world and humankind:

Exodus 15:11: 'Who among the gods is like you, O LORD? Who is like you – *majestic in holiness*, awesome in glory, working wonders?'

1 Samuel 2:2: *'There is no one holy like the LORD; there is no one besides you; there is no Rock like our God.'*

Isaiah 8:13: 'The LORD Almighty is the one you are to regard as holy; he is the one you are *to fear*, he is the one you are *to dread*.'

Isaiah 57:15: 'For this is what the high and lofty One says – he who lives forever, *whose name is holy*: 'I live in a high and holy place, but also with him who is contrite and lowly in spirit." '

Hosea 11:9: 'I am God and not man – the Holy One among you.'

Ezekiel 22:26: Complaining that Israel's priests had backsliden, God declares:

[They] do violence to my law and profane my holy things; they do not distinguish between the holy and the common; they teach that there is no difference between the clean and the unclean, and they shut their eyes to the keeping of my Sabbaths, so that I am profaned among them.

In regard to God's transcendent or majestic holiness Geerhardus Vos insightfully writes:

Taking the divine holiness in this form, we can easily perceive that it is not really an attribute to be coordinated with the other attributes distinguished in the divine nature. It is something co-extensive with and applicable to everything that can be predicated of God: he is holy in everything that characterizes Him and reveals Him, holy in His goodness and grace, no less than in His righteousness and wrath [transcendently holy even in his holiness – RLR].[2]

'Holiness' [in this sense, Vos continues] teaches what ought not to be done [to God], i.e. come too familiarly near [to him]. 'Unapproachableness' would best express it.[3]

Louis Berkhof echoes Vos's words:

[The] fundamental idea [of God's holiness] is that of a *position* or *relationship* existing between God and some person or thing. In its original sense it denotes that He is *absolutely distinct* from all his creatures, and is *exalted above them in infinite majesty*. So understood, the holiness of God is one of his transcendental attributes, and is sometimes spoken of as His central

---

[2]Geerhardus Vos, *Biblical Theology* (Grand Rapids: Eerdmans, 1949), 266.
[3]Vos, *Biblical Theology*, 265.

and supreme perfection. It does not seem proper to speak of one attribute of God as being more central and fundamental than another; but if this were permissible, the Scriptural emphasis on the holiness of God would seem to justify its selection. It is quite evident ... that holiness in this sense of the word ... is ... something that is co-extensive with, and applicable to, everything that can be predicated of God. He is holy in everything that reveals Him, in His goodness and grace as well as in His justice and wrath. [Again, this means that God is even *transcendently* holy in his holiness. – RLR] It may be called the 'majesty-holiness' of God [and] this holiness ... includes such ideas as 'absolute unapproachability' ... or 'aweful majesty.' It awakens in man a sense of absolute nothingness, a 'creature-consciousness' or 'creature-feeling,' leading to absolute self-abasement.[4]

An understanding of and appreciation for God's holy 'unapproachableness,' I would contend in passing, have virtually passed out of the worship life of the contemporary church as we have made God too familiar to us – we have made him 'the man upstairs,' our 'buddy' and our 'pal' – which familiarity has bred contempt for his awful character and transcendence.

In the second instance, and flowing out of the former, God is also *ethically* or *morally* holy. For just as he, the infinite Creator, is *transcendentally separate* from men as creatures, so also he is *ethically separate* from them as *sinful* creatures. He is morally pure – infinitely, eternally, and unchangeably so – with respect to his nature, his thoughts, and his actions. There is not the slightest taint of evil desire, impure motive, or unholy inclination in him. His ethical holiness is the very antithesis of all moral blemish or defilement. And humankind's sin and transgression – coextensive with the race but which some individuals among us have developed to

---

[4]Louis Berkhof, *Systematic Theology* (New combined edition; Grand Rapids, Eerdmans, 1996), 73, emphasis supplied.

a frightful enormity – he regards as unmitigatingly inexcusable, utterly indefensible, and fully deserving of his punishment. He views our sins – the violation of his holy law and rebellious self-deification – as not only real evil, morally wrong, and therefore, in his sight detestable, odious, ugly, disgusting, filthy, loathsome, liable to punishment, with no right to be, but they are also the contradiction of his perfections, cannot but meet with his undiluted disapproval and wrath, and are damnable in the strongest sense of the word because they so dreadfully *dishonor* him. God *must* react with holy indignation against sinners. He *cannot* do otherwise. The Scriptures are replete with this representation of God:

Psalm 5:4-6: 'You are a God who takes no pleasure in evil; with you the wicked cannot dwell. The arrogant cannot stand in your presence; you hate all who do wrong. You destroy those who tell lies; bloodthirsty and deceitful men the LORD abhors.'

Psalm 11:5-7: 'The LORD examines the righteous [and acquits them], but the wicked and those who love violence his soul hates. On the wicked he will rain fiery coals and burning sulfur; a scorching wind will be their lot. For the LORD is righteous, he loves justice; upright men will see his face' (See also Pss. 15; 33:5).

Habakkuk 1:13: 'Your eyes are too pure to look on evil [with any degree of approval]; you cannot tolerate wrong.'

1 John 1:5: 'God is light; in him there is no [moral] darkness at all.'

In ancient Israel, Jehoshaphat appointed the temple singers to 'praise the beauty of [God's] holiness' (2 Chron. 20:21). Hence, Stephen Charnock states: As 'power is [God's] hand and arm; omniscience, his

181

eye; mercy, his bowels; eternity, his duration; [so] his [ethical] holiness is his beauty.'[5] Thus we read of 'the beauty [nô'am] of the LORD' (Ps. 27:4) that is none other than the 'splendor [hadhrê(y)] of holiness' (Ps. 110:3). Now because God is both majestically transcendent and ethically pure, it 'becomes important to [him who is jealous for his holiness to teach mankind so, and to] draw a circle of holiness around Him, which shall bar out the "profane".'[6] Accordingly, he declares heaven to be holy, Mount Sinai due to his presence there holy, Mount Zion upon which his temple rests holy, the temple itself and its services holy, the temple's vessels holy, the high priest's garments holy, his commandments holy, and his Sabbaths holy. And God also demands, because he is holy, that his people be holy:

Leviticus 11:44-45: 'I am the LORD your God. Consecrate yourselves therefore, and be holy; for I am holy.... For I am the LORD, who brought you up from the land of Egypt to be your God; thus you shall be holy for I am holy.'

Leviticus 19:2: 'Speak to all the congregation of the sons of Israel and say to them, "You shall be holy, for I the LORD your God am holy."'

1 Thessalonians 4:3: 'This is the will of God, even your holiness....'

1 Thessalonians 4:7: 'God did not call us to impurity but to holiness.'

Hebrews 12:14: 'Pursue ... holiness, without which no man shall see the Lord.'

1 Peter 1:15-16: '...like the God who called you, be yourselves holy in all your behavior, because it has been written: "Be holy, because I am holy."'

---

[5]Stephen Charnock, *The Existence and Attributes of God* (Reprint; Grand Rapids: Baker, 1996), 2:113.

[6]Vos, *Biblical Theology*, 268.

We may summarize our doctrine to this point this way: with respect to his transcendent holiness God is the '*Wholly* Other' (with a 'W') in his unapproachability; with respect to his ethical or moral holiness he is the '*Holy* Other' (with an 'H') in his opposition to every sinful thought and deed of mankind. If, then, men are to live in God's approving presence at all they must not wantonly seek to stray across the holy barriers he has drawn between him and them or, what is the same thing, transgress his holy laws that delineate these barriers.

We must make one more point: God's twofold holiness evokes a twofold response in people who are really confronted by it.[7] The important book, *The Idea of the Holy*,[8] by Rudolf Otto (1869–1937), a Lutheran scholar and student of comparative religions, may prove helpful in explaining what I mean here. Otto, designating the core, irreducible presence of the transcendentally holy that all men experience in rare, vague, but very real moments when the soul is captured by an 'ineffable Something' – as the *numinous*, that is, an *awareness* of 'divinity', describes this *numinous* by his now-famous formula *mysterium tremendum et fascinans* ('a tremendous and fascinating mystery') that is experienced religiously by 'creature feeling', the sense of dependence upon that which stands over man as the 'Wholly Other' with a 'W.' Now if we use Otto's formula for our present purpose,

---

[7]I am indebted to Donald Macleod, *Behold Your God* (Ross-shire: Christian Focus, 1990), 90-1, for several of the ideas in this paragraph.

[8]Rudolf Otto, *The Idea of the Holy* (Original German edition, 1917; London: Penguin, 1959), 26ff. John Calvin in *Institutes*, 1.1.3 says something similar to Otto: 'Hence that dread and astonishment [*horror ille et stupor*] with which Scripture commonly represents the saints as stricken and overcome whenever they felt the presence of God. Thus it comes about that we see men who in his absence normally remain firm and constant, but who, when he manifests his glory, are so shaken and struck dumb as to be laid low by the dread of death – are in fact overwhelmed by it and almost annihilated.' (See Gen. 18:27; Judg. 6:22-23; 13:22; Isa. 6:2; Ezek. 1:28-2:1; Job 42:5-6.)

this means that God is, first, *tremendous* – not to be construed here in the modern sense of being 'unusually or astonishingly great or large' but in the original sense of the Latin root, namely, 'tremendous' in the sense of *exciting the person who experiences the numinous to tremble,* to *feel dread or awe* (remember Isaiah 8:13: 'The LORD Almighty is ... *holy*; he is the one you are *to fear,* he is the one you are *to dread'*). Because he is 'Wholly Other' than the creature, awesome, absolutely over-powering, even threatening in his transcendent holiness,[9] God's presence awakens in the awe-stricken creature a feeling of total dependence, incompetence, of being no longer in control, even 'undoneness', and the creature's instinct, unless reassured by God's *fascinating* grace, is to turn and flee from him lest he die. Jacob's Bethel experience evoked this response: When he awoke from his sleep, Moses tells us in Genesis 28:16-17: '[Jacob] thought, "Surely the LORD is in this place, and I was not aware of it." He was afraid and said: 'How *awesome* [*nôrā',* literally 'fearsome'] is this place!"' Job confessed: 'My ears had heard of you but now my eyes have seen you; therefore I despise myself and repent in dust and ashes' (Job 42:5-6). Manoah said to his wife, 'We shall surely die, for we have seen God' (Judg. 13:22). Isaiah's experience in Isaiah 6:5 was the same: Confronted with the transcendent holiness of God, he felt dreadfully vulnerable and cried: 'Woe is me! I am destroyed!' For the same reason God is called the 'Fear of Isaac' (Gen. 31:42), and both the Yahwism of the Old Testament and the Law of God are called the 'Fear of the LORD' (Prov. 1:7; Ps. 19:9).

Otto's formula means, second, that God is not only *tremendous,* exciting awe and dread; he is also *fascinating* and *enchanting.* The threatened person, paradoxically, you see, is also *fascinated* and *enchanted* – even *entranced* – by both the very unapproachableness

---

[9]The *Westminster Confession of Faith,* XIV.II, speaks of Christians as 'trembling at [God's] threatenings.'

of God and the compelling beauty of his stainless purity. Even as he would take flight, he looks back, *obsessed* with the object of his fear. And when he learns through the 'good news' of the gospel that in his grace this 'Unapproachable One' arranged a way in the Old Testament whereby he might be approached, namely, the elaborate protocol of its typical sacrificial system, and arranged in the New Testament the simpler yet richer, more glorious antitypical 'Way', namely, the high priestly work of his own beloved Son, he is not put off by such exclusivity and finality but rather is fascinated and enchanted, even *entranced*, by that Way. And when he becomes a Christian, he is captivated by the beauty of God's holiness and continues to be entranced by it in the same way David longed to gaze upon the beauty or holiness of the Lord and to seek him in his temple (Ps. 27:5), in the same way the sons of Korah, like the deer panting for streams of water, thirsted for God, for the living God, and longed to go and meet him (Ps. 42:2), in the same way Paul longed to see Christ face to face (1 Cor. 13:12; Phil. 1:23), in the same way John longed to see Christ as he is (1 John 3:2), so that he joyously sings with Frederick W. Faber:

My God, how wonderful thou art,
thy majesty how bright!
How beautiful thy mercy seat,
In depths of burning light!

How dread are thine eternal years,
O everlasting Lord,
By holy angels, day and night,
Unceasingly adored!

How wonderful, how beautiful,
The sight of thee must be,
Thine endless wisdom, boundless power,
And aweful purity!

O how I fear thee, living God,
With deepest, tend'rest fears;
And *worship thee with trembling hope,*
And penitential tears.

No earthly father loves like thee,
No mother half so mild
Bears and forebears, as thou hast done
With me, thy sinful child.

Yet I may love thee, too, O Lord,
Almighty as thou art;
For thou has stooped to ask of me
The love of my poor heart.

Father of Jesus, love's reward,
What rapture will it be
Prostrate before thy throne to lie
And gaze and gaze on thee!

This rapt, intense 'gazing' upon or fascination with God is what we intend when we speak of the 'beatific vision' – that clear and direct knowledge of God enjoyed ultimately only by the *beati,* the blessed in heaven.

To sum up, the twofold response that God's twofold holiness induces in people is this: first, they will fear him and acknowledge their creaturely 'undoneness' and repent of their sin; second, they will desire to draw near to him and trust and adore him and joyously express their willingness to obey the 'barrier laws' he regards as essential to the 'protection' of his twofold holiness from all profanation.

This then is the doctrine of God's holiness that Holy Scripture and the *Catechism* espouse: our God is *transcendently* withdrawn and separate from his creation as its infinite Creator, and he is *ethically* and *morally* separate from sinful mankind because we fell in Adam's transgression and have become, all of us, transgressors of his laws. As Isaiah declared: 'The LORD's ear is not too dull to hear, but *your iniquities have separated you from your God*; [it is] your sins [that] have hidden his face from you so that he will not hear' (Isa. 59:1-2). Let's apply now this teaching on God's holiness to *our* lives.

Application

I have only one point of application to make this morning, although it is an extended one, and it has to do with the all-important matter of our worship of God. We have seen in our series thus far that the one living and true Lord God Almighty, whom the heaven of heavens *cannot contain*, is *self-contained* and *self-sufficient* and has need of nothing. And as we have seen today, he is unapproachable in his transcendent 'majesty-holiness' and ineffaceable exaltation and is stainlessly perfect in his ethical holiness and flaming purity.

Now all this creates an insurmountable problem for mankind who attempt to approach the unapproachable God in worship in a self-willed way, for finite sinful creatures could sooner create a world out of nothing than find a way on their own either to approach God successfully or to produce an offering that would meet the approval of his stainless purity. In order to get to the one holy God they have to get past the cherubim, the guardians of God's holiness, and the flaming sword of his justice flashing back and forth that guard the way to God and the tree of life (see Gen. 3:24). Furthermore, unless the Holy Scripture has instructed them these people will not know how serious their spiritual condition is. Moreover, they will never know how broad the great divide is[10] between them and the true God and

---

[10]Humanity struggles with its sin and depravity. True, people may not describe their struggle in such terms but they are all conscious that there is a great divide between what they know they *actually are* and what they *ought to be* – a psychological 'Fall' as it were. And they are troubled by that divide and they struggle to remove or at least to reduce its breadth. In their heart of hearts they all wish they were better and want to improve themselves morally. All one has to do to

how impossible by their own efforts is their removal or reduction in the slightest of the breadth of this divide. These people may conclude that my last assertion is quite intemperate, but this is because they do not know that the Word of God provides a lengthy list of moral 'cannots' that are true of them. For example,

♦ they do not know that 'a bad tree *cannot bear* good fruit' (Matt. 7:18), and that they are, as we all are natively, 'bad trees' (see Rom. 3:9-18, especially 3:10: 'There is no one righteous, not even one').

♦ They do not know that unless a person is born from above, he *cannot* even *see*, much less *'enter* the kingdom of God' (John 3:3, 5).

♦ They do not know that *'no one can come* to Jesus Christ unless the Father draws him' and 'enables him' to come (John 6:44, 45).

♦ They do not know that they *'cannot accept* the Spirit of truth, because they neither see him nor know him' (John 14:17).

♦ They do not know that they cannot bear any true moral fruit on their own, for according to Jesus: 'No branch can bear fruit by itself; it must remain in the vine. *Neither can you bear fruit unless you remain in me.* I am the vine ... apart from me *you can do nothing*' (John 15:4-5).

♦ They do not know that 'the sinful mind ... *does not submit* to God's law [this is what theologians call moral depravity]; nor *can it do so* [this is what they call moral inability]. Those controlled by the sinful nature *cannot please* God' (Rom. 8:7-8).

♦ They do not know that 'the person without the Spirit *does not accept* the things that come from the Spirit of God, for they are foolishness to

confirm this fact is to go to the shelves of self-help books either in Borders or Barnes & Noble and there one will find scores and scores of titles on such matters. Yes, moral self-improvement is indeed a major concern with people.

him [there it is again: moral depravity], and he *cannot understand* them [there it is again: moral inability], because they are discernable only through the Spirit's enabling' (1 Cor. 2:14).

♦ They do not know that 'no one can say, "Jesus is Lord,"' and really mean it, 'except by the Holy Spirit' (1 Cor. 12:3).

♦ They do not know that they 'cannot [even] tame their [own] tongues' that are 'restless evils, full of deadly poison' (Jas. 3:8).

♦ They do not know that *no one can learn* the 'new song' that is sung around the throne of God until one is redeemed (Rev. 14:3).

♦ And they do not know that it is as impossible for them to improve their character or act in a way that is distinct from their native corruption as it is for 'the Ethiopian to change his skin or the leopard to change his spots' (Jer. 13:23).

In sum, without being aware of it, these people are incapable of the understanding, the affections, and the will to act that, taken together, enable one to be subject to the law of God, to respond to the gospel of God, and to love and to approach God in acceptable worship.

So they go on struggling against the powers of sin that rage and wage war within them and that make them captive to the law of sin that dwells within them (Rom. 7:23). And the extreme and horrible irony in their go-it-alone struggle to approach God in worship, again unknown to them, is that *their very struggle is itself sinful* in that the very essence of their anxious concern to improve themselves morally on their own is their imagining that they must do for themselves what God is unwilling to do or incapable of doing for them. What is this but their going to their own 'broken cisterns that can hold no water' rather than to the Lord who is the 'fountain of living water' (Jer. 2:13)? And if they continue seriously and long enough in their struggle to find God, they will be brought by their weariness to the spiritual and emotional depths where they cry with the convicted Saul of Tarsus:

'O wretched man that I am! Who will deliver me from this body of death?' (Rom. 7:24)

There it is, dear friends: The Bible's maturest expression of the weariness of the soul that comes from trying to improve and better oneself in the struggle against sin. And if you are here today and are in that self-help struggle, please know that I feel sorry, very sorry, for you. My heart goes out to you, I weep for you, for I know that you will never improve yourself to your own satisfaction, that you will wear yourself out in your struggle, that you will never find a way to God that is acceptable to him, and that you will die a spiritual failure, regardless of what other successes you may achieve in life, if you continue on your own to struggle to remove the breach between God and you. According to Scripture, even to attempt to do so is fraught with peril for your immortal soul, for you will after death appear before God and find yourself indicted for your self-willed attempt to save yourself, and you will find your mouth stopped, unable to answer God's charges against you once in a thousand times.

The Bible plainly teaches that God himself must direct mankind in its worship of him. And, thank God, this he has done by and in Holy Scripture. Reformed churches speak of this approach to worship as the 'regulative principle' of worship, and by it they have much to teach the contemporary church about worship. According to this Reformation principle of worship, true worship will include only those matters that God has either expressly commanded in Scripture or that may be deduced from Scripture by good and necessary consequence such as first-day Sabbath worship[11] and infant baptism,[12] while false worship is anything done in worship that God has not expressly prescribed. The Scriptures sternly warn against worshiping God in ways that he has not expressly prescribed. Moses instructed Israel in Deuteronomy 12:29-32:

> When you have driven [the nations] out and settled in their land, and after they have been destroyed before you, be careful not to be ensnared by inquiring about their gods, saying, 'How do these nations serve their gods? We will do the same.' You must not worship the LORD your God in their way, because in worshiping their gods, they do all kinds of detestable things the LORD hates. They even burn their sons and daughters in the fire as sacrifices to their gods. *See to it that you do all I command you; do not add to it or take away from it.*

Consider the following illustrations of this 'regulative principle' being 'lived out' in biblical history:

♦ God looked with favor on Abel's blood offering, offered in faith, and rejected Cain's produce offering (Gen. 4:4-5; Heb. 11:4).

♦ Nadab and Abihu were consumed by fire from the Lord because they 'offered unauthorized fire ... contrary to his command' (Lev. 10:1-2).

♦ Korah, Dathan, Abiram, and On were swallowed up in an earthquake because, declaring 'that the whole congregation [of Israel] is holy ... [and that Moses and Aaron had] set themselves above the LORD's assembly' by their religious prescriptions, these men attempted to burn incense before God apart from Aaronic priestly mediation. After their judgment God instructed Eleazar the high priest

---

[11]See my article, 'Lord's Day Observance: Man's Proper Response to the Fourth Commandment,' *Presbyterion: Covenant Seminary Review* (Spring 1987), Vol. XIII, Num. 1, 7-23.

[12]See my *A New Systematic Theology of the Christian Faith* (Second edition; Nashville, TN: Thomas Nelson, 2002), 935-50.

to take the censers of 'the men who sinned', to hammer them into sheets, and to overlay the bronze altar of the Tabernacle with them as a sign to Israel that 'no one except a descendent of Aaron should come to burn incense before the LORD' (Num. 16:36-40; see also the lesson of the budding of Aaron's staff in Numbers 17).

♦ God smote King Uzziah with leprosy because he ignored this prohibition and attempted to usurp the priestly privilege to burn incense in the temple (2 Chron. 26:16-19). In this poor man's self-willed worship, we see what happens to the sinful creature who dares to walk into God's holy presence uninvited, acting as though it were his perfect right to be there. This is true of us as well. Just as we cannot look for a moment at the brilliant, boiling light of the sun with our naked eyes without destroying them, so also we cannot in our raw state look at the God who dwells in the unapproachable light of his all-consuming holiness without doing irreversible and eternal harm to ourselves.

♦ Israel's building high places and offering its sons and daughters on them to Baal Jeremiah described as doing 'something [God] did not command or mention, nor did it enter [his] mind' (Jer. 19:5).

New Testament teaching is as clear as the Old Testament's teaching about this matter:

♦ Jesus himself declared – mark Jesus' words well – that when men in their worship of God 'let go of the commands of God' and 'hold on to the traditions of men,' their worship is 'in vain [matēn]' (Mark 7:7-8).

♦ To the Samaritan woman Jesus spoke of the character of true worship:

You Samaritans worship what you do not know; we worship what we do know, for salvation is from the Jews. Yet a time is coming and has now come when the true worshipers will worship the Father in spirit and truth, for *they are the kind of worshipers the Father seeks.* God is spirit, and *his worshipers must worship him in spirit and truth* (John 4:22-24)

Jesus' phrase 'in spirit and truth' surely means at the very least that God's worshipers must worship him as he has prescribed.

♦ Paul admonished the Colossians against self-willed asceticism in worship:

Since you died with Christ to the basic principles [in light of Colossians 2:18 these 'basic principles' are most likely worship regulations alleged to have come from angelic powers] of this world, why, as though you still belonged to it, do you submit to its rules: 'Do not handle! Do not taste! Do not touch!'? These are all destined to perish with use, because they are based on human commands and teachings. Such regulations indeed have an appearance of wisdom, with their self-imposed worship, their false humility and their harsh treatment of the body, but they lack any value in restraining sensual indulgence (Col. 2:20-23).

♦ And we must never forget that over-arching all of God's worship requirements is the all-important exclusivity of biblical salvation through faith in Christ alone that is explicitly asserted in John 14:6 when Jesus declared: 'I am the way [or there is no going] and the truth [or there is no knowing] and the life [or there is no growing]. No one comes to the Father except through me'; in Acts 4:12 when Peter stated: 'Salvation is found in no one else [not Moses, not Muhammad, not Buddha, not Mary or the 'saints'], for there is no other

> name under heaven given to men [except Jesus] by which we must be saved'; in 1 Timothy 2:5 when Paul affirmed: '...there is ... one mediator between God and men, the man Christ Jesus'; and in 1 John 5:12 when John asserted: 'He who has the Son has life; he who does not have the Son of God does not have life.'

You see, God the Father cannot have direct fellowship with any of us. The *only* man with whom the infinitely holy God can have *direct* fellowship is Jesus Christ, whose perfect and obedient manhood rendered him an acceptable sacrifice to God. So we must come to God through the saving virtues of Christ's obedient life and substitutionary death, and *in him* we may enjoy fellowship with the all-holy God.

Therefore, because Holy Scripture is so clear about this principle it has received creedal status in the *Westminster Confession of Faith*, XXI.I, being expressed there this way:

> The acceptable way of worshipping the true God is instituted by himself, and so limited by his own revealed will, that he may not be worshipped according to the imaginations and devices of men, or the suggestions of Satan, under any visible representations, or any other way not prescribed in the Holy Scripture.

The *Larger Catechism* also states this principle unambiguously:

> Question 108: The duties required in the second commandment are, the receiving, observing, and keeping pure and entire, all such religious worship and ordinances, as God hath instituted in his Word....

> Question 109: The sins forbidden in the second commandment are, all devising, counselling, comm-

anding, using, and any wise approving, any religious worship not instituted by God himself....

The *Shorter Catechism* also states the principle and states it with equal clarity:

Question 50: The second commandment requireth the receiving, observing, and keeping pure and entire, all such religious worship and ordinances as God hath appointed in his Word.

Question 51: The second commandment forbiddeth the worshipping of God by images, or any other way not appointed in his Word.

For mankind's spiritual health and well-being, then, the Reformed church must inform the world and other church communions that because God the Creator is majestically transcendent and ethically holy – infinitely, eternally, and unchangeable so – they can approach him in worship only in the manner he has prescribed. All other worship efforts will prove futile and will be spurned by him. And they must do in worship only those things he has prescribed and reject the *dictum* that 'what is not expressly forbidden is permissible'.

What then should such worship include? *First*, and above everything else, acceptable worship to God must include, both initially and always continually thereafter, approaching him by faith only through the substitionary atoning work of Jesus Christ as he is offered in the gospel. The entire Bible teaches this. Public *corporate* worship will also include in due proportion, *second*, singing God's praises and encouraging one another in psalms and hymns and spiritual songs; *third*, the reading and contemplation both of God's holy law as our covenant norm of life and the 'good news' of the gospel; *fourth*, public and private prayers of adoration, confession of sin, thanksgiving, and supplication for only those things approved by Scripture, all to be offered in Christ's name alone; *fifth*, biblically-based, hermeneutically-sound preaching of God's Word; *sixth*, proper observance and administration of the church's two sacraments, baptism and the Lord's Supper; and *seventh*, the giving to God of offerings. And while the worship of God should be joyous and filled with gladness (Ps. 149:2), true worshipers must never forget that their God is a 'consuming fire' and that worship of him must be conducted in truth and sincerity (1 Cor. 5:7-8) and 'with reverence and awe' (Heb. 12:28-29).

Reformed worship will also stress Sabbath observance, not only because the Fourth Commandment requires it, but also because it takes seriously Charles Hodge's insight: 'If men wish the knowledge of [Jesus' resurrection from the dead] to die out, let them neglect to keep holy the first day of the week; if they desire that event to be everywhere known and remembered, let them consecrate that day to the worship of the risen Saviour.'[13]

The triune God of the Reformed faith is an awe-inspiring, absolutely sovereign, infinitely just and infinitely gracious, incomprehensible Deity, but he will not long be known as such or served as such by a people fed rote ritual or emotional choruses and 'Finneyesque' revivalistic preaching. Reformed theology, like all systems of theology, must have a form of worship through which it is expressed. If we neglect that form of worship our theology will cease to be meaningful to us. So let us diligently strive to insure that our worship efforts will meet the approval of him who seeks true worshipers to worship him in spirit and truth, for only such worship is acceptable to him who is the Holy One of Israel and our holy God as well. If you attend a church whose worship efforts seriously fall short of or diverge from his instructions concerning his worship, I would counsel you to labor mightily to fix its lapses and, should your efforts prove futile, to leave it for a

---

[13]Charles Hodge, *Systematic Theology* (Reprint: Grand Rapids: Eerdmans, 1952), 3:330.

church whose worship efforts are more in agreement with the prescriptions of Holy Scripture.

Dear seminarians, I must close now, but before I do let me say that unless the beauty of the Lord, *even his holiness*, rests upon and establishes the work of your hands, both now at the seminary and later in your several ministries, the stench – no, that is putting it too euphemistically – the putrifying *stink* of death will rise from your labors. So ever pray, as did Moses, that the beauty of the holiness of the Lord our God will rest upon your labors, and pray that he will 'establish the work of your hands' in holiness (Ps. 90:17).

Let us pray:
Almighty God, you who are ever holy and therefore ever to be adored and praised: We have considered your majestic and ethical holiness this morning, and we have seen that you have surrounded yourself with 'holy barriers' that make it impossible for such poor unworthy ones as we to approach you by our own efforts or according to what seems appropriate to us.

So like Isaiah each of us cries out: 'Woe is me! I am ruined! For I am a person of unclean lips, and I live among a people of unclean lips.'

Dispatch then to each of us in this moment the mighty 'Seraph of Calvary' with a live coal taken from his altar there, and touch our hearts and mouths and take away our sin and guilt before you.

Enable us to live lives this day and every day that are filled with praise and adoration as we gaze with eyes of faith on the beauty of your holiness.

And grant us the grace to 'pursue that holiness of life, without which no man will see you.'

These things we pray in the only name that has any currency in heaven, even the holy majestic name of Christ our Lord. Amen.

Eighth Address

'Infinite, Eternal, and Unchangeable in His Justice'

From the sixth hour until the ninth hour darkness came over all the land. About the ninth hour Jesus cried out in a loud voice, 'Eloi, Eloi, lama sabachthani?' – which means, 'My God, my God, why have you forsaken me?'

When some of those standing there heard this, they said, 'He's calling Elijah.'

Immediately one of them ran and got a sponge. He filled it with wine vinegar, put it on a stick, and offered it to Jesus to drink. The rest said, 'Now leave him alone. Let's see if Elijah comes to save him.'

And when Jesus had cried out again in a loud voice, he gave up his spirit (Matt. 27:45-50).

But now a righteousness from God, apart from law, has been made known, to which the Law and the Prophets testify. This righteousness from God comes through faith in Jesus Christ to all who believe. There is no difference, for all have sinned and fall short of the glory of God, and are justified freely by his grace through the redemption that came by Christ Jesus. God presented him as a sacrifice of atonement, through faith in his blood. He did this to demonstrate his justice, because in his forbearance he had left the sins committed beforehand unpunished – he did it to demonstrate his justice at the present time, so as to be just and the one who justifies those who have faith in Jesus (Rom. 3:21-26).

Introduction

Good morning once again, esteemed colleagues, students, and friends of the Seminary. Because I take seriously Peter's teaching that it is through the *knowledge* of God that grace and peace may be ours in abundance (2 Pet. 1:2) and that it is through the *knowledge* of him who called us by his glory (does he not mean by 'glory' here his grace?) and goodness that everything that we need for life and godliness comes to us (2 Pet. 1:3), I regard these opportunities afforded me to speak to you about our great and awesome God and his attributes a rare privilege indeed. My prayer this week has been that we will not waste this morning's opportunity to grow in our knowledge of his justice, for nothing is more needful for us at this hour, as I trust you will see before this address is concluded. Let us pray together now for this much-needed knowledge.

Prayer

Blessed heavenly Father, compassionate Lord Jesus Christ, merciful Holy Spirit, we thank you for the opportunity to study your precious Word together, to discern what it has to say about your Being and perfections, and specifically this morning about your attribute of justice. Grant that we may clearly perceive that vain will be our efforts unless we grow in grace, increase in knowledge, and labor to make ourselves more ready for that great Day of Harvest awaiting us.

By our attendance upon your Word this morning, enable us to know you more perfectly, to love and adore you more fully, and to determine to serve you more single-mindedly.

We bring our hungry hearts to you and implore you to fill them with your choicest gifts, not the least of which by any just judgment is wisdom and understanding.

We bring our blind understanding to you and plead that you would drive away our ignorance.

Guide us this morning, we pray, lest we become entangled in error.

We dare to believe, as we ask these things, that you will answer our prayer, because Jesus is our Savior from sin. So purify our hearts, cleanse and clear our minds, that we may learn more about you who called us to yourself by your grace and goodness.

I ask all these things in that name that draws you, our heavenly Father, away from wrath to rapturous overtures of grace, even Jesus Christ our Lord. Amen.

* * *

This morning we take up the *Catechism*'s statement that our God is just or, what is the same thing, righteous[1] – infinitely, eternally, and unchangeably so. What does this mean according to Holy Scripture? What comes to *your* mind when you reflect upon the justice and/or the righteousness of God? Does God's justice frighten you? Does his righteousness console you? Well, we shall see that it may and can do both, depending upon your standing before him.

Justice as retributive righteousness

To begin our exposition, God's justice first means that he is necessarily righteous (*tsedheq* [Heb]; *dikaios* [Gr]) in all his judicial judgments, *always* rewarding his rational creatures directly proportional to their works, showing partiality to none (Deut. 10:17) and *always* acquitting (that is, 'declaring righteous') the righteous and *always* condemning the guilty (Exod. 23:7).

The Bible describes him as the Judge (*shôphēt*) of all the earth (Gen. 18:25). Moses declares that the Lord is 'the Rock, his works are perfect, and *all his ways are just* [*mishpāt*]. A faithful God who does no wrong; *just*

---

[1] In Holy Scripture the terms 'justice' and 'righteousness' can scarcely be distinguished from each other. This is the reason that close attention must be paid to the contexts in which the terms occur if one is to discern their proper intent.

[*tsadhîq*] and *upright* [*yāshār*] *is he*' (Deut. 32:4). But whereas human judges are righteous judges if and when they adhere to the righteous law *above* them, God as the righteous Judge of all the earth knows no standard of law above him in conformity to which he must render his judicial decisions. The criterion of justice to which he conforms his every judgment is *innate* and *intrinsic* to him, namely, his own holy, perfect, and righteous knowledge of the truth. Accordingly, the creature need have no fear that he will be judged someday by the arbitrary fiat of an unjust divine tyrant. He may rest assured that God's justice is grounded in his infinite wisdom and knowledge, his commitment to truth, and the demand for just judgments that his own holy nature imposes on him. His decisions at the Great White Throne Judgment will be so just and righteous that no one will be able to question them, not once in the billions and billions of times that human beings will appear before him. This is the reason, I would suggest, that Paul declares: 'every mouth will be silenced' (Rom. 3:19) at the judgment bar of God. 'Does God pervert justice? Does the Almighty pervert what is right [*tsedeq*]?' (Job 8:3) Never! 'Will not the Judge of all the earth do right [[*mishpāt*]?' (Gen. 18:25) Yes, always! His judgments are and will ever be unquestionably, incontrovertibly, unassailably right and just.

What we have been describing thus far highlights the fact that God's justice is *retributive* or punitive in nature. Acting retributively, God 'reacts to human conduct, both good and evil, with absolute propriety. He condones nothing; and He overlooks no mitigating or extenuating factor.'[2] Since dishonoring the infinite God by sinning against him is worse than destroying countless worlds, even the impenitent's smallest sin has infinite disvalue for which no created good can compensate God by

---

[2]Donald Macleod, *Behold Your God* (Ross-shire: Christian Focus, 1990), 74.

way of satisfaction. So God in retributive justice or righteousness *judges the impenitent wicked*. And the Bible teaches this very plainly:

Retributive righteousness texts

Psalm 7:11: 'God is a righteous judge, a God who expresses his wrath every day.'

Psalm 9:7-8: 'The LORD reigns forever; he has established his throne for judgment. He will judge the world in righteousness; he will govern the peoples with justice.'

Psalm 62:12: '...you, O Lord,.... Surely you will reward each person according to what he has done.' (See also Proverbs 24:12)

Psalm 94:1-3: 'O LORD, the God who avenges, O God who avenges, shine forth. Rise up, O Judge of the earth; pay back to the proud what they deserve. How long will the wicked, O LORD, how long will the wicked triumph?'

Psalm 96:10, 13: 'Say among the nations, "The Lord reigns." ...He will judge the peoples with equity.... He will judge the world in righteousness and the peoples in his truth.'

Isaiah 5:16: '...the LORD Almighty will be exalted by his justice, and the holy God will show himself holy by his righteousness.'

Daniel 9:14: 'The LORD our God is righteous in everything he does.'

Romans 2:5-6: 'You are storing up wrath against yourself for the day of God's wrath, when his righteous judgment will be revealed. God "will give to every person according to what he has done".'

Romans 3:5-6: 'What shall we say? That God is unjust in bringing his wrath on us?... Certainly not! If that were so, how could God judge the world?'

2 Thessalonians 1:5-7: 'God's judgment is right.... God is just; he will pay back trouble to those who trouble you and give relief to you who are troubled.'

The doctrine

Perhaps someone is asking at this juncture, 'Do you expect me to believe that God will *really* judge in retributive righteousness the impenitent sinner for his sin?' I will only say here that it is all too clear from Holy Scripture that *he will indeed do so*, for according to Scripture he has already demonstrated that he will. God cast the angels who sinned against him out of heaven and delivered them into everlasting chains of darkness, to be reserved until the great judgment day when he will consign them to the lake of fire forever (Jude 6). He destroyed the entire antediluvian world of mankind, with the exception of Noah and his family, because the wickedness of mankind against him then became great in the earth, with every inclination of the thoughts of every person being only evil continually (Gen. 6:5; Gen. 6–8). He rained down fire and brimstone upon Sodom because the Sodomites were wicked and exceedingly evil before the Lord (Gen. 19:24; see 2 Pet. 2:6-8; Jude 7). And someday he will turn all the nations who have forgotten him, spurned his law, and rejected his overtures of grace into hell (Ps. 9:17). You see, my friends, our sin infuriates God, and one day, so say the prophets Nahum (1:2, 5, 8) and Malachi (4:1), God

> will take vengeance on his adversaries and pour out his wrath upon his enemies ... the mountains will quake at him, the hills will melt, the earth will burn at his presence, the world, and all that dwell therein. Who will stand before his indignation? Who will abide the fierceness of his anger? For he will pursue his enemies into darkness.... Behold, the day will come that will burn as an oven, and all the proud and

those that do wickedly will become stubble and that day will burn them up, says the LORD of hosts.

But *just as clearly as all these examples of God's retributive justice* – now please hear me, dear colleagues and seminarians – *just as clearly as all these Old Testament examples* that God will judge the sinner in retributive justice for his sin, Jesus' cry of dereliction from the cross, 'My God, my God, why have you forsaken me?' and his agonizing death on the tree of Calvary show this age, I say, *as clearly*, if not more so, that God *will* indeed judge impenitent men for their sin.

I say 'if not more so' because if ever there were a time when one might expect that God would have withheld his retributive justice, it would have been against his own beloved Son because there was no one anywhere in all existences so dear to God as his own Son and because his Son had no sin of his own. But when God made his Son the Sinbearer for his elect, it 'pleased the LORD to bruise him' (Isa. 53:10). This is why I say that if any single event demonstrates to our age that God will retributively judge the lawbreaker it is the crucifixion of his own dear and sinless Son when he stood in the stead of sinners, bearing their sin, and died on the tree under the curse of God (Deut. 21:23; Gal. 3:13). *If anything in all the world is an exhibition to our age of retributive justice on earth against sin, that is, of the sinner's damnation under the curse of Almighty God, it is the crucifixion of Jesus Christ, God's own beloved Son, at Calvary!* Thomas Kelly, the hymn writer, understood this:

Tell me, ye who hear him groaning, was there ever grief like his?
Friends thro' fear his cause disowning, foes insulting his distress;
Many hands were raised to wound him, none would interpose to save;

But the deepest stroke that pierced him was the stroke
that Justice gave.

Jonathan Edwards also understood – better than
most preachers today – the terror of God's *retributive*
righteousness. In his sermon, 'Sinners in the Hands
of an Angry God,' he proclaimed to the congregation at
Enfield:

> The God that holds you over the pit of hell, much as
> one holds a spider or some loathsome insect over the
> fire, abhors you and is dreadfully provoked: his wrath
> toward you burns like fire; he looks upon you as worthy
> of nothing else but to be cast into the fire; he is of purer
> eyes than to bear to have you in his sight; you are ten
> thousand times more abominable in his eyes than the
> most hateful venomous serpent is in ours. You have
> offended him infinitely more than ever a stubborn rebel
> did his prince; and yet it is nothing but his hand that
> holds you from falling into the fire every moment. It is
> to be ascribed to nothing else that you did not go to hell
> last night; that you were allowed to awake again in this
> world after you closed your eyes to sleep. And there is
> no other reason to be given why you have not dropped
> into hell since you arose in the morning but that God's
> hand has held you up. There is no other reason to be
> given why you have not gone to hell since you have sat
> here in the house of God provoking his pure eyes by
> your sinful manner of attending his solemn worship.
> Yea, there is nothing else that is to be given as a reason
> why you do not this very moment drop down into hell.
> O sinner! Consider the fearful danger you are in: it is
> a great furnace of wrath, a wide and bottomless pit, full
> of the fire of wrath, that you are held over in the hand
> of that God whose wrath is provoked and incensed as
> much against you as against any of the damned in hell.
> You hang by a slender thread, with the flames of divine
> wrath flashing about it, and ready every moment to singe
> it, and burn it asunder; and you have no interest in
> any Mediator, and nothing to lay hold to save yourself,

nothing to keep off the flames of wrath, nothing of your own, nothing that you ever have done, nothing that you can do, to induce God to spare you one moment.... Your wickedness makes you as it were heavy as lead and to tend downwards with great weight and pressure towards hell, and if God should let you go you would immediately sink and swiftly descend and plunge into the bottomless gulf; and your healthy constitution and your own care and prudence and best contrivance and all your righteousness would have no more influence to uphold you and keep you out of hell than a spider's web would have to stop a falling rock.[3]

---

[3]Given Edwards' graphic descriptions of eternal punishment I believe I should comment on the nature of hell as the 'second death'. I will make three points.

First, the word in the Greek that is translated 'hell' ('Gehenna') is the Aramaic word for 'Valley of Hinnom,' the site name mentioned in 2 Kings 23:10, an idolatrous worship center from the time of Ahaz to Manasseh located south of Jerusalem at which site children were burned in fire as an offering to the god Molech (2 Chron. 28:3, 33). It was later destroyed by Josiah and made a refuse dump for the city's garbage. Since fire burned continuously in the valley, Gehenna became a symbol of and provided the imagery for the 'unquenchable fire' of hell. Then Topheth that was in the valley of Ben Hinnom (2 Kings 23:10) became a synonym for the site as a whole: 'Topheth has long been prepared; it has been made ready [writes Isaiah].... Its fire pit has been made deep and wide, with an abundance of fire and wood; the breath of the LORD, like a stream of burning sulphur, sets it ablaze' (Isa. 30:33). This then is apparently the source of the New Testament description of hell as 'unquenchable fire'.

As for its description of hell as a 'lake of fire' (*limnē tou puros*) this phrase occurs six times in five verses and only in the Revelation. It has no precedent either in the Old Testament or anywhere else in Jewish literature. But three of these six occurrences add 'and brimstone [or sulfur]' (*kai theiō*), a combination that is found elsewhere in the Bible (Gen. 19:24; Ps. 11:6; Ezek. 38:22; Luke 17:29; Rev. 9:17-18; 14:10). Perhaps John's imagery of hell as a 'lake' of fire should be traced to the depiction in the Old Testament verses of God '*raining down* fire and brimstone'. It is the final place of eternal punishment for the beast and false prophet (Rev 19:20), for Satan (20:10), for Death and Hades (20:14, two times), for those whose names are not written in the book of life (20:15), and for all evildoers (21:8), all of

Dreadful indeed is Edwards' description of the sinner's plight before the righteous Judge of all the earth but it is also very true! So mankind should and must take God's *retributive* justice or righteousness very seriously.

---

whom are cast into 'the lake that burns with fire and brimstone, which is the second death'.

Second, I do not think that we must maintain that hell is a place of actual, literal flame as we know flame since it is difficult, if not impossible, for us to comprehend how Jesus could then speak of the impenitent's end as 'the outer darkness' (*to skotos to exōteron*) in Matthew 8:12, 22:13, and 25:30, how 2 Peter 2:17 and Jude 13 could describe hell as a 'forever place' of 'the blackness of darkness' (*ho zophos tou skotous*), and how literal fire could torment demonic spirits or disembodied spirits as in Luke 16. Doubtless at least some of the language of Scripture describing the world of the afterlife must be understood figuratively. But figurative language, if it has any meaning at all, intends something literal, and it is my contention that the figures of 'unquenchable fire' and 'the lake of fire and brimstone where [there is] torment day and night forever and ever,' in light of all the Scripture references, intend at the very least unimaginable *unending conscious torment and misery*.

Third, we should take no comfort in the prospect that hell may not be literal fire, for if the scriptural imagery of hell is only symbolic, then the reality the Bible seeks to represent with its verbal imagery can only be understood by us to be *more* – not less – horrible than the imagery it depicts just as a real 'perfect storm' in which one would find himself would be unspeakably more terrible than any verbal depiction of it.

Nor should we hope that all mankind will eventually be saved, for the New Testament teaches or implies the *eternal* bifurcation of the saved and the unsaved in more than fifty passages. I will cite three of them as examples of this division:

'Let the [the good seed and the weeds] both grow together until the harvest [Jesus said]. At that time I will tell the harvesters: First collect the weeds and tie them in bundles to be burned; then gather the wheat and bring it into my barn.... The harvest is the end of the age, and the harvesters are angels. As the weeds are pulled up and burned in the fire, so it will be at the end of the age. The Son of Man will send out his angels, and they will weed out of his kingdom everything that causes sin and all who do evil. They will be thrown into the fiery furnace, where there will be weeping and gnashing of teeth. Then the righteous will shine as the sun in the kingdom of their Father' (Matt. 13:30, 38-43).

Justice as distributive righteousness

What most of mankind, even most professing Christians, are not aware of, however, is that, far and away, *throughout Scripture God's righteousness is represented as distributive, that is, as salvific righteousness.* In fact, while the Scriptures certainly cast God's justice in a retributive sense, as we have seen, John Calvin notes that the divine righteousness is that 'by which the faithful are preserved and most benignantly cherished'.[4] Herman Bavinck quite properly notes that the punishment of the wicked 'is usually derived from God's *wrath,*' with God's righteousness being 'usually represented as the principle of the salvation of God's people', that is, as the 'attribute by virtue of which God justifies [or acquits] the righteous, and exalts them to glory and honor'.[5] Louis Berkhof affirms that God's distributive righteousness, as both an expression of the divine love and the reflection of his gracious covenant that he has established with his own, deals out its bounties according to his promises.[6] And Geerhardus Vos speaks

---

'When the Son of Man comes in the glory of his Father, and all the angels with him, he will sit on his throne in heavenly glory. All the nations will be gathered before him, and he will separate the people one from another as a shepherd separates the sheep from the goats. He will put the sheep on his right hand and the goats on his left.... Then [they on his left hand] will go away to eternal punishment, but the righteous to eternal life' (Matt. 25:31-33, 46).

'...an hour is coming, in which all who are in the tombs shall hear [my] voice, and shall come forth; those who did good to a resurrection of life, those who committed evil to a resurrection of judgment' (John 5:28-29).

No amount of exegetical magic can overturn this final division of mankind that is plainly taught throughout Scripture. One's exegesis would be perversely inept to conclude otherwise.

[4]John Calvin, *Institutes*, 1.10.2.

[5]Herman Bavinck, *The Doctrine of God* (Grand Rapids: Baker, 1977), 216, 217.

[6]Louis Berkhof, *Systematic Theology* (New combined edition; Grand Rapids: Eerdmans, 1996), 75.

of God's distributive righteousness as 'a righteousness of vindication, and a righteousness of salvation', rising from the fact that the adjudged righteous, looking to him for protection and redress, commonly expect their judge to be their savior.[7]

Distributive righteousness texts
Accordingly, the Old Testament portrays the people of God with respect to their salvation as

> long[ing] for the future, for the Messiah, who will be the *righteous* branch, Jer. 23:5, who will be righteous, Zech. 9:9; and who will not judge after the sight of the eyes, but with righteousness, Is. 11:3-5; and whose judgment, therefore, will consist in this: that 'he will have pity on the poor and needy (who were now neglected and suppressed), and the souls of the needy he will save,' Ps. 72:12-14. Hence, [God's] exercising [of his] righteousness would consist especially in delivering the needy; doing justice becomes with reference to these needy ones a deed of grace and compassion, as it were.[8]

Therefore, as their *righteous* Judge, God grants salvation to the pious

> because he establishes them [in his righteousness], Ps. 7:9; helps them [in his righteousness], 31:1; answers them [in his righteousness], 65:5; hears them [in his righteousness], 143:1; delivers them [in his righteousness], 143:11; revives them [in his righteousness], Ps 119:40; acquits them [in his righteousness], 34:22; [and] grants unto them [in his righteousness] the justice due unto them, 35:32; etc.; while the wicked do not come into his righteousness, 69:27, 28.[9]

---

[7]Geerhardus Vos, *Biblical Theology* (Grand Rapids: Eerdmans, 1949), 271, 273-4.

[8]Bavinck, *The Doctrine of God*, 217.

In his grace the Lord is their righteousness (Jer. 23:6: *Yhwh tsidhqēnū*) who enrobes his people with his righteousness (Isa. 61:10; Rom. 1:16-17; 3:25: Gal. 2:16; 2 Cor. 5:21). And his people, singing the Song of Moses and the Song of the Lamb, affirm: 'Great and marvelous are your deeds, Lord God Almighty. Just and true are your ways, King of the ages. Who will not fear you, O Lord, and bring glory to your name? For you alone are holy ... for your righteous acts have been revealed' (Rev. 15:3-4).

The doctrine

In multitudes of Old and New Testament passages the Lord's *righteousness* does not stand *in contrast with* his lovingkindness, as does his wrath (Ps. 69:24ff.), but *is synonymous with his lovingkindness* (Pss. 22:31; 33:5; 35:28; 40:10; 51:15; 89:14; 145:7; Isa. 45:21; Jer. 9:24; Hos. 2:18; Zech. 9:9). Indeed, the manifestation of God's righteousness is often at the same time *the showing forth of his grace* as in Psalms 97:11-12, 112:4, 116:5, and 119:15-19. *Even the forgiveness of sins is due to God's righteousness* according to Psalms 51:14, 103:17, and 1 John 1:9. Hence, deeds of redemption and of salvation and deliverance are revelations of God's righteousness according to Judges 5:11, 1 Samuel 12:7, Psalm 103:6, Isaiah 45:24-25, and Micah 6:5.[10] Now do you understand better the oft-quoted Johannine statement: 'If we confess our sins, he is faithful and [distributively] *just [dikaios]* to forgive us our sins, and to cleanse us from all unrighteousness'? God's justice grants here, you see, our salvation!

But how can the righteous Judge of all the earth in *righteousness* forgive and in *righteousness* show compassion toward undeserving sinners? His distributive

---

[9]Bavinck, *The Doctrine of God*, 218.
[10]Bavinck, *The Doctrine of God*, 218.

righteousness must be traced to the fact that he is governed, as Berkhof rightly observes, by his eternal covenant with his elect people, both Jews and Gentiles, particularly as that covenant came to expression in the terms of the Abrahamic covenant.[11] As Donald Macleod observes:

> ...the gods of the [other] nations [round about Israel] were capricious and unpredictable and their devotees lived in constant dread of their malevolent and irrational intrusion into their daily lives. But this was not true of Israel's God. He was reliable and predictable and stood in a stable relationship both with the world and with His people... This was very largely the result ... that all God's dealings with men occurred within the framework of covenant.[12]

---

[11]See my *A New Systematic Theology of the Christian Faith* (Second edition; Nashville, Tennessee: Thomas Nelson, 2002), 512-18.

[12]Donald Macleod, *Behold Your God*, 41. I should add that the pagan religions of the nations surrounding Israel had room for conquest and coercion that included forcing their gods upon the conquered and imposing the death penalty upon any who refused to worship their gods (see Dan. 3). This is because the god-worlds of these pagan religions were mirrors of this world with its warfares, love affairs, jealousies, and murders. These pagan religions could also be and in fact were open to religious syncretism that often absorbed the gods of the conquered into their pantheons. But *what these pagan religions could not do was to make a sincere effort to bring other nations to faith in their gods simply by bearing a spiritual witness.*

This is possible only within the framework of the covenant that God made with Abraham that foresaw and proclaimed that God would justify the Gentiles by faith along with Abraham (Gal. 3:8-9). Since Yahweh was Israel's God only by virtue of his gracious covenant with it, Israel had no special and peculiar claim upon him; it enjoyed its privileged covenant position only because of God's electing grace since it was not intrinsically or inherently better than other nations (see Deut. 7:7-8 and 9:4-6). And because this was so, it was entirely conceivable – indeed, God declared it would come to pass – that his covenant with Abraham could and would eventually encompass people not only within Israel but also within the other nations as well (Gen. 12:3: 'All peoples on earth will be blessed through you'),

Therefore, because of his covenant fidelity God does not turn destructively on his elect who have placed their confidence in him. Because the covenant threat would and ultimately did exhaust itself in Christ's suffering at Calvary, God's people are immune to his wrath, and his *rectitude* or righteousness in covenant-keeping leads him to save and to vindicate them. In Christ's obedience and suffering they have met all the demands of God's justice (*dikē*), and their forgiveness is a matter of covenant right. So while his children are guilty of all manner of iniquity, they in faith, as those with whom he has entered into covenant,

> delight in the covenant itself. It is an unfailing source of consolation to them.... They delight to contemplate *the antiquity* of that covenant, remembering that before the daystar knew its place, or planets ran their round, the interests of the saints were made secure.... It is peculiarly pleasing to them to remember *the sureness* of the covenant, while meditating upon 'the sure mercies of David'.... It often makes their hearts dilate with joy to think of its *immutability*, as a covenant which neither time nor eternity, life nor death, shall ever be able to violate.... They also rejoice to feast upon *the fulness* of this covenant, for they see in it all things provided for them.... More especially it is the pleasure of God's people to contemplate *the graciousness* of this covenant. They see that the law was made void because it was a covenant of works and depended upon merit, but this [covenant] they perceive to be enduring because grace is the basis, grace the condition, grace the strain, grace the bulwark, grace the foundation, grace the topstone.[13]

Therefore, they

---

not by force but rather by means of preaching and the Spirit's accompanying persuasion.

[13]C. H. Spurgeon, *Morning and Evening*, August 26, morning.

favor [God's] righteous cause, they trust in the Lord, and they expect that he will grant them justice [or righteousness], that he will fight their battle, and will give unto them the victory of salvation, Ps. 17:1ff; 18:20, 21; 34:15; 103:6; 140:12. This salvation [consists] in this, that God grants unto his people forgiveness of sins, that he pours his Spirit into their hearts, that he grants unto them a new heart, and that he writes his law in their hearts, so that they walk perfectly before his countenance..., Is. 43:25; Is. 31:33, 34; 32:39, 40; 33:8; Ezek. 11:19; 36:25; Joel 2:28ff. [They are sinful and they know it, but they realize that] no one else than Yahweh can deliver [them] from this sin; 'only in Jehovah ... is righteousness and strength,' Is. 45:24.[14]

These forgiven ones recognize that only as the Lord is righteous in his *faithfulness* to his covenant and that only as they are by his grace 'in the LORD will all the descendents of Israel be found righteous' (Isa. 45:25). They apprehend that it is only as the Lord brings his covenantal righteousness near to them that their salvation will not be delayed (Isa. 46:13).

In sum, the Old Testament portrays the righteousness of God far more vividly in its *distributive* or salvific sense than in its *retributive* sense, setting the stage for the New Testament revelation of the righteousness of God in Jesus Christ who is Jeremiah's promised 'Righteous Branch' (Jer. 23:5: *ts^{e}mach tsaddîq*), the Branch who takes away Joshua's filthy robes and enrobes him in garments of righteousness (Zech. 3:4, 8; see Isa. 61:10), the Branch who builds the Lord's Temple (Zech. 6:12-13). In the gospel a *distributive* righteousness of God is revealed that comes by faith alone (Rom. 1:17; 3:21). By virtue of Christ's righteous life and substitutionary death God is able to forgive sin and to distribute or impute Christ's active righteousness to believers' accounts who

---

[14]Bavinck, *The Doctrine of God*, 218.

'are justified freely by his grace through the redemption that came by Christ Jesus' (Rom. 3:24). Ultimately, the atoning work of Jesus Christ is the ground upon which God the righteous Judge 'passes over [that is, forgives] sins committed [by the elect]' as that work 'demonstrates God's [retributive] justice..., making it possible for him ever to be both [retributively] just and the [distributive] justifier of the one who has faith in Jesus' (Rom. 3:25-6).

This then is the doctrine of God's infinite, eternal, and unchangeable justice worked out biblically and theologically. God's justice is impartially *retributive* as he shows partiality to none (Deut. 10:17) – *always* acquitting the righteous and *always* condemning the guilty (Exod. 23:7), meting out his righteous wrath upon the impenitent evildoer. His justice is also salvifically *distributive* as it freely bestows his bounty upon and justifies all who place their trust in the atoning work of His Son, Jesus Christ.

We will turn now to what I regard as the most significant point of application of what we have just observed about this attribute of God.

Application
My brothers and sisters, it takes no daring on my part to say that not only mankind in general but also even most professing Christians, to their own hurt, have *never* grasped the distinction I just made for you between God's *retributive* righteousness and his *distributive* or salvific righteousness. Mankind in general and even most professing Christians understand God's righteousness only in its retributive sense but not in its distributive sense and as a result believe that in order to escape his retributive justice and finally to achieve heaven they must gain God's approval by performing righteous deeds. Of course, most people believe that they perform such deeds and that all they have to do to be justified is to die, that is to say, they believe, as R. C. Sproul has often

said, not in justification by faith but in justification by death! Which is just to say, neither mankind in general nor most professing Christians understand the biblical doctrine of justification by faith alone – the heart and core of the one true 'law-free' gospel.[15] As a result they hold a Pelagian or Semi-Pelagian plan of salvation that is 'another gospel' that cannot save.

The Roman Catholic Church, claiming over half of those who profess to be Christians as its adherents, has repudiated the one true law-free gospel of Jesus Christ in favor of the Decrees and Canons of the counter-Reformation Council of Trent that confuse justification and sanctification, thereby bringing in human works as part of the ground of their final acceptance before God.[16]

---

[15]By the term 'law-free' we intend what Paul intended when he declared that 'a man is justified by faith apart from observing the law' (Rom. 3:28) and that a 'man is not justified by observing the law, but by faith in Jesus Christ ... because by observing the law no one will be justified' (Gal. 2:16). We do not intend by the term 'law-free' that the gospel delivers the Christian from the obligation to obey God's moral law as that law comes to expression in the Ten Commandments, in their summary in the two love commandments, and in Christ's pattern of life. Clearly the Christian lives under the law of God as the covenant way of life, but *his* obedience to God's law is *no* part of the ground of his justification; Christ's obedience alone is the ground of the believer's justification before God (Rom. 5:18-19).

[16]We reject the 'Regensburg-esque' expressions of the doctrine of justification advanced by the North American documents 'Evangelicals and Catholics Together' and 'The Gift of Salvation' and the 'bi-dimensional' European document, 'The Joint Declaration on the Doctrine of Justification,' all written and endorsed by those who, in the interest of church unity, are willing to settle for an ecumenical 'compromise' between Rome and the Magisterial Reformation in which Rome actually concedes nothing, with Trent's false deliverances on justification still standing as binding dogma for the Roman church, while the *sola fide* of the Reformation doctrine of justification is either obscured or abandoned altogether.We also reject the Sanders/Dunn 'New Perspective on Paul' that argues that Martin Luther and John Calvin at the time of the Reformation

More recently, a good many theologians even within Protestantism, following the lead of Norman Shepherd and N. T. Wright, have abandoned the doctrine of justification as enunciated by the sixteenth-century Magisterial Reformers and the historic Protestant Confessions and are teaching that the Christian's justification is not by faith alone in the all-sufficient work of Jesus Christ but is rather the *eschatological* result of the *believer's* faithfulness to Christ that includes his imperfect works of obedience. These teachers have rejected the Apostle Paul's clear teaching that justification is an act of God's free grace by which the moment a penitent sinner truly places his faith in Christ God forgives that believer of all his sins and imputes to him the perfect obedience of his Son Jesus Christ (see Acts 13:38-39; Gal. 2:16; Rom. 1:16-17; 3:21-22, 28; 4:4-15; 2 Cor. 5:21; Eph. 2:8-10), thereby constituting and declaring him righteous in his sight. Either minimizing or denying altogether the imputation of Christ's active or preceptive obedience to the believer, they teach that justification is not a purely forensic declaration but a spiritually transforming activity in which the believer's obedience is necessary for his full and final justification before God. But the Apostle Paul warned that those who intermingle to any degree their obedience with Christ's obedience as the ground of their final justification before God (1) stand under apostolic condemnation (Gal. 1:8-9), (2) have made Christ's cross-work of no value to them (Gal. 5:2), (3) have alienated themselves from Christ (Gal. 5:4a), (4) have set aside (Gal. 2:21) and have fallen away from grace in the sense that they have placed themselves once again under the Law as the way of salvation (Gal. 3:10; 5:4b), and (5) have

---

misunderstood what the Apostle Paul taught about justification and so constructed an erroneous and misleading doctrine of justification that Protestantism has enshrined in its national Confessions and unwittingly follows to this day.

abolished the offense of the cross (Gal. 5:11) because they are trusting in a 'different gospel [from Paul's] that is no gospel at all' (Gal. 1:6-7); indeed, their false 'gospel' requires them to 'continue to do everything written in the Book of the Law' (Gal. 3:10) perfectly as the ground of their justification before God.

To make what I mean here clear I will take you on a brief excursion into church history, beginning with a citation from Martin Luther on his spiritual struggles as an Augustinian monk in the early sixteenth century:

> ...in the same year [1519] I had begun to lecture on the Psalms again, believing that with my classroom experience in lecturing on the letters of Paul to the Romans, to the Galatians, and on the Letter to the Hebrews, I was now better prepared. All the while I was aglow with the desire to understand Paul in his letter to the Romans. But up till then it was ... the single expression in Chapter 1:17 concerning 'the righteousness of God' that blocked the way for me. For I *hated* that expression 'righteousness of God,' *since I had been instructed by the usage and custom of all the teachers to understand it according to the scholastic philosophy as the 'formal and active righteousness' by which God proves himself righteous by punishing sinners and the unjust.*
>
> Although I was a holy and blameless monk ... I did not love, indeed, I hated the righteous God ... and ... murmuring greatly, I was angry with God, and said: 'As if, indeed, it is not enough that miserable sinners, eternally lost through original sin, are crushed by every kind of calamity by the law of the Decalogue, *without having God add pain to pain ... by the gospel also threatening us with righteousness and wrath!'* Thus I raged with a fierce and stubborn conscience. Nevertheless, I beat importunately upon Paul at that place [Romans 1:17], most ardently desiring to know what Paul wanted.

These words Martin Luther wrote twenty-six years later in 1545 in his 'Preface' to the Latin edition of his *Works*, to which 'Preface' we will return later.

Now if we can associate Romans 13:13-14 with the conversion experience of Augustine and 1 Timothy 1:19 with Jonathan Edwards' conversion, we can surely associate Romans 1:17 in a very special way with the life of the great Protestant Reformer, Martin Luther, which verse teaches so clearly that the gospel's 'good news' is that God's righteousness, which we sinful human beings so desperately need because we have none of our own, he freely gives to anyone and everyone who trusts in the preceptive and penal obedience of the Lord Jesus Christ alone. I want us to consider the influence of this verse on Martin Luther's life. We shall see that in a real way it became his life text.

Having been frightened almost to death during his law-school days by a terrifying thunderstorm during which he vowed to St. Anne that he would become a monk, and to prepare himself for that awful meeting someday with God, Luther, against all the pleadings of his astonished friends, on August 17, 1505, then twenty-one years old, suddenly left the university at Erfurt and entered the Augustinian Cloister there, not so much to study theology, he tells us, as to save his soul.

Immediately Luther gave himself rigorously and with unflagging zeal to the monastic life. He fasted and prayed, he tortured himself and devoted himself to the most menial of tasks. Above all, he adhered to the medieval church's sacrament of penance, confessing even the most trivial of perceived faults for hours on end until his superiors wearied of his soul-searching exercises and ordered him to cease confession until he had committed some sin worth talking about. Luther would write later to the Duke of Savoy:

> I was indeed a pious monk and followed the rules of my order more strictly than I can express. If ever a monk

could obtain heaven by his monkish works, I should certainly have been entitled to it. Of this all the friars who have known me can testify. If it had continued much longer, I should have carried my mortifications even to death, by means of my watchings, prayers, reading and other labor.

Still, Luther found no peace of heart or mind. When the monkish wisdom advised him to satisfy God's righteous demands by meritorious works, he thought: 'But what works can come from a heart like mine? How can I stand before the holiness of my Judge with polluted works – polluted as they are at their very source?'

During this period of spiritual agonizing, God gave to Luther a wise spiritual father in the person of John Staupitz, the vicar-general of the Augustinian Order for all Germany. 'Why are you so sad, brother Martin?' Staupitz asked him one day. 'Ah,' replied Luther, 'I do not know what will become of me.... It is vain that I make promises to God; sin within me is ever the stronger.' To this Staupitz rejoined:

[Dear Martin,] more than a thousand times have I sworn to our holy God to live piously, and I have never kept my vows. Now I swear no longer, for I know that I cannot keep my solemn promises. If God will not be merciful towards me for the love of Christ and grant me a happy departure when I must quit this world, I shall never with the aid of all my vows and [Now note!] *all my good works* stand before him. I must perish.

Why, dear Martin, do you torment yourself? Look at the wounds of Jesus Christ, to the blood that he has shed for you; it is there that the grace of God will appear to you. Instead of torturing yourself on account of your sins, throw yourself into the Redeemer's arms. Trust in him – *in the righteousness of his life* – in the atonement of his death. Do not shrink back.... Listen to the Son of God. He became a man to give you the divine favor.

But how, Luther asked, could he hear the Son of God? Where could he hear *his* voice? In the church's tradition? 'In the Bible,' said the vicar-general. 'Let the study of the Scriptures be your favorite occupation.' And it was thus that Luther, who had only first seen a Bible in his law-school days shortly before entering the cloister, began to study the Scriptures, especially the letters of Paul, a privilege that you and I take so much for granted today.

But the divine work begun by Staupitz was not finished. The conscience of the young Augustinian monk, in spite of all his efforts in self-denial, had still not yet found peace with God. In 1510, five years after he had become a monk and two years after he had, upon Staupitz's recommendation, begun to teach the Bible at Elector Frederick of Saxony's new university at Wittenberg, Luther was sent to Rome on church business by his Order.

Going not only as an emissary for his Order but also as a pilgrim, when Luther caught sight of Rome in the distance – the site to which Paul's letter to the church at Rome was written and the capital city of Roman Catholicism – he tells us that he fell to his knees and raised his hands, exclaiming: 'I greet you, holy Rome, thrice holy from the blood of the martyrs.' No sooner did he arrive than he began, as time and official business permitted, to make the rounds of the churches, shrines, and relics, believing all the superstitions that were told to him at each site, and even regretting, he says, that his parents were not already dead because he could then have assured them against purgatory by all of his acts of penance.

Yet Rome was not the city of light and piety Luther had imagined it would be. Very quickly he perceived that the Mass, at which he thought the body and blood of Christ were being offered up by the priests as a sacrifice for sin – still the center of his religious devotion – was being made a laughing stock by many priests. Once, while he was repeating one Mass, the priests at the adjoining altar rushed through seven of them, calling out to Luther: 'Quick, quick, send our Lady back her Son.' In the company of some distinguished ecclesiastics, Luther heard them ridiculing the rite, laughing and with apparent pride boasting how, when they were standing at the altar repeating the words that were, according to Roman Catholic teaching, supposed to transform the bread and wine into the very body and blood of Christ, they said instead, no doubt in solemn intonations: *'Panis es, et panis manebis; vinum es, et vinum manebis'* ('Bread you are, and bread you will remain; wine you are, and wine you will remain.'). Then they laughingly explained that they would elevate the host and the people would bow down and worship the creaturely elements. Luther was shocked beyond words at what was to him at that time such freely confessed blasphemy!

In Rome also occurred the famous incident told many years later by Luther's son, Dr. Paul Luther, and preserved in a manuscript in the library at Rudolfstadt. In the Church of St. John Lateran in Rome there is a set of medieval stone stairs, said to have been the stairs leading up to Pilate's house in Jerusalem and thus once trod upon by the Lord himself, which stairs Luther was told had been miraculously transported to Rome. For this reason they were called the *Scala Sancta* or 'Holy Stairs'. It was customary for pilgrims to ascend these steps on their knees, praying as they ascended and kissing the bloodstains of Christ that reputedly appeared at certain intervals. Remission of years of punishment in Purgatory was promised to all who performed this arduous exercise.

His father, Paul Luther writes, began to crawl up those stairs as many others had done before him. But as he ascended the staircase, the words of Romans 1:17: 'The righteous will live by faith,' suddenly came forcefully to his mind. They seemed to echo over and over again: 'The righteous will live by faith.' 'The righteous will live by faith.' The old superstitions and the new biblical theology began to wrestle within him:

'By fear,' argued Luther. 'By faith,' said Paul.

'By meritorious works,' the scholastic fathers had taught him. 'By faith,' said the Apostle.

'By agonizing suffering,' argued Luther and those on the steps beside him by their actions. 'By faith,' spoke God the Holy Spirit, the Author of Scripture, to his heart.

Luther rose in wonder from the steps, up which he had been dragging himself, shuddering at the superstition and folly in which he had been engaged. Now he began to realize that God justifies sinners by faith in Christ alone. Slowly he turned on 'Pilate's Staircase' and returned to the bottom. He went back to Wittenberg, and while not without still some spiritual struggle, in time, as his son writes, 'He took, "The righteous will live by faith," as the foundation of all his doctrine.'

Of that 'staircase experience' J. H. Merle D'Aubigné, the great nineteenth century historian of the Reformation, writes:

This powerful text [Romans 1:17] [had] a mysterious influence on the life of Luther. It was a *creative* sentence both for the reformer and for the Reformation. It was in these words God then said, 'Let there by light; and there was light' ... when Luther uprose from his knees on Pilate's staircase, in agitation and amazement at those words which Paul had addressed fifteen centuries before to the inhabitants of that metropolis, Truth, till then a melancholy captive, and fettered in the church, uprose also to fall no more.[17]

This was the real beginning of the sixteenth-century Reformation because Luther's *personal* reformation

---

[17]J. H. Merle D'Aubigné, *History of the Reformation of the Sixteenth Century*, translated by H. White (New York: American Tract Society, n. d.), I, 207-8.

necessarily had to precede his effort to reform medieval Christendom's false theology. The latter began seven years later, on October 31, 1517 when he posted his 'Ninety-Five Theses' on the door of the Castle Church at Wittenberg, which act eventually led to his excommunication from the Roman Catholic Church by Pope Leo X in January 1521, and which brought him before Emperor Charles V at the Diet of Worms in April of that same year, at which assembly, in response to the two questions: 'Are these your writings? And will you, or will you not, recant?' after an all-night vigil in prayer he put both the world's and the church's mighty ones to flight with his immortal declaration:

> Since your most serene majesty [Charles V] and your high mightinesses require from me a clear, simple, and precise answer, I will give you one with neither horns nor teeth [that is neither offensive nor biting], and it is this: I cannot submit my faith either to the pope or to the councils, because it is clear as the day that they have frequently erred and contradicted each other. Unless therefore I am convinced by the testimony of Scripture, or by the clearest reasoning – unless I am persuaded by the passages I have quoted – and unless they thus render my conscience bound by the Word of God, I cannot and I will not retract, for it is unsafe for a Christian to speak against his conscience. Here I stand, I can do no other; may God help me! Amen!

Several things in Luther's declaration greatly impress me. First, his commitment to the Reformation's *sola Scriptura* principle is clearly evident. Second, he affirmed the validity of the laws of logic[18] and therefore, because

---

[18]In *What Luther Says*, compiled by Ewald M. Plass (St. Louis, MO: Concordia, 1959), Luther declares: '...we are certain that the Holy Spirit cannot oppose and contradict Himself' (216), and 'Passages of Scripture that are opposed to one another must, of course, be reconciled, and to one must be given a meaning which agrees with

popes and councils contradicted each other, he rejected their authority over him. Third, I have also been struck for a good many years now by Luther's words, 'I cannot and I will not retract for it is unsafe....' Unsafe? Did he not understand that 'it was unsafe' for him to oppose the imperial power of the Emperor and authorities of the Church? Had he forgotten that they had the power to have him burned alive. But he had believed the gospel that had delivered him from bondage to sin, he believed that God had imputed to him the preceptive righteousness of Christ and had imparted to him as well the peace within that passes all understanding, and he knew that all that these petty Caesars could do to him was kill the body but not the soul. So he resisted their tyrannical demands, declaring that 'it is unsafe for a Christian to speak against [the] conscience' that has been captured by the truth of God.

Do you remember how I began this application of God's attribute of justice – citing Luther's ragings against God because he thought not only the righteousness of God in the law but also the righteousness of God in the gospel condemned him? I will now complete his remarks:

At last, by the mercy of God, meditating day and night, I gave heed to the context of the words, namely, 'He who *by faith* is righteous shall live.' There I began to understand that the righteousness of God is that by which the righteous lives by the gift of God, namely, by faith ... [that] the righteousness of God revealed by the gospel is the righteousness with which the merciful God justifies us by faith.... Here I felt that I was altogether born again and had entered Paradise itself through open gates.... And as previously I had detested with all my heart these words, 'the righteousness of God,' I began from that hour to value and to love them, as the sweetest and most consoling words in the Bible. In very

the sense of the other; for it is certain that Scripture cannot disagree with itself' (220).

truth, that place in Paul [Romans 1:17] was for me truly the gate to Paradise.

Dear friends, the burning question for Martin Luther in the sixteenth century was *Wie kriege ich einen gnädigen Gott?* ('How can I find a gracious God?'), or as Job puts it: 'How can a mortal be righteous before God?' (Job 9:2) or as Bildad's ancient question phrases it: 'How can a man achieve right standing before God?' (Job 25:4). The church of the Middle Ages had taught for centuries that right standing before God was achieved through the Spirit's *inward* work of grace in the human heart, that is to say, through the sacrament of baptism, inner renewal, works of penance to address post-baptismal sins, and the grace of sanctification that is never complete in this life and thus Christians must go to Purgatory when they die – if they do not go directly to Hell for unrepented-of 'mortal sins' – to make final expiation for their sins. And candor requires that I inform you that that church is still with us today, with no change for the better in its false soteriology, in spite of Vatican II, from that time to our own, declaring again as recently as its 1994 *Catechism of the Catholic Church* that 'justification is ... the sanctification and renewal of the interior man'.

Luther had struggled for an answer to Bildad's question and at first had tried to find the answer in his own works of penance that never brought peace. Finally he came to a true and proper understanding of Romans 1:17 and found the very gates of heaven opened wide to him in that verse. Through his struggles and careful study of Scripture he (as well as the other Magisterial Reformers) came to understand that

♦ the *only* man with whom the infinitely holy God can have *direct* fellowship is the perfect Godman, the only mediator 'between God and man, the man Christ Jesus' (1 Tim. 2:5) – the *solus Christus* of the Magisterial Reformation – and that it is only as sinful people place their trust in Christ's saving work and are thereby regarded by God as *en Christō* ('in Christ') that the triune God can have any fellowship with them; that

♦ the only way to protect the *solus Christus* ('Christ alone') of salvation is to insist upon the *sola fide* ('faith alone') of justification, and the only way to protect the *sola fide* of justification is to insist upon the *solus Christus* of salvation; that saving faith is to be directed to the doing and dying of Christ alone and not to the good works or inner experience of the believer; that

♦ the Christian's righteousness before God today is *not on earth* within the believer but *in heaven* at the right hand of God in Jesus Christ; that

♦ the ground of our justification is the vicarious work of Christ *for* us, *not* the gracious work of the Spirit *in* us; that

♦ the faith-righteousness of justification is *not retributive but distributive*, not personal but vicarious, not infused but imputed, not experiential but forensic, not psychological but legal, not our own but a righteousness alien to us, and not earned but graciously given through faith in Christ, which faith is itself a gift of grace – all which means

♦ that justification by faith is not to be set off over against justification by works *per se* but over against justification by *our* works, for justification is indeed grounded in Christ's preceptive and penal obedience in our stead that we receive by faith alone.

While I trust that all of you here are genuinely converted and true Christians, I must urge you to examine yourselves to make sure that you are trusting solely in the preceptive and penal obedience of Jesus Christ for God's forgiveness and imputed distributive righteousness. For make no mistake about it, the day will come when you and I will stand naked before God, and in that day the issue of in whom or in what we trusted here for our salvation will be all-important. And 'though [we may] wish to dispute with him,' as Job states, 'we will [be unable to] answer him one time out of a thousand' (9:3), for you and I in that Great Day will be stripped of all the things in which we may have placed our confidence in this world. We will stand before the throne of the Judge of all the earth in that day without earthly title, without money, without property, without earthly reputation, without personal prestige – in utter poverty in ourselves. And unless we have been forgiven of our sins and are enrobed in the glorious dress of the imputed righteousness of Jesus Christ, God will consign us to eternal perdition for our sins.

Beloved friends, if you have never completely repudiated your own self-help efforts at self-salvation and have never totally trusted the Savior's righteous life and sacrificial death alone for your salvation, I beg of you, *do both right now*! You need a righteous Advocate who can legitimately say to the Father on your behalf, like Paul said to Philemon on Onesimus' behalf (Philem. 17-19):

> ...if you consider me a partner, welcome him as you welcome me [that is, reckon to him my merit]. If he has done you any wrong or owes you anything, charge it to me [that is, reckon to me his demerit]. I ... will pay it back.

Wouldn't you want and don't you need an Advocate like that when you appear before God? Christ alone *is* such an Advocate, and you need him more than you need anything else in this life. For not by works of righteousness that you will ever do will you be saved (Titus 3:5). Christ's bearing your imputed sin on the tree and the Father reckoning Christ's imputed righteousness to you through faith in him is your only hope of heaven, your only acceptable righteousness with God! Trust him now, for it is only by faith alone in Christ's righteous doing and sacrificial dying that you will receive forgiveness and the imputed distributive righteousness of God. Only then can you truly sing from the heart:

> Jesus, thy blood and righteousness
> my beauty are, my glorious dress;
> 'midst flaming worlds, in these arrayed,
> with joy shall I lift up my head.

Let us pray:
O righteous God, our heavenly Father, today we bless you for your *retributive* righteousness exhibited against your beloved Son, in whose death for our sin you vicariously punished him who paid our debt, bore our curse, died our death, and delivered us thereby forever from the sufferings of hell.

Eternity will be too short to praise you sufficiently for your Son's distributive or imputed righteousness that you freely give to all who entrust themselves to him.

We thank you that when we confess our sins to you, you are faithful and *distributively just* to forgive us our sins and to cleanse us from all unrighteousness.

We pray even now, if anyone here in this place has not cast himself by faith solely, wholly, and only upon your distributive righteousness revealed in Jesus Christ, that your Holy Spirit will quicken in that person a genuine fear of your retributive justice and move him or her to trust your Son's justifying death and distributive righteousness. For Jesus' glory and cause, we pray. Amen.

NINTH ADDRESS

'INFINITE, ETERNAL, AND UNCHANGEABLE IN HIS GOODNESS'

Moses said to the LORD, 'You have been telling me, "Lead these people," but you have not let me know whom you will send with me. You have said, "I know you by name and you have found favor with me." If you are pleased with me, teach me your ways so I may know you and continue to find favor with you. Remember that this nation is your people.'

The LORD replied, 'My Presence will go with you, and I will give you rest.'

Then Moses said to him, 'If your Presence does not go with us, do not send us up from here. How will anyone know that you are pleased with me and with your people unless you go with us? What else will distinguish me and your people from all the other people on the face of the earth?'

And the LORD said to Moses, 'I will do the very thing you have asked, because I am pleased with you and I know you by name.'

Then Moses said, 'Now show me your glory.'

And the LORD said, 'I will cause all my goodness to pass in front of you, and I will proclaim my name, the LORD, in your presence. I will have mercy on whom I will have mercy, and I will have compassion on whom I will have compassion. But,' he said, 'you cannot see my face, for no one may see me and live.'

Then the LORD said, 'There is a place near me where you may stand on a rock. When my glory passes by, I will put you in a cleft in the rock and cover you with my hand until I have passed by. Then I will remove my hand and you will see my back; but my face must not be seen' (Exod. 33:12-23).

Introduction

Good morning, beloved brothers and sisters, loved by God the Father, by Jesus Christ his only Son, our Lord, and by the Holy Spirit, our indwelling Comforter.[1]

I have deeply appreciated over the last several weeks your many kind expressions of gratitude for these addresses. I sincerely thank you for them, but you know, do you not, that more than your words of appreciation I earnestly desire that you will grow in grace and in the knowledge of our wonderful triune Savior God who is omnibenevolent in himself and who desires to make known the Alpine dimensions of his inexhaustible goodness to us in Jesus Christ? So let us pray that through my words today we all will be prompted by

---

[1]God the Holy Spirit deigns to inform us only once that he loves us, namely, in Romans 15:30, though he hints at it also in James 4:5, which paucity of expression is so, I would suggest, because the Holy Spirit much more desires that we know that the Father and the Son love us – truths that he inspired the Bible writers to tell us many times.

In Romans 15:30 the genitive, *tou pneumatos*, in the phrase, *agapēs tou pneumatos*, admittedly, could be either subjective ('through the Spirit's love for you') or objective ('through your love for the Spirit'). I would urge the former because of its parallelism with 'through our Lord Jesus Christ' and because it is more likely that Paul would invoke the Spirit's love for the Roman Christians than their love for the Spirit as the reason for striving together in prayer for him. But I admit a case can be made for the latter view.

James 4:5 reads: 'With jealousy longs the Spirit who dwells within us [for our undivided affection].' Because James states that the Scripture says this, we must assume that he had such verses as Exodus 20:5 in mind. And it is because of his jealous love for our affections, I would suggest, that our dalliances with sin grieve the Holy Spirit (Isa. 63:10; Eph. 4:30).

his grace to greater love and devotion for our good and gracious God.

Prayer

Our gracious God and loving heavenly Father: We come to you this morning, having been drawn *by your grace* away from the folly of thinking that we can live without you, having been drawn back *by your mercy* to your consolations which are new every morning, and having been kept *by the wonder* of your love which has forgiven us so very much.

I pray that you will prosper my address this morning about your incomparable goodness. Grant once again that your blessed Holy Spirit, our precious Comforter, will work by and with the preached Word in restless hearts and transform them into hearts that love you more earnestly, praise you more ardently, desire to serve you more sincerely, and long to be with you more fervently.

For these things I pray in the precious name of our merciful Savior. Amen.

* * *

The *Shorter Catechism* informs us that God has always been and always will be infinitely and unchangeably good, ascribing to him thereby that perfection of the divine nature that prompts him to deal bountifully and kindly with all his creatures.[2] If it is God's attribute of majestic holiness that exhibits his *transcendence over* his *finite* creation, it is his attribute of goodness that manifests his *condescendence toward* his *sinful* creation. For just as the *Catechism* subsumes God's omnipresence under the infinitude of his Being and his knowledge under the rubric of his wisdom, so also it intends this single beautiful word 'goodness' as the

---

[2]Louis Berkhof, *Systematic Theology* (New combined edition; Grand Rapids: Eerdmans, 1996), 70-1.

subsuming category under which God's love, common and special grace, mercy, pity, patience, compassion, longsuffering, kindness, gentleness, benevolence, generosity, faithfulness, joy when the sinner repents, grief when his child sins, and other such expressions of his tender and fatherly character are to be placed. Wayne Grudem correctly observes that 'God's mercy is his goodness toward those in distress, his grace is his goodness toward those who deserve only punishment [and] his patience is his goodness toward those who continue to sin over a period of time.'[3] And I would add, his pity is his goodness stirred by the spectacle of temporal and spiritual human misery, his grace is his goodness in action in the very presence of sin, and his love is his goodness manifested for us particularly in the sacrifice of Jesus Christ at Calvary.

Among the hundreds of Scripture verses that could be cited that testify to these 'good' characteristics of God's infinite nature are the following:

Texts

Genesis 1:31: 'God saw all that he had made, and it was very good.' The creation of the universe in its original 'very good' [*tōbh me'ōdh*] condition and man in his original state of integrity (*status integritatis*) (Eccles. 7:29) was the original display of God's intrinsic goodness.

Exodus 33:19: 'I will cause all my goodness to pass in front of you, and I will proclaim my name, the LORD, in your presence. I will have mercy on whom I will have mercy, and I will have compassion on whom I will have compassion.' Here God defines his goodness in terms of his sovereign mercy and compassion.

Psalm 33:5: '...the earth is full of his *unfailing love* [*hesed*].'[4]

---

[3]Wayne Grudem, *Systematic Theology* (Grand Rapids: Zondervan, 1994), 198.

Psalm 34:8: 'Taste and see that the LORD is good.'

Psalm 73:1: 'Surely God is good to Israel, to those who are pure in heart.' God's goodness in this psalm is his restraining grace that kept the psalmist's foot from slipping all the way away from him.

Psalm 103:1-6, 7-17, 22: 'Praise the LORD, O my soul; all my inmost being, praise his holy name. Praise the LORD, O my soul, and forget not all his benefits – who forgives all your sins and heals all your diseases, who redeems your life from the pit and crowns you with love and compassion, who satisfies your desires with good things so that your youth is renewed like the eagle's. The LORD works righteousness and justice for all the oppressed....

The LORD is compassionate and gracious, slow to anger, abounding in love. He will not always accuse, nor will he harbor his anger forever; he does not treat us as our sins deserve or repay us according to our iniquities. For as high as the heavens are above the earth, so great is his love for those who fear him; as far as the east is from the west, so far has he removed our transgressions from us. As a father has compassion on his children, so the LORD has compassion on those who fear him; for he knows how we are formed, he remembers that we are dust. As for man, his days are like grass, he flourishes like a flower of the field; the wind blows over it and it is gone, and its place remembers it no more. But from everlasting to everlasting the LORD's love is with them who fear him and his righteousness with their children's children...

Praise the LORD, O my soul.'

---

[4] *hesed*, because of its fullness of meaning, is not an easy word to translate. It is most often translated 'lovingkindness' or 'unfailing love' but even these fall short of capturing all that it means for in many contexts it alludes to God's 'covenant mercy'.

Psalm 106:1, 44-46: 'Give thanks to the LORD, for he is good; his love endures forever... [In spite of Israel's debauchery and rebellion], he took note of their distress when he heard their cry; for their sake he remembered his covenant and out of *his great love* [*rōbh hᵃsādhāw*] he relented. He caused them to be pitied by all who held them captive.' Here God's covenant faithfulness is subsumed under his goodness.

Psalm 107 in its entirety, particularly the recurring expression in verses 1, 8, 15, 21, 31: 'Give thanks to the LORD, for he is good...; his love endures forever... Let [men] give thanks to the Lord for his unfailing love and his wonderful deeds for men.'

Psalm 118:1, 29: 'Give thanks to the LORD, for he is good; his loves endures forever.' The body of this psalm expands upon his goodness and concludes with the refrain with which it began: 'Give thanks to the LORD, for he is good; his loves endures forever.'

Psalm 119:68: 'You are good, and what you do is good.'

Psalm 145:7-9, 13, 15, 16: '[The generations of your people] will celebrate your abundant goodness and joyfully sing of your [distributive] righteousness. The LORD is gracious and compassionate, slow to anger and rich in love. The LORD is good to all; he has compassion on all he has made ... the LORD is loving toward all he has made.... The eyes of all look to you, and you give them their food at the proper time. You open your hand and satisfy the desires of every living thing.' Here God's 'abundant goodness' entails his justifying righteousness, compassion, and love, as well as his common goodness to all living things.

Isaiah 55:6-7: 'Seek the LORD while he may be found; call upon him while he is near. Let the wicked forsake his way and the evil man his thoughts. Let him turn to the LORD, and he will have mercy on him, and to our God, for he will freely pardon.' Here God's goodness is exhibited by his merciful longing to pardon the sinner.

Ezekiel 33:11: 'As surely as I live, declares the sovereign LORD, I take no pleasure in the death of the wicked, but rather that they turn from their ways and live. Turn! Turn from your evil ways! Why will you die, O house of Israel?' Here God's goodness is displayed in his intense longing to see the sinner forsake his sin and turn to him.

Micah 7:18: 'Who is a God like you, who pardons sin and forgives the transgression of the remnant of his inheritance? You do not stay angry forever but delight to show mercy.' Here we learn that God who takes no delight in the sinner's death delights to show him mercy.

Matthew 5:45-48: '[Your heavenly Father] causes his sun to rise on the evil and the good, and sends rain on the righteous and the unrighteous.... Be 'all-inclusive [in your goodness]' [*teleioi*], therefore, as your heavenly Father is 'all-inclusive [in his].'

Here Jesus speaks of God's common goodness to all mankind. This is my translation, by the way, bringing out the fact from the context that *teleioi* does *not* mean 'morally perfect' as most Christians take it to mean but rather 'all-inclusive in the administration of one's goodness'. For additional support for my translation see its Lukan parallel in Luke 6:36: 'Be merciful just as your Father is also merciful.')

Mark 10:18: 'No one is good – except God alone.' See my *Jesus, Divine Messiah: The New and Old Testament Witness*,[5] for my treatment of this statement of Jesus where I show that he is neither confessing by

---

[5]Robert L. Reymond, *Jesus, Divine Messiah: The New and Old Testament Witness* (Ross-shire, Scotland: Mentor, 2003), 274-6.

implication that he is a sinner nor is he denying his deity.

Acts 14:17: 'He has shown kindness by giving you rain from heaven and crops in their season; he provides you with plenty of food and fills your hearts with joy.' Here again is highlighted God's common goodness to all his creatures.

Romans 2:4: '...do you show contempt for the riches of his kindness, tolerance, and patience, not realizing that God's kindness leads you toward repentance?'

Romans 8:28: 'In all things God works for the good of those who love him.' I should say as a passing comment here that if you reserve for yourself the prerogative to determine what the content of this 'good' is in this verse, you will always have a problem with Romans 8:28. For you will include in 'the good' many things that you will never get, and you will exclude from 'the good' many things that will come your way. The context makes it clear that 'the good' is your ultimate conformity to Christ's likeness, and God will continue that 'good work' in you until he has completed it, even though that 'good work' may entail at times hardship, pain, and great suffering.

James 1:17: 'Every good and perfect gift is from above, coming down from the Father of the heavenly lights.'

1 John 4:8: 'God['s very essence] is love. This is how God showed his love among us: He sent his one and only Son into the world that we might live through him. This is love: not that we loved God, but that he loved us and sent his Son as an atoning sacrifice for our sins.'

The doctrine
All these and the myriad other verses that speak, first, of God's goodness to all men – the evil and the good, the righteous and the unrighteous – that provides

food for them and moves him to relieve their human misery and distress with the loving care of a father and the compassionate succor of a mother (designated by theologians as God's 'common grace'), and second, of God's love for the world that prompted him to give his one and only Son for it (John 3:16; 1 John 4:9-10) and his unmerited grace that moves him still to extend forgiveness to the undeserving elect sinner (designated by theologians as God's 'special grace') – all these verses, I say, affirm each in its own way the *infinite* goodness of God. And even when he does what many of his rational creatures regard as the ultimate misdeed of condemning the impenitent sinner to hell, he is not being bad (he is still good – more on this point later); he is simply being *retributively* just. It is simply impossible for him to be bad or to take any pleasure in the horrible end of the impenitent.

Let's develop the meaning of this *Catechism* assertion further. These Scriptures would have us understand that our God is intrinsically good in and of himself. The creature's good – but an infinitesimal drop in comparison to God's goodness – is a derivative of God's goodness that is the infinite ocean, for goodness in God is an intrinsic characteristic of his infinite Being. What the Greeks sought for by their philosophies, namely, the 'highest good', they could have had in Israel's God for he is, if you will pardon the Latin neuter as a description of him, man's *Summum Bonum*, his *highest* Good. God is not just the 'Good' or the 'Better than Most'; he is the Best, the *highest* Good! And all that proceeds from him – from his eternal purpose and its execution by his works of creation and providence to the dropping of the final curtain on earth history in the Eschaton – is good. From the simplest living cell to man, his crowning act of creation, one may see on display the goodness of God. And the more closely one examines the crowning act of God's creation, namely, man, God's *imago*, the more one is filled with awe and wonder at God's beneficence to him. With the psalmist one has to say: 'I praise you because I am fearfully and wonderfully made; your works are wonderful, I know that full well' (Ps. 139:14). For not only does everything about our bodies attest to the goodness of their Maker – how well-suited, with their opposable thumbs, are our marvelous hands to perform their allotted tasks; how beneficial are their lids and brows to our eyes that can distinguish over seven million colors; indeed, how wonderful are all our senses and all the natural things that gratify them such as glorious sunsets, breath-taking panoramic vistas, and beautiful flowers for our sense of sight, rapturous orchestral and organ music and the melodious songs of birds for our sense of hearing, tantalizing aromas of flora for our sense of smell, delicious foods for our sense of taste[6] – but also he has deigned not only to speak to us,

---

[6]If the unbeliever would require the Christian to have a satisfying answer to the problem of evil before he turns to God the Christian in turn may require the unbeliever to have a satisfying explanation for both the 'natural good' that is on majestic and panoramic display everywhere in the natural world that he himself experiences and without which he could not survive and the 'ethical [or "compassionate"] good' that mankind displays toward those in need not only in times of natural crisis but also constantly through the world's charitable organizations. His experience and witness of the good is a major theological problem for the unbeliever. How does he explain the Western world's altruism and massive acts of charity in response to the Asian tsunami in December 2004, the world's hospitals and voluntary caregivers, the Red Cross, and even simple friendship? Andree Seu, senior writer for *World*, drives home my point with an illustration from C. S. Lewis in 'The problem of good' in *World* (August 14, 2004), 39:

The problem of good is what rallied Puddleglum (in Lewis's *The Silver Chair*) from the brink of deadly soul sleep by the witch's evil enchantment in her dungeon kingdom. Prince Rilian, Scrubb, Jill, and he had nearly succumbed to her specious logic disproving the Overworld, or Narnia: 'Your sun is a dream; and there is nothing in that dream that was not copied from the lamp. The lamp is the real thing; the "sun" is but a tale, a children's story.'
But the Marshwiggle, in his finest moment, would not deny what he had seen: 'I know I was there once. I've seen the sky full of stars,

thereby ennobling us and honoring us above all other living creatures, but also even to enter into covenant with us that we might receive some fruition from him as our blessedness and reward for obedience. And we could continue itemizing examples of God's exhibitions of goodness to mankind indefinitely here were that our present purpose.

One other point must be made. If the one infinite God is the original Good and if goodness is intrinsic to his nature, then he is the *ultimate* good. And if he is the ultimate good then he is the ultimate *standard* of good, and we now possess what the Greek philosophers also sought by their philosophies, namely, the means to discern what is man's 'good', this 'good' being whatever God approves and declares is good; and the 'bad' being whatever he disapproves and declares is bad. If one asks: 'Why is what God approves good?' we must simply say: 'Because he approves it; there is no higher standard of good than God's own character.' And he has informed us what the standard of *moral* goodness for man is, namely, his holy law, the covenant norm for human behavior. So much for the doctrine. Let's turn now to application.

Application
By way of application I want to ask you to consider in some detail with me this morning two divine attributes

---

the sun coming up out of the sea of a morning and sinking behind the mountains at night. And I've seen him in the midday sky when I couldn't look at him for brightness.'

Puddleglum added an interesting twist: 'Suppose we have only dreamed, or made up, all those things – trees and grass and sun and moon and stars and Aslan himself. Suppose we have. Then all I can say is that, in that case, the made-up things seem a good deal more important that the real ones. Suppose this black pit of a kingdom of yours *is* the only world. Well, it strikes me as a pretty poor one.'

Which strikes me as another bit of evidence for God's reality. All are road signs, all pointing to God – the True, Omniscient, the Good.

that are usually subsumed by our theologians under his attribute of 'goodness', namely, his patient longsuffering and his immeasurable love. Our *Shorter Catechism*, as you know, teaches us: 'God is a Spirit, infinite, eternal, and unchangeable in his being, wisdom, power, holiness, justice, goodness, and truth.' Now you know I love the Reformed faith and I love the *Shorter Catechism*, and I can certainly appreciate and understand that a children's catechism should be a model of brevity, but we have reached the point in its definition of God where I must say that I believe the *Catechism*, first, is not as sensitive as it should be to its intended audience, namely, to 'such as are of a weaker capacity,' as the Scottish General Assembly put it in the Act approving it, and second, is indeed 'shorter' than it should be by at least these two attributes.

With respect to its insensitivity to its intended audience, why, I ask, should children have to reach the tenth term of the *Catechism* description of the biblical God before they learn that he is 'good'? And just good? How about loving? For however beautiful the single word 'goodness' is as an attribute of God – and it *is* both a beautiful and subsuming biblical word – the *Shorter Catechism*, in my opinion, should not have subsumed the attributes of God's longsuffering toward and love for sinful children under his 'goodness' but should have given them equal and separate billing for our children's sake.

But then, even the *Larger Catechism* definition of God for the more mature – have you noticed? – fails to mention his love. And there is no chapter on God's love either in Stephen Charnock's *The Existence and Attributes of God* or in Herman Bavinck's *The Doctrine of God*, both being content to subsume God's love under his goodness. Louis Berkhof, defining God's love as 'that perfection of the divine nature by which he is eternally moved to self-communication' also subsumes it under God's goodness and devotes *one* sixteen-line paragraph to it.[7] Heinrich Heppe in his *Reformed Dogmatics*, defining God's love as 'a certain benevolent and beneficent propension towards the creatures' – subsumes it under God's attribute of holiness, and he too devotes only one paragraph to it.[8]

I ask you now: Do such definitions of God's love as the two I just read to you – that perfection by which he is 'eternally moved to self-communication' and 'a certain benevolent and beneficent propension towards the creature' – do definitional justice to the immeasurable love of God?

Gerald Bray, even though he declares that God's love is the 'greatest of his personal attributes,' devotes only about two pages of his *The Doctrine of God* to God's love for the creature.[9] In my own *Systematic Theology* I too treat God's love under his attribute of goodness but only because I had determined to use the *Shorter Catechism*'s handling of God's attributes as my matrix for treating the topic as I am doing in this current series of addresses on God's attributes.

But, my brothers and sisters, such handling of this divine attribute, in my opinion, does *not* do justice to the New Testament's emphasis, for in the writings of the New Testament God's love is the very essence of his nature (1 John 4:8), the source of our election (see '…in love he predestined us,' Eph. 1:4-5), the fountain from which flows all of his gracious redemptive activity (John 3:16), and the supreme message of Calvary. Does not the Apostle John inform us in 1 John 4:8-10 that 'God['s very essence] is love,' and does he not go on to say: 'This is how the love of God was manifested among us: He sent his one and only Son into the world that we might live through him. This is love: not that we loved God, but that he loved us and sent his Son as an atoning

---

[7]Louis Berkhof, *Systematic Theology* (Fourth revised edition; Grand Rapids: Eerdmans, 1949), 71.

[8]Heinrich Heppe, *Reformed Dogmatics* (Reprint; Grand Rapids: Baker, 1978), 95-6.

[9]Gerald Bray, *The Doctrine of God* (Downers Grove, Ill.; InterVarsity, 1993), 220-4.

sacrifice for our sins'? Twice in these three verses the Apostle John singles out God's sending his Son, first into the world and then to Calvary, as the tangible, concrete, revelational expression of God's great love for Christians. Does not the same Apostle also inform us: 'God so loved the world that he gave his one and only Son' (John 3:16)? And does not the Apostle Paul say virtually the same thing: 'God demonstrated his own love for us in this way: While we were yet sinners, Christ died for us' (Rom. 5:8)? And does he not also say that 'Christ loved me and gave himself for me' (Gal. 2:20) and that 'Christ loved the church and gave himself up for her' (Eph. 5:25)? All of these statements regarding divine love's self-expression focus our attention on God's love-gift to mankind of the cross of Christ.

So, in my opinion, our Reformed tradition's dogmatic pronouncements have been guilty of 'heresy by dispro-portion' when they subsume God's patient longsuffering and his redeeming love under his 'goodness' and fail to mention them in their definitions of God.[10] Therefore, I want to spend a few minutes this morning rectifying this disproportion and to expound upon these two mar-velous attributes of God that are on such prominent display throughout Holy Scripture. For if I have one crusade left in me it is to elevate the New Testament emphasis on the love of God exhibited for sinners at Calvary to its rightful place in the dogmatic declarations and expressions of the Reformed church.

God's patient longsuffering
Think with me, first, about the patient longsuffering of God, that is, his patient slowness to anger.[11] Now,

---

[10]Donald Macleod in his *Behold Your God* (Ross-shire: Christian Focus, 1990), 13, also contends that our Reformed statements are guilty of shortchanging God's love in their definitions and descrip-tions of him.

[11]Of course, one must not say that God's patient longsuffering is eternal and unchangeable toward all sinners, for times do come

of course, when we speak of God's longsuffering, our little one-syllable English word 'God' is the obvious grammatical subject of this longsuffering. But if we move too quickly over this little word, because of our familiarity with it, thinking of it only in terms of its being a point of grammar or a mere phoneme and do not reflect upon its content before we take up his attribute of longsuffering, we shall not take the first needful step in understanding the Bible's message. We must endeavor to appreciate this word with regard to its intended referent. In other words, when we see the noun 'God', our minds should be immediately flooded with the wondering awareness that the God about whom the writers of Scripture speak is the one living and true Lord God Almighty, infinite in his majesty and ineffaceable exaltation, stainlessly perfect in his holiness, justice, and flaming purity – whom the heaven of heavens cannot contain, to whom this earth is as the small dust on the balance, and before whom all the nations are like a drop in a bucket, indeed, before whom, Isaiah 40:17 states, all the nations are like nothing, and who regards them as worthless and as less than nothing. Quite properly does John Calvin attempt to assist us to understand the moral purity of this God before whom we all will someday stand in judgment when he writes:

> Let us envisage for ourselves that Judge, not as our minds naturally imagine him, but as he is depicted for us in Scripture: by whose brightness the stars are darkened; by whose strength the mountains are melted; by whose wrath the earth is shaken; whose wisdom catches the wise in their craftiness; beside whose purity all things are defiled; whose righteousness not even the

---

when his patient longsuffering toward some impenitents comes to an end and his judgment falls upon them. Perhaps this is one reason that the framers of the *Shorter Catechism* did not specifically mention this attribute of God in its definition of God that speaks of attributes that are 'infinite, eternal, and unchangeable'.

angels can bear; who makes not the guilty man innocent; whose vengeance when once kindled penetrates to the depths of hell. Let us behold him, I say, sitting in judgment to examine the deeds of men: Who will stand confident before his throne? 'Who ... can dwell with the devouring fire? ... Who ... can dwell with everlasting burnings? He who walks righteously and speaks the truth.' But let such a one, whoever he is, come forward. Nay, that response causes no one to come forward. For, on the contrary, a terrible voice resounds: 'If thou, O Lord, shouldst mark iniquities, Lord, who shall stand?' (*Institutes*, 3.12.1)

[And] ... if the stars, which seem so very bright at night, lose their brilliance in the sight of the sun, what do we think will happen even to the rarest innocence of man when it is compared with God's purity? For it will be a very severe test, which will penetrate to the most hidden thoughts of the heart.... This will compel the lurking and lagging conscience to utter all things that have now even been forgotten.... They who do not direct their attention to such a spectacle can, indeed, for the moment pleasantly and peacefully construct a righteousness for themselves, but one that will soon in God's judgment be shaken from them, just as great riches heaped up in a dream vanish upon awakening. But they who seriously, and as in God's sight, will seek after the true rule of righteousness, will certainly find that all human works, if judged according to their own worth, are nothing but filth and defilement. And what is commonly reckoned righteousness is before God sheer iniquity; what is adjudged uprightness, pollution; what is accounted glory, ignominy. (*Institutes*, 3.12.4)

And as we have said more than once in this series, this God has need of nothing, nor can his unsullied blessedness be in any way affected – whether by way of increase or decrease – by any act of the creatures of his hand. Apparelled in the light of unapproachable holiness and majesty and girded with matchless strength, his will is the resistless law of all existences to which their every motion conforms. Righteousness and judgment, as we saw last week, are the foundations of his throne. Now although our sin infuriates God, Moses informs us – wonder of wonders! – that *this* God – *this* God, mind you – is 'slow to anger ['*erek 'appayim*, lit. 'long of nostrils, that is, 'slow to snort in anger']' (Num. 14:18). So does Nahum (1:3). Moreover, God himself (Exod. 34:6), David (Pss. 86:15; 103:8), Joel (Joel 2:13), Jonah (Jonah 4:2), and Nehemiah (Neh. 9:17) all tell us that Yahweh is 'slow to anger and *abounding in steadfast lovingkindness* [*rabh hesedh*].' In Psalm 145:8 David also informs us that God is 'slow to anger and *rich* [or 'great'] *in steadfast lovingkindness* [*gᵉdhol hesedh*].' Employing a bold figure in Hosea 11:8-9 God deliberates with Ephraim:

> How can I give you up, Ephraim? How can I hand you over, Israel? How can I treat you like Admah? How can I make you like Zeboiim? [Admah and Zeboiim, two cities of the plain, you may recall, were destroyed along with Sodom and Gomorrah according to Deuteronomy 29:23.] My heart is changed within me; all my compassion is aroused. I will not carry out my fierce anger, nor will I turn and devastate Ephraim. For I am God, and not man – the Holy One among you. I will not come [to you] in wrath.

Micah asks: 'Who is a God like you, pardoning and passing over transgressions for the remnant of his inheritance? He *does not retain his anger for ever* because he delights [*hāphēts*] to show lovingkindness [*hesedh*]' (Mic. 7:18). Ezekiel states twice that the Lord 'takes no pleasure in the death of the wicked, but rather [is pleased when] they turn from their ways and live' (Ezek. 18:32; 33:11). Jeremiah strikingly declares that the Lord does '*acts of kindness* [*hesedh*] *and [distributive] righteousness* [*tsᵉdhāqāh*] *in the earth,* for in these [God states] *I delight* [*hāphatstî*]' (Jer. 9:24), and that he 'does *not from his heart* [*lō'...millibbō*] bring affliction or grief to the children of men' (Lam. 3:33). That is to say, because the Lord delights to show them his lovingkindness, his heart is not in afflicting the sons of men as if it brought him any positive joy. And Peter asserts that the Lord 'is patient with you, not wanting any [of you] to perish but everyone [of you] to come to repentance' (2 Pet. 3:9).

All these declarations mean that we must never think of the biblical God as eagerly and longingly panting to judge sinners. He is *not* in haste to slay; he is *not* swift to condemn. If only ten righteous people could have been found in Sodom, he declared he would have spared even Sodom and Gomorrah, Admah and Zeboiim (Gen. 18:32). His hand of mercy is ever outstretched toward the sinner, remembering that he is but dust. He never smites without first warning. Does he not first dig around and fertilize the barren tree that simply encumbers the ground before he removes it (Luke 13:8-9)? Does he not give warnings by acts of providence such as natural disasters and lengthy and chronic illnesses to remind us of our mortality (see Luke 13:4-5)? And from the world's evangelical pulpits does he not often tell the sinner of his sins, urging him to repent, and of the judgment that will follow after death? And only after much sin has stirred the Lion from his lair does he make hell with all its dreadful terror stare the sinner in the face in order to frighten him. And even then, how slow he is, after such warnings, to punish the criminal! He informs him first that he will punish him unless he repents, but oh, *how long* a time does God normally give the impenitent to do so. He is *not* swift to execute judgment. He is indeed a reluctant judge. His judgment of sinners is what Charles Haddon Spurgeon called God's 'strange work'; it is not 'from his heart' in the sense that it brings him any pleasure. And all of us should be very grateful that it is so. We should realize that the riches of his kindness and his patience with us were intended to lead us to repentance (Rom. 2:4). For if he had judged us as soon as we deserved it he would have cast all of us already into hell. As I said in the address on God's immutability, no earthly father in this world would ever endure the rebellion of his children had his sons and daughters provoked him even a nano-amount as much as we, the sons of Jacob, corporately and individually, have provoked the one holy living and true God. Even in the state of grace our best works are 'mixed with so much weakness and imperfection, that they cannot endure the severity of God's judgment,' are in themselves 'blameable and reprovable in his sight' (*Westminster Confession of Faith*, XVI.V, VI), and are accepted by God as 'good' only because we are 'in Christ' and therefore God imputes Christ's righteousness to our works, Christ's 'vicarious repentance' expressed in his accepting John's baptism of repentance[12] to our poor, imperfect repentance, and Christ's perfect prayers of intercession to our frivolous, silly, lazy, soon-forgotten prayers of adoration, confession, thanksgiving, and supplication.

This nation is also the beneficiary of God's longsuffering. Its iniquities are great and it is liable to divine judgment. No nation, with the exceptions of Israel and the United Kingdom, has played so fast and loose with bestowed divine truth as the United States of America. But God is 'slow of anger and abounding and rich in his steadfast love', and he keeps the sword of his wrath sheathed. That sword, I can imagine, struggles to get free, but God's patient longsuffering puts its hand on the sheath and says, 'Stay! Not yet!' And so he continues to give this nation, along with all the other nations of the world, as well as the Mafia dons and their goons and the Usama bin Ladens and the terrorists of this world who would destroy us, time to learn of him and to repent in order that he may bring all of his chosen ones to himself. And this is all *because* he is 'longsuffering', *because* he

---

[12]See Geerhardus Vos, *Biblical Theology* (Grand Rapids: Eerdmans, 1948), 344, for his discussion of Jesus' vicarious repentance for his people.

takes no pleasure in punishing the sinner but rather in showing him mercy (Mic. 7:18), and *because* he is so great. Little people, Charles Spurgeon observes, are always swift to anger; the great are not so. The silly cur dog barks at every passer-by and tolerates no insult; the lion bears a thousand times as much. While the little and the puny are always swift to show anger, God, just because he is so graciously magnanimous toward us sinners, is slow in being stirred to wrath and takes no delight in condemning us.

Someone may object and point out that as part of the 'curse section' of the Deuteronomic Covenant in Deuteronomy 28:63 Moses informed Israel: 'Just as it *pleased* [*sās*] the LORD to make you prosper and increase your number, so [because you will not obey the Lord your God] it *will please* [*yāsîs*] the LORD to ruin and destroy you.' But God's statement here does not contradict his later statements in Ezekiel 18:32 and 33:11. As Keil and Delitzsch observe in their commentary on Deuteronomy:

> With this bold anthropomorphic expression Moses seeks to remove from the nation the last prop of false confidence in the mercy of God. Greatly as the sin of man troubles God, and little as the pleasure may be which He has in the death of the wicked, yet the holiness of his love demands the punishment and destruction of those who despise the riches of His goodness and longsuffering; so that He displays His glory in the judgment and destruction of the wicked no less than in blessing and prospering the righteous.[13]

Robert Lewis Dabney, the Southern Presbyterian theologian who served for a time as a senior staff officer under General 'Stonewall' Jackson during the American

---

[13]C. F. Keil and F. Delitzsch, 'The Pentateuch,' in *Biblical Commentary on the Old Testament* (Grand Rapids: Eerdmans, n.d.), III, 444-5.

Civil War, provides a fitting story from the life of George Washington that I offer here as a helpful analogy to what I mean regarding God's 'pleasure to destroy' in Deuteronomy 28 not standing in contradiction to his later statements that he takes 'no pleasure in the death of the wicked.'[14] John Marshall, third chief justice of the United States Supreme Court, writes of President Washington's signing the death-warrant of a certain Major André whose 'rash and unfortunate' acts of treason had jeopardized the safety of the young nation:

> 'Perhaps on no occasion of his life,' Marshall writes, 'did the commander-in-chief obey with more reluctance the stern mandates of duty and policy.'

Washington had plenary power to execute or to spare; his compassion for the criminal was genuine and profound. Yet he signed the major's death-warrant. 'Washington's volition to sign the death-warrant,' writes Dabney,

> did not arise from the fact that his compassion was slight or feigned, but from the fact that [his compassion] was counterpoised by a complex of superior judgments and propensions of wisdom, duty, patriotism, and moral indignation.... The pity was real, but was restrained by superior elements of motive. Washington had official and bodily power to discharge the criminal, but he had not the sanction of his own wisdom and justice.

So it is, I would submit, with God: *The absence in him of a will to spare a particular sinner does not imply the absence in him of profound pity toward him even as he consigns him to perdition.* Did you hear what I just said? Even as God with moral indignation consigns impenitent sinners to hell he pities them. His pity is

---

[14]Robert Lewis Dabney, 'God's Indiscriminate Proposals of Mercy, as Related to His Power, Wisdom, and Sincerity,' in *Discussions: Evangelical and Theological* (Reprint; London: Banner of Truth, 1967), I, 285-6.

genuine and profound; he takes no pleasure in the death of the wicked; he judges the wicked retributively only reluctantly. But because God as the just Judge of all the earth is also governed by his wisdom, his duty to his offended holiness, and his moral indignation against sin, it 'pleases' the Lord to punish the impenitent,[15] although he takes no positive delight in punishing them, just as it 'pleased' (*hāphēts*) the Lord, when he made his Son a sin-offering for the elect, to forsake him and to execute him at Calvary under his curse (Isa. 53:10), a 'pleasure' that we may be sure also caused the Father infinite sorrow.

Now right here I want to address what I think is a grave misunderstanding that has been perpetuated in the church by such Christian thinkers of the past as Thomas Aquinas in the supplement to his *Summa Theologicae*, Dante in his *Inferno*, and Jonathan Edwards in his sermon, 'The Torments of the Wicked in Hell No Occasion of Grief to the Saints in Heaven,' who suggest that at the last judgment the eternal torment of the wicked will become a matter of eternal song to the redeemed because we in that day will 'have the mind of God on the matter of justice' and will therefore rejoice with him in their eternal destruction. But wait. God has plainly declared that he 'takes no pleasure in the death of the wicked', that he judges the creature made

---

[15]Nothing I have said in this section should be construed to mean that I believe that God will not punish the sinner for his sin, because the Scriptures are too clear that his wrath against sin is also a perfection of the divine nature (see Deut. 32:39-41; Rom. 1:18; 1 Thess. 1:10). For not only does God swear by his holiness (Ps. 9:35) but he also swears by his wrath (Ps. 95:11). A perusal of a good concordance will show that there are more references to his anger, fury, and wrath than there are to his love and tenderness. Leon Morris in his article, 'Propitiation,' in *Evangelical Dictionary of Theology*, edited by Walter A. Elwell (Grand Rapids: Baker, 1984), 888, notes that the idea of the wrath of God is 'stubbornly rooted in the Old Testament, where it is referred to 585 times' by no less than twenty different words that underscore God's indignation against sin and evil.

in his image because it is right and just to do so, but he does so reluctantly and not because he relishes it as something in which he takes any positive delight. *So what gives God no pleasure, then, should give Christians no pleasure either,* and the more Godlike we become the less will we take personal pleasure in the thought of anyone suffering in hell. *Never* should we ever say to any person with malice: 'Go to hell!' *Never* should we wish *any* man or woman were in hell, *not even our worst enemy.*[16] In that Great Day, *precisely because*

---

[16]Someone may object that Revelation 18:20 and 19:1-3 represent the 'great multitude in heaven' as doing precisely what I have here declared that Christians should never do, namely, rejoice that God has consigned the wicked to eternal suffering in hell: 'Hallelujah! ... for his judgments are true and just; for he has judged the great prostitute who corrupted the earth with her immorality and has avenged on her the blood of his servants.... Hallelujah! The smoke from her goes up forever and ever.' But to say, as the Scriptures clearly state, that the church will someday rejoice that God's true and just judgments have vindicated both his own honor and their faith and that the punishment of the wicked is absolutely final is to say one thing; to say that the church will someday rejoice that the wicked will *suffer* in hell forever is to say something else – something that the Scriptures do not affirm here. Robert H. Mounce comments in his *The Book of Revelation* (NICNT, revised edition; Grand Rapids: Eerdmans, 1998): 'Some writers feel that [18:20] is a call to the church to rejoice over the suffering of the unrighteous. The call, however, is ... addressed to heaven' and 'the church victorious is to rejoice that God the righteous judge has turned back the evidence laid against believers and in turn has served to bring judgment upon the accuser himself.... The outburst of praise rests upon the fact that the judgments of God ... are both true and just [and] because the destruction of the wicked city is absolutely final' (336, 342-43). And G. K. Beale declares in his *The Book of Revelation: A Commentary on the Greek Text* (NIGTC; Grand Rapids: Eerdmans, 1999): 'The focus is not on delight in Babylon's suffering but on the successful outcome of God's execution of justice, which demonstrates the integrity of Christians' faith and of God's just character' (916). So while Christians should surely rejoice that someday God will vindicate his offended honor by judging sin and by bringing their salvation to its final consummation I would stand by my insistence that Christians should take no positive pleasure in the suffering of the impenitent in hell.

I will understand better the mind of God on the matter of justice, I who deserve hell as much as those who will be consigned there forever will be doxologically singing, in the words of Robert Murray McCheyne, not of their destruction and suffering, but of God's grace shown to me in Jesus Christ:

> When this passing world is done,
> When has sunk yon setting sun,
> When we stand with Christ in glory,
> Looking o'er life's finished story,
> Then, Lord, shall I fully know,
> Not till then, how much *I* owe.

> When I hear the wicked call
> on the rocks and hills to fall,
> When I see them start and shrink
> on the fiery deluge brink,
> then, Lord, shall I fully know,
> not till then, how much *I* owe.

> When I stand before the throne,
> dressed in beauty not my own,
> When I see thee as thou art,
> Love thee with unsinning heart,
> Then, Lord, shall I fully know,
> Not till then, how much *I* owe.

> When the praise of heav'n I hear,
> Loud as thunder to the ear,
> Loud as many waters' noise,
> Sweet as harp's melodious voice,
> Then, Lord, shall I fully know,
> Not till then, how much *I* owe.

God's love

Think with me now about God's attribute of love. I have already called your attention to the fact that the Apostle John informs us in 1 John 4:8-10 that

God['s very essence] is love. This is how God showed his love among us [he writes]: He sent his one and only Son into the world that we might live through him. This is love: not that we loved God, but that he loved us and sent his Son as an atoning sacrifice for our sins.

And, as I observed earlier, twice in these three verses John singles out God's sending his Son, first into the world and then to Calvary, as the tangible evidence of God's great love for us.

Someone has well opined that God's special grace is simply his redeeming love in Christ in action in the very presence of sin. Thomas Manton (c.1620–77) provides us with a wonderful analysis of love that I believe passes biblical muster: love, he declares, consists of three parts: first, it is a 'desire' to become one with an object; second, it 'delights' when that union occurs; and third, it exhibits itself in a 'deluge' of generous giving in order both to attain and to retain that union. Manton's analysis beautifully describes God's love: he desires to become one with his own (2 Tim. 2:19), rejoices when that union is realized (Zeph. 3:17; Luke 15:7, 10, 24, 32), and provides both his Son to attain it and his Spirit to retain it.[17] Oh, the gracious love of God, the marvelous, matchless, immeasurable love of God! Can we ever sound its depths? We can appreciate it only in light of the two indices of the quite extraordinary object of its affection and the expensive costliness of its bounteous sacrifice. Think with me about these two features of God's love.

First, what is the quite extraordinary object of God's affection? What does John 3:16 tell us? John tells us

---

[17]Thomas Manton, *Complete Works* (Worthington, PA: Maranatha, n. d.), Vol. 22, see Index under 'Love'. I am indebted to Henry Krabbendam, professor of biblical studies at Covenant College, Lookout Mountain, Tennessee, for steering me to Manton's analysis.

that the great and holy God loved *this world*! But, you ask, what is so strange or extraordinary about that? Why wouldn't God love this world, for consider how many people there are who live in it? Would not the sheer *number* of people – some six and a half billion of us today – move the great heart of God to love this world? No, dear friends, not at all, for

> the mere uncounted multitudes of men are hardly a reason for God's loving it, for as great as this conception is, the mere measure of the number of mankind cannot compel the love of God to action. All the multitudes of humankind – what is their mere finite sum, however immense, [compared] to the infinitude of God? Do we praise the blacksmith's brawn [in the slightest] by declaring it capable of supporting a mustard seed in his outstretched hand? Of course not. Similarly, the mere *number* of people in this world is too small to be the standard for measuring the greatness of God's love. Conceive of the multitudes of mankind as vastly as you may, their number remains ever a poor measure – an inadequate index – by which to comprehend the immeasurable love of God.[18]

Well, you ask, if it is not the *number* of mankind that is the index for measuring the greatness of God's love, what is? And for this,

> ...we must ... let the Scriptures themselves tell us; and primarily that Apostle to whom we owe the great declaration that God loved this world. Nor does he fail to tell us; and that without the slightest ambiguity. The 'world,' he tells us, is just the synonym of all that is evil and noisome and disgusting. There is nothing in it that can attract God's love.... It is not that [God's love] is so great that it is able to extend over the whole of a

---

[18]This is a paraphrase of Benjamin B. Warfield, 'God's Immeasurable Love,' *Biblical and Theological Studies* (Philadelphia: Presbyterian and Reformed, 1952), 506.

big world; it is [rather that his love is] so great that it is able to prevail over his own hatred and abhorrence of sin [and love] the world that lies in the evil one.... ['World' in John 3:16] is not a term of [demographic] extension so much as [it is] a term of [ethical] intensity. Its primary connotation is ethical, and *the point of its employment is not to suggest that the world is so big that it takes a great deal of love to embrace it all, but that the world is so bad that it takes a great kind of love to love it at all,* and much more to love it as God ... loved it when He gave His Son for it.... [John 3:16] is intended to arouse in our hearts a wondering sense of the marvel and the mystery of the love of God for the sinful world – conceived here, not quantitatively but qualitatively as, in its very distinguishing characteristic, sinful ... search the universe through and through ... and you will find no marvel so great, no mystery so unfathomable, as this, that the great and good God, whose perfect righteousness flames in indignation at the sight of every iniquity and whose absolute holiness recoils in abhorrence in the presence of every impurity, yet loves this sinful world, – yes, has so loved it that He has given His one and only Son to die for it. It is this marvel and this mystery that [John 3:16] would ... carry home to our hearts.[19]

God's love is indeed a very *extraordinary* thing, I say then, when we take due note that it set itself upon *this* lost, ruined, guilty world. For what was in this world that should or would compel him to love it so? There was *nothing* lovable in it. *No* fragrant flower of corresponding love for him grew in it anywhere but rather only the weeds of human enmity toward him, hatred toward his truth, disregard of his law, and rebellion against his commandments. *Nothing and no one* upon the face of the earth, save his own beloved Son, ever *merited* his love. Humankind *deserves* only his displeasure. And there are some six and a half billion reasons living

---

[19]B. B. Warfield, 'God's Immeasurable Love,' *Biblical and Theological Studies*, 514-17, emphasis supplied.

today why he *still* should detest it. Yet God loved this world, dominated as it is by the flesh and the devil and organized specifically in opposition to his will, with a love that was so deep, so wide, so long, so high, so strong, so incredible, so immeasurable, so beyond all human imagining that even inspiration found it difficult to compute its measure in human terminology, and hence the Holy Spirit gave us that wondrous little word 'so' *houtōs* – 'God *so* loved' – and left it to us to attempt to comprehend the measurement of it.

One could even justly speak here of the holy *humility* of God the Father that he would condescend to such depths that he would love *this* unworthy world! Indeed, it seems to me that one may appropriately speak here of the entire Godhead's humility as just one more of God's *'countless* attributes' (E. Lange),

♦ in light of God the Father's condescension, in keeping with the eternal covenant of redemption,[20] in entering into covenant with Adam in Genesis 2 that we might receive some fruition from him as our blessedness and reward for obedience (*Westminster Confession of Faith*, VII/i), his 'wisdom that... is first of all pure; then peace-loving, considerate, *willing to yield* [*eupeithēs*] [as evidenced by his patient longsuffering toward Israel throughout the Old Testament and toward sinners in general], full of mercy and good fruit [as evidenced by his willingness to send his beloved Son to die for sinners], impartial and sincere' (Jas. 3:17), and his gracious, condescending love for this undeserving sinful world – and primarily for those within it who are the 'foolish,' the 'weak,' the 'base,' the 'despised,' and 'those that are not' whom he chose and effectually calls to himself (1 Cor. 1:26-28);

---

[20]See my *A New Systematic Theology of the Christian Faith*, Second edition (Nashville, Tenn.: Thomas Nelson, 2001), 462-67.

♦ in light of God the Son's willingness, in keeping
with the eternal covenant of redemption, to be
sent by his Father on his mission of mercy;
the *preincarnate* Son as the Angel of the Lord
accommodating his omnipotent strength to Jacob
allowing him to 'best' him in the wrestling match
(Gen. 34:24-28); his tabernacling in a portable tent
with his idolatrous, stiff-necked people during the
wilderness years, foreshadowing his 'tabernacling'
among sinful men in his incarnation; his declaring
that he not only lived 'in a high and holy place,'
but also condescendingly 'with him who is contrite
and lowly in spirit' (Isa. 57:15); Psalm 45, singing
of God the Son's might, splendor, and majesty
(45:3), then saying: '...in your majesty ride on
victoriously, for the cause of truth, *humility*
[*'anwāh*], and righteousness' (45:4); the *incarnate*
Son, as Isaiah's Servant of Yahweh (Isa. 53),
taking 'the form of a bond-slave' (Phil. 2:7) and
'tabernacling' among men (John 1:14), being
'born of a woman, born under the Law' (Gal. 4:4);
as the Bread of Life experiencing hunger and
as the Fountain of Living Water experiencing
thirst, saying of himself: 'I am gentle and *humble*
[*tapeinos*] in heart' (Matt. 11:29), a virtue he not
only displayed in the washing of his disciples' feet
(John 13:3-17) and at Calvary but also a virtue
that he will display at his Second Advent when 'he
will dress himself to serve, will have [his faithful
servants] recline at the table and will come and
wait on them' (Luke 12:37), implying that there
will never be a moment when Christians will not
need *him* – *ever* in his role of servant – to serve
them; the Pharisees characterizing Jesus as 'a
friend of tax-collectors and "sinners"'(Matt. 11:19;
Luke 7:34), a characterization that they intended
derisively and condemningly but that was indeed
true: he did associate himself with the lowly ones

of this world; Paul declaring that God the Son, though he was rich, yet for [our] sakes, became poor (2 Cor. 8:9), and though being in the 'form of God,' that is, whose very nature is deity, '*humbled* [*etapainōsin*] himself and became obedient to death – even death on a cross' (Phil. 2:6, 8) – the greatest act of humility imaginable since hanging as he did on a tree meant that he died under the wrath and curse of God; his disciples then entombing the Good Shepherd who had laid down his life for his sheep – all this *Westminster Shorter Catechism* Question 27 summing up in the following words:

> Christ's humiliation consisted in his being born, and that in a low condition, made under the law, undergoing the miseries of this life, the wrath of God, and the cursed death of the cross; in being buried, and continuing under the power of death for a time. Finally,

♦ in light of God the Holy Spirit, in keeping with the eternal covenant of redemption, being willing to be sent by both the Father and the Son on his mission of mercy to this world; his striving [*yādhōn*] with men (Gen. 6:3) and permitting himself to be resisted by the non-elect (Acts 7:51), and to be stricken with grief by the sins of Christians (Isa. 63:10; Eph. 4:30) and his overtures of guidance to be quenched or 'put out' (*sbennute*) by backsliding Christians (1 Thess. 5:19) resulting in their chastisement; his always speaking more about God the Father and God the Son than about himself, inducing believers to their filial consciousness of God as their Father (Rom. 8:15-16; Gal. 4:6) and their perception of Jesus as their Lord (1 Cor. 12:3); all in accordance with the decretive will of God.

Such divine humility amazes the angels of God but it lies at the heart of what saved a wretch like me.

The second index by which we must measure God's love is the unspeakably expensive cost of its sacrifice. God spared *no* expense to redeem us; do you recognize that? He spared *no* cost to save us! Indeed, Paul speaks of Christ as God's 'indescribable gift' (2 Cor. 9:15). For *he 'did not spare his own Son but gave him up for us all'* (Rom. 8:32). God so loved this world that he gave his one and only Son to save sinners. And who is his Son? Now listen carefully, dear ones. None of us will ever have such a son as our heavenly Father has who ever delights to do his Father's will. Ours are the sinful sons of men; his the pure Son of God, the Father's other Self, One with himself. When God gave his Son, he gave God himself, for Jesus is because of his divine nature not less or other than God. As such he is

> the [visible] image of the invisible God, the first-born of all creation; for in him all things were created, in heaven and on earth, visible and invisible ... all things were created through him and for him. He is before all things, and in him all things hold together. He is the head of the body, the church; he is the beginning, the first-born from the dead, that in everything he might be preeminent. For in him all the fullness of God was pleased to dwell ... in [him] are hid all the treasures of wisdom and knowledge ... in him the whole fullness of deity dwells bodily (Col. 1:15-19; 2:3, 9).

He is also

> the heir of all things, through whom [God] made the world. He reflects the glory of God and bears the very stamp of his nature, upholding the universe by his word of power. [And] when he had made purification for sins, he sat down at the right hand of the Majesty on high, having become as much superior to angels

as the name he has obtained is more excellent than theirs (Heb. 1:2-4).

So when God gave God for us he gave himself. What more then could he give? He gave his all; he gave his infinite self. Who can measure – how can *we* measure, how can *any* mortal measure – such wondrous condescending love!

Judge, you fathers here, how you love your sons. Could you give them to die for your enemies? Judge, you fathers who have only one son, does it not seem that God loved us even better than he loved his one and only Son? For many a father has given a son to the service of his country and many a mother's son has become a casualty of war. But we regard theirs as honorable deaths. But to what did God give his Son – to some profession in the pursuit of which he might still enjoy his company? To some service that all mankind would respect? To an honorable death? No! He gave his Son to exile among men; he sent him down to hunger and thirst amid poverty so dire that he had no place to lay his head; he sent him down to the scourging and the crowning with thorns; to the giving of his back to wicked smiters and his cheeks to those who plucked out his beard. And finally, the Father gave his Son up to death on the cross – a type of execution so ignoble and reprehensible that it was reserved for the meanest and lowest criminal types. And on the cross he gave him up, still further, to the awful forsakenness expressed in 'the strangest utterance that ever ascended from earth to heaven' (Murray) – that cry of dereliction: 'My God, my God, why have you forsaken me?' We hesitate to say it, but say it we must: in those hours at Calvary, God the Father became a sonless Father, and God the Son a fatherless Son – for us men and for our salvation. Oh, wondrous, immeasurable reach of his love that God would give his one and only Son to the divine abandonment to and the cursed suffering of a Roman cross for us – the last place in the whole wide world where one would look to find his God and expect that *there* a saving deed occurred by which Christ expiated our sins, propitiated God's wrath, removed God's alienation due to our sin, thereby reconciling him to us, and redeemed us from the curse of the law and the power of sin!

To sum up, nothing relates more closely and needfully, dear hearts, to the dire plight of our earthly condition than does the love of God. We are tiny, lonely specks on the face of a vast universe, quantitatively insignificant, involved in sequences of events and activities in which all is vanity, and constantly threatened by nature and the inexorable march of history over which we have little and no *ultimate* control. Yet into our insignificance, our insecurity, our inability to save ourselves, our loss of true identity intrudes the gracious, redeeming love of God. And *suddenly* the lights go on for us, for we learn because of his love that *we matter immensely, we matter titanically to God!* God's love illumines our darkness, redeems our lives from sin and the threat of meaninglessness, and places his family name upon us, thereby granting us as children of God an identity that causes our hearts to make melody always and in every circumstance. God's love is the most stupendous, and truly his ultimate, word to us. It is his 'Yes' to us, and the gospel of Christ is his 'Amen'! Christ's going to Calvary that we may have eternal life, his dying for us while we were weak, sinners, and God's enemies, his bearing our curse, his dying our death, his paying our debt that he did not owe because we owed a debt we could not pay – all of these, above and beyond everything else, are exhibitions of God's immeasurable love. I would urge, therefore, that we are being unfaithful to the biblical witness if we define God's love merely as a subset of some other aspect of God's character, even his goodness. It deserves the prominence commensurate with the clarity with which the Scriptures declare it and with which the hill of Calvary exhibits it. So let us exult today in God's redeeming love that, in its Christian form, is totally unexpected and undeserved, utterly amazing and marvelous, incomprehensibly matchless and immeasurable! And may we never allow it to become a subset to anything else in our thinking! Rather, may the love of God and of Christ for us always be that which constrains us to love and to serve our God all our days with purity, holiness and faithfulness,[21] for

> Were the whole realm of nature mine,
> that were a present far too small;
> Love so amazing, so divine,
> demands my soul, my life, my all!

Let us pray:
Our loving heavenly Father, in whose great heart of love our salvation originated:

In this moment in our lives we thank you for your immeasurable love for us that you revealed in your beloved Son when he died for us at Calvary.

In response to your great love, we would flee to no other refuge than your Son Jesus, we would wash in no other fountain than his redeeming blood.

We would build on no other foundation than his perfect righteousness, we would receive from no other our fullness.

We would rest in no other for our souls' relief from sin and sin's misery, and we would hope in no other for the bliss and joys of heaven.

Grant that all who have heard this address are indeed trusting in your beloved Son, the world's only Savior.

But if someone here is not yet trusting him, draw him or her by your Spirit now, we pray, to your great salvation through trust in Jesus.

In whose matchless name we pray, Amen.

---

[21]I have borrowed some of the thoughts in this paragraph from Donald Macleod, *Behold Your God*, 143.

TENTH ADDRESS

'INFINITE, ETERNAL, AND UNCHANGEABLE IN HIS TRUTH'

Jesus answered, 'You are right in saying I am a king. In fact, for this reason I was born, and for this I came into the world, to testify to the truth. Everyone on the side of truth listens to me.'

'What is truth?' Pilate asked. With this he went out again to the Jews and said, 'I find no basis for a charge against him' (John 18:37b-38).

Introduction

Good morning once again, my dear friends, and more importantly, dear friends of God. It truly has been a rich experience for me to prepare these addresses for these chapel services. We have treated many issues in them but, given the cultural climate today in which the widespread rejection of absolute truth, and specifically biblical truth, is more and more manifesting itself, I would assert that the greatest crisis of our time is the one that surrounds this issue of the fact and nature of biblical truth; therefore, no topic is more important for Christianity's future than the one we address this morning, namely, God's truth as being 'infinite, eternal, and [absolutely] unchangeable'.

A while back I sat beside a woman on a flight from Fort Lauderdale to Boston and when she found out that I was a preacher of the gospel, her first question to me after I had disclosed that fact was surprisingly this: 'Tell me, are things really as bad as I am told they are?' Talk about a conversation opener! I immediately replied: 'Things are much worse than that!' When she asked me to explain what I meant, I replied: 'I believe that conditions in America are much worse that either of us can even begin to imagine, not because I think that abortion, although it has been legalized as a constitutional right, is still murder of the unborn, or because I think that homosexuality, although it also has been legalized as a civil right, is still a deviant, sinful, and not simply a variant, lifestyle, or because I think that child pornography, although its right to exist on the internet has also been legalized as a First-Amendment right, not only undermines this nation's morals but also places every child in America in danger of predatory pedophiles – so much for the secularized wisdom of this nation's highest court! These are symptoms of a far more dangerous condition. Such moral drift in our nation simply reflects the fact that large segments of both the church and our nation's judiciaries, no longer subscribing to the teaching of the Holy Scripture upon which this nation was founded, believe that no final or absolute truth exists; rather, they believe that truth is relative. But relative truth is no truth at all.' She simply looked at me in silence, not understanding what I meant.

Dear men and women, the same answer I gave her I would give to you, and I trust that you *do* understand that without absolute truth *all* moral absolutes go by the board and as a result anything may be legalized under the citizenry's current clamor for their civil rights. And I would contend, if we are ever going to reclaim this nation and to evangelize our world to any significant degree for Christ, that we must instill once again in the minds of the general population the fact that truth is final and absolute and that believing that truth is relative has dire consequences. To believe that truth is relative is to commit not only national, societal, and religious but also epistemological suicide for it is to hold to a 'truth system' that is self-defeating. So I want you to think seriously this morning with me about the God of the Bible as being infinite, eternal, and unchangeable in his truth and the implications of this fact. Let us now pray for understanding.

Prayer
Almighty God, our heavenly Father, whose Word is truth, whose Son is the Truth, and whose Spirit is the Spirit of truth: Grant to this assembly this morning that special set of ears about which Jesus spoke when he said: 'he who has an ear to hear, let him hear.' For no topic is more basic to the future ministries of these students than the topic of this chapel hour.

Give to me clarity of expression beyond what is normally mine, and give to these auditors attentiveness beyond what is normally theirs. And grant that what I say this morning and what they take into their minds and reflect upon this morning will contribute in everlasting ways to the health and benefit of their future ministries. These things I pray, for Jesus' glory and cause and for the sake of their future ministries to needy men and women. Amen.

* * *

Francis Bacon begins his essay on truth by declaring that too many people, like jesting Pilate, ask: 'What is truth [*alētheia*]?' and then do not wait for an answer before they act. Since I trust that none of you here is of that ilk, I will begin this morning's address on God's infinite, eternal, and unchangeable truthfulness by reading the following verses:

Texts:
Psalm 31:5: 'Yahweh is [the] *true God* [*'ēl 'ᵉmeth*].'

Jeremiah 10:10: '...the LORD is the *true God* ['*elōhîm*
'emeth]; he is the living God, the eternal king.'

John 1:17: '...grace and *truth* [*hē alētheia*] came through
Jesus Christ.'

John 14:6: 'I am ... *the truth* [*hē alētheia*].'

John 17:3: 'Now this is eternal life: that they may know
you, *the only true God*, and Jesus Christ, who you
have sent.'

John 18:37: '...for this reason I came into the world,
to testify to the truth. Everyone on the side of truth
listens to me.'

1 John 5:6: '...the Spirit is *the truth* [*hē alētheia*].'

1 John 5:20: '...we are in him *who is true* – even in his
Son Jesus Christ. He [Jesus Christ] is *the true God*
and eternal life.'

The Doctrine and its Application

As I set forth the doctrine implicit in these verses and
this morning's *Catechism* statement ('infinite, eternal
and unchangeable in his truth'), please note that I
will not be postponing its application to the end of the
address as I have done in previous addresses but will be
applying it as I move through the address. You will see
what I mean as we proceed.

The God of the Bible is the one living and *true* God,
that is, the only God who is 'really there', the only God
whose opinion about anything truly counts. When the
Bible speaks of God, as in Jeremiah 10:10, as 'the true
God; ...the living God, the eternal King',[1] it intends
that we understand that, as the *true* God, he stands off
over against all the false gods and idols of this world,
all of whom the Scriptures appropriately describe by
the word 'lies' (Pss. 96:5; 97:7; 115:4-8; Isa. 44:9-10,
20; Jer. 10:2-16; Amos 2:4; Jon. 2:9). Here the words

---

[1]John 17:3 refers to the Father and 1 John 5:20 refers to the Son
as the 'true God.'

'truth' and 'lies' are depicted in their ultimate and final metaphysical and theological senses: The biblical God is the *true* God; by contrast, all the gods of this world are 'lies' or false gods conjured up by godless and immoral persons of darkened understanding reacting to the true God's revelation of himself in nature. The biblical God alone has perfect knowledge of what true 'Godness' entails. And as the one living and true God, the God of Scripture perfectly conforms in his being and character to his understanding of what true 'Godness' should be. Let's take this one step further.

Because he alone knows what true 'Godness' is, his knowledge of true 'Godness' means that his knowledge is *perfectly* and *completely* true – Job 37:16 tells us, you may recall, that God is 'perfect in knowledge' – and thus *his* true and perfect knowledge is, as such, *the standard of truth* for mankind.[2] We do indeed hold to a 'correspondence view of truth' but not the classic correspondence view of truth, most famously linked with John Locke, that naturalistic philosophers espouse. They state that truth is what corresponds to reality. But the question then arises: 'Reality as perceived and determined by whom?' And these naturalistic philosophers answer: 'Reality as perceived and determined by man and his sciences! You see, what man can't catch in his net isn't fish, that is to say, it doesn't exist until he catches it.' Thus man becomes the standard of truth and the measure of all things. But we say that truth is that which corresponds to reality as God defines it, for just as God is love so also is he truth. His truth is firmly rooted and grounded in his immutable nature. It is not a construction of men; it is not variable, not relative, and not dependent upon social or cultural conditions. Thus that which God knows and tells us in his Word is the perfect standard of absolute truth. For example, God's ordinance concerning the

---

[2]I am indebted to Wayne Grudem, *Systematic Theology* (Grand Rapids: Zondervan, 1994), 195, for these thoughts.

institution of marriage as the lifelong union between one man and one woman is unalterably binding upon all human societies at all times. It cannot be altered by human legislative, judicial, or cultural action without doing irreparable harm to human society, and God will hold those whom he has placed in positions of authority accountable if they try to do so.

Moreover, God's truth came incarnationally with Jesus Christ (John 1:17) who claimed to be the Truth (John 14:6). Indeed, as we just read, Jesus declared: '...for this reason I came into the world, to testify to the truth.' We seldom think about this reason for Christ's coming. We are more inclined to say, when asked for a reason for his Advent, that he came to die on the cross, that he came to save sinners, that he came to pay the penalty for sin, that he came to forgive us, and so on and so forth, and *we forget that before every other purpose he came to bear witness to God's truth* and that his entire ministry did so. Jesus, the divine Son of the God of truth, had a passion for God's truth; and he was prepared to die for God's truth (Matt. 26:53-54). Therefore, because he said, 'Everyone who is on the side of truth *listens to my voice*' (John 18:37),[3] no Christian should ever assume a cavalier attitude toward God's truth as revealed in Holy Scripture. For as Jesus had a passion for God's truth, so we his disciples should also have a passion for God's truth revealed in Holy Scripture; it should become our passion to know it, our passion to obey it, our passion to propagate it.

Truth Univocal for God and Man
Now some evangelical theologians in our time, who ought to know better, have contended that, while God knows all truth and his Word is certainly true, we can never possess more than an *analogical* comprehension of his

---

[3]Jesus' statement suggests that only a minority portion of mankind is on the side of truth today since only a relatively small minority of mankind 'listens to his voice'.

truth because we are finite in knowledge and therefore there will always be a *qualitative* difference between the truth content of God's mind and the truth content of our minds. That is to say, not only is God's knowledge prior to and necessary to man's knowledge that is always secondary and derivative, not only is God's knowledge self-validating whereas man's knowledge is dependent upon God's prior self-validating knowledge for its validation, not only is God's knowledge infinite whereas man's knowledge is finite (with these I concur), but also, these theologians contend, God's and man's knowledge of truth is such that man's knowledge of truth will never be more than an analogy of God's knowledge of truth, indeed, they say, man will never univocally know anything as God knows a thing.[4]

---

[4]Even John Calvin errs here. While he does not go as far as these theologians he does move perilously close to this position with respect to human knowledge of God when explaining the Bible's anthropomorphic descriptions of God. Calvin contends that not only does God speak 'sparingly' of his essence but also even when he does do so his 'forms of speaking *do not so much express clearly what God is like* as accommodate the knowledge of him to our slight capacity' (*Institutes*, 1.13.1). In a similar vein he contends in *Institutes*, 1.17.13, that '...because our weakness does not attain to his exalted state, *the description of him that is given to us must be accommodated to our capacity so that we may understand it. Now the mode of accommodation is for him to represent himself to us not as he is in himself, but as he seems to us*. Although he is beyond all disturbance of mind [Calvin is expressing his understanding of God's impassibility here, which expression I happen to think is erroneous], yet he testifies that he is angry toward sinners. Therefore whenever we hear that God is angered, we ought not to imagine any emotion in him, but rather to consider that *this expression has been taken from our own human experience*; because God, whenever he is exercising judgment, exhibits the *appearance* of one kindled and angered' (emphasis supplied). Calvin appears to mean by these comments that because of our finitude God could not given to us a univocal verbal depiction of himself as he is in himself. Rather, what we possess in the main, if not exclusively, is at best only a finite (analogical?) representation of God and thus ours is an understanding of him 'as he seems to us' and not as he is in himself. We should be hesitant about following Calvin here.

With this I strongly disagree, for what these theologians of analogy fail to realize is that the success of any analogy turns on the strength of the univocal element in it. That is to say, the basis for any analogy is non-analogical, that is, univocal. An 'analogy' that has no univocal element in it is really not an analogy at all but an equivocation. Cornelius Van Til, one such theologian of analogy, writes:

> All human predication is analogical re-interpretation of God's pre-interpretation. Thus the incomprehensibility of God must be taught with respect to any revelational proposition.[5]

And in his 'Introduction' to Warfield's *The Inspiration and Authority of the Bible* Van Til declares:

> When the Christian restates the content of Scriptural revelation in the form of a 'system,' such a system is based upon and therefore analogous to the 'existential system' that God himself possesses. Being based upon God's revelation it is, on the one hand, fully true and, on the other hand, *at no point identical* with the content of the divine mind.[6]

Indeed, if I have understood him properly I would urge that we should *not* follow him since we *can* know on the basis of God's verbal self-revelation many things about him in the *same* sense that he knows them.Where Calvin made his mistake is in his explaining the Bible's anthropomorphisms by resorting to linguistic accommodation. It were better had he construed them simply as figures of speech – metaphors designed, in light of God's spiritual essence, to drive home the truth that God is indeed personal.

[5]Cornelius Van Til, *In Defense of the Faith*, volume 5 in *An Introduction to Systematic Theology* (Nutley, New Jersey: Presbyterian and Reformed, 1976), 171.

[6]Cornelius Van Til, 'Introduction' to *The Inspiration and Authority of the Bible* by Benjamin B. Warfield (Philadelphia: Presbyterian and Reformed, 1948), 33 (emphasis original).

In a Complaint filed against the presbytery that voted to sustain Gordon H. Clark's ordination examination, to which Van Til affixed his name as a signatory (which Complaint was not upheld by the way), it was declared a 'tragic fact' that Clark's epistemology 'has led him to obliterate the qualitative distinction between the contents of the divine mind and the knowledge which is possible to the creature'.[7] The Complaint affirmed: 'We dare not maintain that [God's] knowledge and our knowledge coincide *at any single point.*'[8]

Against this strange notion we can and must pit Jesus' teaching that contradicts it. In John 12:49-50 Jesus declared:

> I did not speak of my own accord, but the Father who sent me commanded me *what to say and how to say it* [*ti eipō kai ti lalēsō*].... So whatever I say, *just as* [*kathōs*] the Father told me, *so* [*houtōs*] I say.

And in John 17:6-17 Jesus prayed:

> I have manifested your name to those whom you gave me out of the world.... Now they know that all things that you have given me are from you, for *I have given to them the words [teaching] that you have given me,* and they have received them.... *I have given them your word....* Your word is truth.

Jesus asserts in these passages that he gave to us the Father's true word that he received from his Father *just as* his Father had given it to him.

Not only is Van Til's position unscriptural but also Gordon H. Clark contended that Van Til's position leads to total human ignorance. He writes:

---

[7] *Minutes* of the Twelfth General Assembly of the Orthodox Presbyterian Church, 1945, 15.

[8] *Minutes*, 14, emphasis original.

> If God knows all truths and knows the correct meaning of every proposition, and if no proposition means to man what it means to God, so that God's knowledge and man's knowledge do not coincide at any single point, it follows by rigorous necessity that man can have no truth.[9]

Clark further argued:

> If God and man know, there must with the differences be at least one point of similarity; for if there were no point of similarity it would be inappropriate to use the one term knowledge in both cases.... If God has the truth and if man has only an analogy [of this truth that contains no univocal element], it follows that he (man) does not have the truth.[10]

Clark illustrated his point this way:

> If ... we think that David was king of Israel, and God's thoughts are not ours, then it follows that God does not think David was king of Israel. David in God's mind was perchance prime minister of Babylon.
>
> To avoid this irrationality, ... we must insist that truth is the same for God and man. Naturally, we may not know about some matters. But if we know anything at all, what we know must be identical with what God knows. God knows the truth, and unless we know something God knows, our ideas are untrue. It is absolutely essential therefore to insist that there is an area of coincidence between God's mind and our mind. One example, as good as any, is the one already used, viz., David was king of Israel.[11]

---

[9]Gordon H. Clark, 'Apologetics' in *Contemporary Evangelical Thought*, edited by Carl F. H. Henry (New York: Harper Channel, 1957), 159.

[10]Gordon H. Clark, 'The Bible as Truth' in *Bibliotheca Sacra* (April 1957): 163.

[11]Gordon H. Clark, 'The Axiom of Revelation' in *The Philosophy of Gordon H. Clark*, edited by Ronald H. Nash (Philadelphia: Presbyterian and Reformed, 1968), 76-7.

Clark concluded:

> If God is omnipotent, he can tell men the plain, unvarnished, literal truth. He can tell them David was King of Israel, he can tell them he is omnipotent, he can tell them he created the world, and ... he can tell them all this in positive, literal, non-analogical [that is, univocal], non-symbolic terms.[12]

I would assert that Clark is correct. And we Christians should be overwhelmed by the magnitude of this simple fact that we take so much for granted – *that the infinite personal God has deigned to share with us in a univocal way some of the truths that are on his mind. He has condescended to elevate us poor undeserving sinners to the status of 'truth-knowers' by actually sharing univocally with us a portion of the truth that he knows.*

But, someone asks, does not Isaiah 55:8-9 teach that an unbridgeable gulf exists between the content of God's knowledge and the content of our knowledge? No, far from it! These verses actually hold out the real possibility that people may know God's thoughts, and they urge the wicked to turn from their thoughts that are fickle and wicked and to learn God's thoughts from him. In Isaiah 55:7 God calls upon the wicked man to forsake his ways and thoughts. Why? 'Because,' says the Lord, 'my thoughts are not your thoughts, neither are your ways my ways' (55:8). The entire context, far from affirming that God's thoughts are beyond the capacity of human beings to know, expressly calls on the wicked man to turn, in repentance and humility, from his thoughts and to seek and to think God's thoughts after him.

Accordingly, Holy Scripture declares that saving faith must be grounded upon true knowledge: '[Evil men] perish,' Paul writes, 'because they refuse to love the

---

[12]Clark, 'The Axiom of Revelation,' 78.

truth [tēs alētheias] and so be saved. For this reason God sends them a powerful delusion so that they will believe the lie [tō pseudei] and so that all will be condemned who have not believed the truth [tē alētheia] but have delighted in wickedness' (2 Thess. 2:10-12). Therefore, the church must vigorously oppose any view of truth, however well-intentioned, that would strip from mankind the only ground of a true knowledge of God and accordingly mankind's only hope of salvation. Against the view of human knowledge that would deny to its truth content univocal correspondence at any point with God's knowledge of truth, it is vitally important that you pastors and aspiring pastors come down on the side of Christian reason and work with an epistemology that insists upon at least some identity between the content of God's knowledge and the content of man's knowledge. Otherwise, you have no truth. And when truth goes, the Scriptures go; and when the Scriptures go, the church's sermons as wellsprings of blessing and benefit to the church and the world also go as surely as night follows day, with the result that the world is left in spiritual darkness. For make no mistake about it: the Christian church is 'the light of the world'.

God's Word of Truth Logically Rational, Ethically Steadfast, Covenantally Faithful

Now assuming all this, the *Catechism*, when it affirms that God is infinitely, eternally, and unchangeable true, intends to say that God's *Word*, because it is the exact univocal expression of God's thought, is, first, logically rational, second, ethically steadfast, third, covenantally faithful, and fourth, has always been so and always will be unchangeably so. I will now develop these ideas.

I. *In regard to God's Word as logically rational*, I want to call your attention to two verses:

John 1:1: 'In the beginning was the Logos [that is, 'the personal, filial Reason [of God]'], and the [filial]

Logos was *'face to face' with* [*pros*] God [the Father; see 1 John 1:2], and the [personal, filial] Logos was God [the Son]....'

John 1:9: '[The personal, filial Reason of God was] the true light who enlightens [with his rationality] every man coming into the world.'

These verses affirm that God is not *above* logic as one often hears some folk piously say (which is not really piety at all but misguided piosity) but that logic is intrinsic to God's nature. If these folk doubt this, let them ask and answer whether it is true for God that if all dogs have teeth, then some dogs – Welsh terriers, for example – have teeth. Or do they mean that for God, according to his logic, all dogs have teeth while Welsh terriers do not? I ask again: Is this what they mean? I hope not. For as the knowing, speaking, eternal God of truth the laws of thought (which are the laws of truth) are *intrinsic* to his thought and reason, and because the laws of thought are intrinsic to and original with him it follows that they are true. Hence, he is innately rational in all that he thinks and says – another of his attributes.

What are these laws of thought to which I refer? Well, the most basic laws of thought are (1) the *law of identity*, that is, 'whatever is, is,' symbolically represented by 'A is A'; (2) the *law of contradiction*, that is, 'a thing cannot both be and not be so and so,' and/or 'contradictory propositions cannot both be true,' symbolically represented by 'A cannot be both A and non-A'; (3) the *law of excluded middle*, that is, 'a thing either is or is not so and so,' symbolically represented by 'A is either A or non-A'; and (4) the laws of the valid syllogism. And I should note in passing, because the God of truth created all things, that these laws of thought are true with regard to all created things as well, for unless these laws of thought are also the laws of things we would be unable to apprehend the nature of things since a thing could then have and not have the same character. The Bible justifies the legitimacy of these laws for us in three ways: first, by the very fact that the God of truth employed languages (Hebrew, Aramaic, Greek), the very use of which presupposes the laws of reason, in order to communicate his truth to the human mind; second, by his many uses of various kinds of logical arguments and logical inferences in his inspired Scripture – Gordon Clark calls our attention, for example, to an enthymematic hypothetical destructive syllogism in Romans 4:2, to a hypothetical constructive syllogism in Romans 5:13, and to the sorites in 1 Corinthians 15:15-18; and third, by John's assertion that every person, because he is the image of God, innately possesses them by virtue of the bestowment of the divine Logos himself. And it is because the Logos of God has enlightened them with rationality (John 1:9) that every rational man in this world thinks and speaks according to the *same* laws of reason, for these laws of logic are actually divine laws of truth. Even the attempt to deny them must presuppose and employ them.

Moreover, because our God is logically *rational*, neither in his understanding nor in what he says is there the slightest contradiction. As the God of truth, for him the laws of logic – *his* innate laws of truth and rationality – are intrinsically and inherently valid because they are intrinsic and inherent to his nature. I would even suggest that we should think of logic, if not as an attribute of God *per se* and just one more of God's 'countless attributes' (E. Lange), as the *epistemological* aspect of God's infinite attribute of wisdom and knowledge.

Now there was a time when it was our Lutheran/ Arminian opponents who castigated us Calvinists for being 'too logical', and we Calvinists bore this witless insult as a compliment. But in our time some neo-Calvinists are using this same absurd accusation against those of us who maintain that God is rational and his Word, the Bible, is non-contradictory. They tell us that faith must curb logic. Even though they ought to know better these theologians compromise God's rationality, telling us that, even after we have understood the Spirit-inspired Bible correctly, it will often represent its inspired truths to the human existent, even the *believing* human existent, in *paradoxical* terms as defined by R. B. Kuiper, professor of practical theology at Westminster Seminary in Philadelphia and president of Calvin Seminary and one such theologian:

> A paradox is not, as Barth thinks, two truths that are actually contradictory. Truth is not irrational. [Amen to that!] Nor is a paradox two truths which are difficult to reconcile but can be reconciled before the bar of human reason. That is a seeming paradox [Amen to that as well!]. But when two truths, both taught unmistakably in the infallible Word of God, cannot possibly be reconciled before the bar of human reason, then you have a paradox [Horrors!].[13]

'What should one do ... with [such an irreconcilable paradox or antinomy]?' asks James I. Packer, another such Calvinistic theologian. 'Accept it for what it is, and learn to live with it. Refuse to regard the apparent contradiction as real.'[14]

George Marston, a third such Calvinistic theologian, informs us that such doctrines as the Trinity, the hypostatic union of the divine and human natures in the one person of Christ, God's sovereignty and human responsibility, unconditional election and the sincere preaching of the gospel to all, and particular redemption and the universal offer of the gospel – all cardinal doctrines of the Reformed Faith – are all biblical 'paradoxes', each respectively advancing antithetical truths unmistakably taught in the Bible that cannot

---

[13]R. B. Kuiper, cited by George W. Marston, *The Voice of Authority* (Philadelphia: Presbyterian and Reformed, 1960), 16.

[14]James I. Packer, *Evangelism and the Sovereignty of God* (Chicago: InterVarsity, 1961), 18-25.

possibly be reconciled by human reason. And right here I will mention another alleged paradox making its rounds today, namely, the contention that the Bible teaches not only that justification is by faith alone but also that justification is by faith and works – the irrational matrix lying at the root of the current Shepherd controversy.

Cornelius Van Til, yet a fourth such theologian, because he believed that human knowledge is 'only analogical' to God's knowledge, even declared that *all* Christian truth will ultimately appear to be contradictory to the human existent.[15]

What must we say about this notion that the Bible will often, if not always, set forth its truths in irreconcilably contradictory terms? To say the least, if this were the case, then every attempt to arrange the Bible's theology systematically is 'dead in the water' before it begins since it is impossible to reduce to a system irreconcilable contradictories that steadfastly resist all attempts at harmonization. One must abandon the effort to systematize the propositions of Scripture and be content simply to live with a veritable nest of theological 'discontinuities'.

Of course, these theologians who believe this are quick to remind us that these paradoxes are not real contradictions but are only *apparently* so to us human existents, for God knows how to and can 'unpack' them. But does this proposed adjustment help us? These people seem to be oblivious to the following problems inherent in their paradigm.

First, Kuiper's definition of paradox is problematical in that it makes an assertion that no one can know. How does he know that such paradoxes even exist in Scripture, that is, that in the Bible contradictory truths exist that no one can reconcile? Has he polled every

---

[15]Cornelius Van Til, *The Defense of the Faith* (Philadelphia: Presbyterian and Reformed, 1955), 61; and his *Common Grace and the Gospel* (Philadelphia: Presbyterian and Reformed, 1973), 9, 142.

biblical scholar who has ever lived, is living now, and will live in the future and has he discovered that not one of them *has been* able, *is* able now, or *ever will be* able to reconcile the alleged contradictions? To ask the question is to answer it. The very assertion that Scripture contains such paradoxes is seriously flawed by the terms of the definition itself. There is simply no way to know that such phenomena are present in Scripture. And to claim that there are is to assert for oneself the attribute of omniscience. And just because a large number of scholars have failed to reconcile to their satisfaction two given truths of Scripture is no proof that the truths cannot be harmonized. And if one scholar claims to have reconciled these alleged paradoxes to his satisfaction, though his efforts may satisfy no one else, this renders the definition both gratuitous and suspect.

Second is the intrinsic problem of *meaning* in paradoxes so defined. What can two true biblical statements that constitute an *unresolvable* contradiction mean? I will explain my point this way: Let us assume that God told us in Scripture that he had created square circles. The fundamental problem for us would be to understand what he *meant* by this. The word 'square' is a useful term, of course, because to say something is square distinguishes it from other objects that are non-squares. But if a square can also be a 'non-square', say, a circle, at the same time, then our ability to conceive of, and thus to identify and discuss, squares is at an end. In short, the term 'square' no longer remains from our point of view a meaningful term. And the same is true of the term 'circle' in this context. But what if God were to inform us – and this is only a hypothetical – that the concept of a square circle is not contradictory from *his* perspective and that to him it is meaningful. Would this help us? Would this clarify anything for us? Well, it would certainly tell us something about God: that he is thinking in other than rational categories. But it would not make the concept of a square circle any more meaningful. Given the categories of meaning with which God created us, the concept itself would remain just as meaningless from *our* perspective as before. In the same way the alleged irreconcilable theological contradictories in the Bible, even though their advocates assure us that they are only apparently contradictory, are meaningless to us.

Third, if actually non-contradictory truths can *appear* as real contradictions that no amount of study or reflection on our part can harmonize, then there is no available means to distinguish between an apparent contradiction and a real contradiction. Since both will *appear* to us in precisely the same form, and since neither will yield up its contradiction to study and reflection, the human existent can never know at any given moment whether he is embracing only a seeming contradiction and not a real one. Accordingly, as Gordon Clark often said to his students, anyone who says that he *can* believe that contrary propositions can both be true at the same time simply has, without realizing it, a 'charley horse [a muscular bruise] between his ears'.

Fourth and finally – and this point should deliver the *coup de grâce* to the entire notion that irreconcilable contradictions exist in Scripture – once one asserts that biblical truths may legitimately assume the form of irreconcilable contradictions, *he has given up all possibility of ever detecting a real falsehood.* Every time he rejects some proposition as false because it contradicts the Bible or because it is illogical, the proposition's sponsor only needs to observe that it only 'appears' to contradict the Bible or to be illogical, that it is just one more of those paradoxes that the theologians of paradox have acknowledged have their rightful place in our man-made 'little systems', to borrow a phrase from Alfred, Lord Tennyson. But this means the end of Christianity's uniqueness as the revealed religion of God since it is then liable to, indeed, must be open to, the assimilation of any and every truth claim of whatever kind, as well as the end of all rational theology. The only solution to this dreadful muddleheadedness is to deny to paradox, understood as *irreconcilable* contradictions that are actually only apparently so to us, a legitimate place in the Christian understanding of truth, recognizing it for what it is – 'truth decay,' the offspring of an irrational age. This view of paradox is destructive of Christianity for, by positing that the Bible contains such irreconcilable contradictions, it makes God the author of confusion, attacks the unity, inerrancy, and perspicuity of Scripture, and renders forever impossible a *rational* faith and a *systematic* theology. And any Bible-believing theologian who claims to have found such irreconcilable truths in the Bible pridefully speaks logical nonsense and deserves to be ignored by the Christian world, for his is not theology but *anti*-theology.

Dear brothers and sisters, if there is to be (and there is) an offense in Christianity's truth claims, it should be the *soteric* and *ethical* implications of the cross of Christ as the only means of salvation and not the irrationality of alleged irreconcilable contradictories being proclaimed to mankind as being both true. Certainly there are biblical concepts that we cannot fully understand. We may never be able to explain how God created the universe out of nothing, how he can raise the dead, or how the Spirit of God can quicken the unregenerate soul. But such concepts are *mysteries* to us; they are *not* contradictions. And certainly God himself upon occasion employed in his written Word paradoxes, understood however as *reconcilable* contradictories, for example, 'Whoever wants to save his life will lose it, but whoever loses his life for me will find it' (Matt. 16:25) or 'So the last will be first, and the first will be last' (Matt. 20:16). But he did so for the same reason we employ them – as rhetorical or literary devices to invigorate the thought being expressed, to awaken human interest, to intrigue and to challenge the intellect, and to shock and to frustrate the lazy mind. But the notion that God's propositional statements will often, if not always, finally appear to the human existent as contradictions must be rejected. Specifically, the contention that the cardinal doctrines of the Faith – the Trinity, the person of Christ, the doctrines of grace, and the doctrine of justification – when proclaimed aright will contain irreconcilable contradictories is a travesty of Scripture interpretation. To affirm otherwise, that is, to affirm that Holy Scripture when properly interpreted can and does teach that which for the human existent is both irreconcilably contradictory and yet still be true, is to make Christianity and the propositional revelation upon which it is grounded for its teaching irrational and absurd. And this strikes at the rational character of the God who speaks throughout its pages. God is Truth itself; he is not the author of confusion. Christ is the Reason of God. The Spirit is the Spirit of truth. None of them can lie. And what they say is internally consistent and non-contradictory. And none of their truth statements were in any way distorted in or by either the revelatory or inspired inscripturation processes. Hence, the Bible, as God's inspired revelation of his mind to man, is true – unqualifiedly and univocally so – and it contains no irreconcilable contradictions!

Let no one conclude from my rejection of paradox, understood as irreconcilable contradictories that are only apparently so, that I am urging upon the church a Cartesian rationalism that presupposes the autonomy of human reason and freedom from divine revelation, a rationalism that asserts that it must begin with itself in its build-up of knowledge. But make no mistake about it: I *am* calling for a *Christian* rationalism that forthrightly affirms that the God of truth is rational, that the promises of his Christ are not both 'Yes' and 'No' (2 Cor. 1:19-20), that he does not, indeed, cannot lie (Titus 1:2; Heb. 6:18), that he is therefore always necessarily truthful, and that his propositional revelation that the true church has made the bed-rock of all its theological predications is internally self-consistent and non-contradictory in what it teaches.

That this view of Holy Scripture is a common Christian conviction is borne out, I would remind you, in the consentient willingness by Christians everywhere to affirm that there are no contradictions in the Bible. I quite frankly cannot understand people who tell me on the one hand that the Bible is God's inspired Word and on the other that it contains irreconcilable contradictions. It is simply unthinkable to me that God, who is Truth itself, could ever reveal irreconcilable contradictions and ask men to believe them. The church as a whole has properly seen that the truthfulness and rational character of the one living and true God would necessarily have to be reflected in any propositional self-revelation that he determined to give to mankind. And for the Christian not to set for himself the goal of quarrying from Scripture its *harmonious* 'big picture' theology devoid of paradoxes is to sound the death knell not only to *systematic* theology but also to *all* theology that would commend itself to thinking men as the truth of the one living, true, and rational God. We must be dogged in our efforts to harmonize the so-called contradictions that some theologians allege are present in Scripture,[16] and we may encounter difficulties as we do so. But this effort and these difficulties are infinitely to be preferred to the epistemological difficulties that confront the theologians of paradox in their pursuit of

---

[16]By this assertion I am simply following the Reformation commitment to the logical nature of truth. In *What Luther Says*, compiled by Ewald M. Plass (St. Louis, MO: Concordia, 1959), Martin Luther declares: '...we are certain that the Holy Spirit cannot oppose and contradict Himself' (216). Therefore, 'Passages of Scripture that are opposed to one another must, of course, be reconciled, and to one must be given a meaning which agrees with the sense of the other; for it is certain that Scripture cannot disagree with itself' (220).

biblical truth. So much then for God's Word containing unresolvable paradoxes.

II. *In regard to the ethical steadfastness of God's Word,* I want to call your attention to the following passages of Scripture:

Psalm 19:7-11:
> The law of the LORD is perfect, reviving the soul.
> The statutes of the LORD are trustworthy, making wise the simple.
> The precepts of the LORD are right, giving joy to the heart.
> The commands of the LORD are radiant, giving light to the eyes.
> The fear of the LORD is pure, enduring forever.
> The ordinances of the LORD are sure and altogether righteous.
> They are more precious than gold, than much pure gold;
> They are sweeter than honey, than honey from the comb.
> By them is your servant warned; in keeping them there is great reward.

Psalm 119:86, 89, 138, 142, 144, 151, 160; Psalm 31:5:
> All your commands are trustworthy;
> Your word, O LORD, is eternal; it stands firm in the heavens.
> The statutes you have laid down are righteous; they are fully trustworthy.
> Your righteousness is everlasting, and your law is true.
> You statutes are forever right; ...all your commands are true.
> All your words are true; all your righteous laws are eternal.

Isaiah 40:8: 'The grass withers and the flowers fall, but *the word of our God stands forever.*'

2 Corinthians 1:18, 20: '*...as surely as God is faithful,* our message to you is not "Yes" and "No." ...For no matter how many promises God has made, *they are "Yes" in Christ Jesus.* And so through him the "Amen" is spoken by us to the glory of God.'

Titus 1:2: '[Our hope of eternal life] ... God, *who does not lie,* promised before the beginning of time.'

Hebrews 6:17-19: 'Because God wanted to make the *unchanging* nature of his purpose very clear to the heirs of what was promised, he confirmed it with an oath. God did this so that, *by two unchangeable things in which it is impossible for God to lie,* we who have fled to take hold of the hope offered to us may be greatly encouraged. We have this hope as an anchor for the soul, firm and secure....'

These verses make it clear that there has always been and always will be a precise equivalence between *what God thinks* and *what God says.* In other words, we may believe that what he is thinking is *infallibly* reflected in what he says and what he says *infallibly* reflects what he is thinking. Since he cannot lie, when he declares things to be of a certain nature, we may be sure that that is what they are. When he makes a promise, we may be sure that he will keep his word. If he were ever to break his promise to me that he will save forever all who trust his Son, all I would lose is my sinful, miserable soul. But he would be the far greater loser for he would lose his honor and thus cease in that moment to be the God of truth. But that can never happen, he being the God that he is, for he cannot and will not go back on his eternal and immutably determined purpose. We may be sure then that he and his Word are *ethically* steadfast. Therefore,

Ye fearful saints, fresh courage take; the clouds ye so
much dread
are big with mercy, and shall break in blessings on your
head.
Judge not the Lord by feeble sense, but trust him for
his grace;
Behind a frowning providence he hides a smiling face.

His purposes will ripen fast, unfolding ev'ry hour;
The bud may have a bitter taste, but sweet will be the
flow'r.
Blind unbelief is sure to err, and scan his work in
vain;
God is his own interpreter, and he will make it plain.

III. *In regard to God's covenantal faithfulness*, I want
to call your attention to the following ten Scripture
verses:

Deuteronomy 7:9: '...the LORD your God is God; he is
the *faithful* [*hann*ᵉ*'emān*] God, keeping his covenant
of love to a thousand generations of those who love
him....'

Psalm 89:8, 33: 'You are mighty, O LORD, and *your
faithfulness* [*'emûnāth*ᵉ*kā*] surrounds you... [The Lord
says] I will not take my love from him, nor will I ever
betray *my faithfulness* [*'emûnāthî*].'

Lamentations 3:22-23: 'Because of the LORD's great love
we are not consumed, for his compassions never fail.
They are new every morning; great is *your faithfulness*
[*'emûnāth*ᵉ*kā*].'

1 Corinthians 1:9: 'God, who has called you into
fellowship with his Son Jesus Christ our Lord, is
faithful [*pistos*].'

1 Corinthians 10:13: 'God is *faithful* [*pistos*]; he will not
let you be tempted beyond what you can bear.'

1 Thessalonians 5:24: 'The one who calls you is *faithful* [*pistos*], and he will [keep you blameless, body and soul, at the coming of our Lord Jesus Christ].'

2 Thessalonians 3:3: '...the Lord is *faithful* [*pistos*], and he will strengthen and protect you from the evil one.'

2 Timothy 2:13: 'If we are faithless, he will remain *faithful* [*pistos*], for he cannot deny himself.'

Hebrews 10:23: 'Let us hold unswervingly to the hope we profess, for he who promised is *faithful* [*pistos*].'

1 John 1:9: 'If we confess our sins, he is *faithful* [*pistos*] ... and will forgive us our sins....'

I told you two weeks ago in my address on God's justice how it is that the righteous Judge of all the earth can be just and yet forgive and show compassion toward sinners. I said then that his steadfast mercies toward his people must be traced to the fact that he is governed by his covenant faithfulness, particularly as that covenant faithfulness came to expression in the terms of the Abrahamic covenant. Unlike the gods of the nations round about it who were capricious and unpredictable and whose devotees lived in constant dread of their malevolent and irrational intrusion into their daily lives, Israel's God was reliable – one may even say predictable – and who stood in a stable relationship both with the world and with Israel, all this resulting from the fact that he had deigned to enter into and commit himself to covenantal stipulations with the Patriarchs and with Israel. And because of God's covenant faithfulness he will never turn against his elect. Because the covenant threat exhausted itself in Christ's suffering at Calvary, God's people are immune from eternal harm, and his irrevocable rectitude in covenant-keeping leads him to save and to vindicate his people.[17]

---

[17]A paraphrase of Macleod, *Behold Your God*, 41.

In sum, because God's Word is ethically steadfast he is *covenantally faithful*. Because there is an exact equivalence on the one hand between that which God the Father covenantally promised his Son in the eternal covenant of redemption and that which he covenantally promised Abraham and his seed, who is Christ, in the covenant of grace, and on the other hand that which he declares he will actually achieve in history, we may be certain that he will actually give to them that which he covenantally promised them.

To see this, all one need do is to recall that the Bible sweeps across the thousands of years between the creation of man and Abraham in only eleven chapters, with the call of Abraham coming in Genesis 12. This suggests that the information given in the first eleven chapters of Genesis was intended as preparatory 'background' to the revelation of the Abrahamic covenant. Revelation subsequent to the Abrahamic covenant discloses that everything that God has done savingly in grace since then is the result and product of that covenant. In other words, once the covenant of grace had come to expression in the salvific promises of the Abrahamic covenant that God would be the God of Abraham and of his descendants and that in Abraham and his seed, even the Christ, all the nations of the world would be blessed, *everything that God has done since then to this present moment he has done in order to fulfill his covenant promises to Abraham.*

If you had asked Mary the reason for Christ's first coming, she would have told you that the 'Christmas miracle' was a vital constituent part of the fulfillment of God's gracious covenant promise to Abraham: 'He has helped his servant Israel, remembering to be merciful to Abraham and his descendants forever, even as he said to our fathers' (Luke 1:54-55). Zechariah, John the Baptist's father, would have told you the same thing. When John was born Zechariah declared: 'Praise be to the Lord, the God of Israel, because he has come ... to remember his holy covenant, the oath he swore to our father Abraham' (Luke 1:68-73). If you were to inquire of Paul the reason even for Christ's death at Calvary he would tell you that Jesus died 'in order that the blessing given to Abraham might come to the Gentiles in Christ Jesus' (Gal. 3:13). He also declared that Abraham is the 'father of all who believe' among both Jews and Gentiles (Rom. 4:11-12), and that all who belong to Christ 'are Abraham's seed, and heirs according to the promise' that God gave to Abraham (Gal. 3:29). In light of such New Testament data I would urge that Christians should celebrate at Christmas time and on Good Friday far more than they do the great truth and 'big picture' theology of God's covenant faithfulness to his people, for that is why God sent his Son into the world and that is why Christ died at Calvary. And if you ask me, 'What in the world is God primarily doing today, this very Thursday morning?' I would say, 'He's in the process primarily of fulfilling his covenant with Abraham by building his church.'

What did God the Father promise his Son in the eternal covenant of redemption? He promised his Son, whom he appointed the Head of his elect, that he would give him, as the reward for his work of redemption an elect seed redeemed out of every tribe and race on the face of the earth for his 'bride'. In Psalm 2:8 the enthroned Son on Zion informs us that his Father said to him: 'Ask of me and I will make the nations your inheritance, the ends of the earth your possession.' In his high-priestly prayer in John 17:1 Jesus speaks of the authority his Father had given him over all people in order that he might give eternal life to all those whom the Father had given him (see also 17:6, 9, 24).

And what did God promise Abraham and his seed in the covenant of grace? He promised that he would be their God and that they would be his people (Gen. 17:7). He promised that Abraham and his people would become heirs of the world (Rom. 4:13). He promised that he would justify them through his gift to them of faith

(Gen. 15:6; see Hab. 2:4). He promised that they would become members of the body of Christ. Therefore the psalmist sings: 'All the ways of the LORD are loving and faithful' (Ps. 25:10). Thus God's covenantal faithfulness is the saint's ground of confidence, the foundation of his hope, the cause of his rejoicing, and the source of his courage.

The *Catechism* affirmation that God is infinite, eternal, and unchangeable in his truth highlights, then, the ground of our only hope in life and in death, namely, the Word of God that stands eternally firm in the heavens. Nothing is more pertinent today for this silly, fickle, inane world in this irrational age of non-reason than the fact that the one living and true God is infinite, eternal, and unchangeable in his truth.

> How firm a foundation, ye saints of the Lord,
> is laid for your faith in his excellent Word!
> What more can he say than to you he hath said,
> You who unto Jesus for refuge have fled?

So let us love his Word of truth more than we ever loved it before, more than life itself; let us cast ourselves wholly upon its promises, proclaim every time we are given the opportunity its amazing message of grace concerning the 'wondrous cross on which the Prince of glory died', and be willing to defend its truthfulness to the death. And let us also never forget that the God of truth hates liars (Prov. 6:16-17) and that all liars will have their part in the lake of burning sulfur (Rev. 21:8).

Let us pray:
Our righteous heavenly Father, our faithful covenant God: We thank you this morning that we have an anchor for our souls, even your infinite, eternal, unchangeable Word of truth that is forever settled in the heavens.

We praise you that you are steadfast in your covenantal commitment both to your Son and to us.

Not a promise that you have ever made to either your Son or to us will you permit to fall to the ground because you are the God of truth and of covenantal fidelity.

Grant that we may live today in the light of your Word of truth; may it indeed become a lamp for our feet and a light for our path.

Enable us by your Spirit to hide your Word in our hearts that we might not sin against you.

These things we ask for the glory and cause of Jesus Christ. Amen.

Eleventh Address

'Trinity – God's "Special Mark" of Distinction'

At that time Jesus came from Nazareth in Galilee and was baptized by John in the Jordan. As Jesus was coming up out of the water, he saw heaven being torn open and the Spirit descending on him like a dove. And a voice came from heaven: 'You are my Son, whom I love; with you I am well-pleased' (Matt. 3:13-17).

'May the grace of the Lord Jesus Christ, and the love of God, and the fellowship of the Holy Spirit be with you' (2 Cor. 13:12).

Confessional Reading

In the unity of the Godhead there be three persons, of one substance, power, and eternity: God the Father, God the Son, and God the Holy Ghost: the Father is of none, neither begotten, nor proceeding; the Son is eternally begotten of the Father; the Holy Ghost eternally proceeding from the Father and the Son (*Westminster Confession of Faith*, II, III).

* * *

Introduction

Good morning, ladies and gentlemen. Thank you for being here this morning; I am honored by your attendance. As we come to this final topic in our series of addresses on the attributes of God I must tell you that I feel so strongly about what I am going to say this morning that I wish every minister in all the Reformed churches of America could hear this address in order to initiate a much-needed discussion among us on Nicaeno/Constantinopolitan Trinitarianism.

Now, of course, no one is more aware than I that I have only scratched the surface in my expositions of God's attributes. I highly recommend to all of you who want to know more about the nature of your God Stephen Charnock's two volumes on God's attributes – the first volume in the 1996 Baker reprint edition 606 pages in length, the second 524 pages in length, the sum total being 1130 pages of truly great theology on God's attributes.[1] This work is indeed a *tour de force* in the field. Yet even Charnock did not do in his work what I am about to do as I conclude this series on God's attributes and that is to treat, as his special mark of distinction, God's triunity. I do this because I take seriously Calvin's insight that I called your attention to in my first address ten weeks ago, namely:

> God ... designates himself [in addition to the attributes of his spiritual essence] by another special mark to distinguish himself *more precisely* from idols. For he so proclaims himself the *sole* God as to offer himself [at the same time] to be contemplated in three persons. *Unless we grasp these, only the bare and empty name of God flits about in our brain to the exclusion of the true God.*[2]

Echoing Calvin's insight, the Dutch Reformed theologian Herman Witsius (1636–1708) with whom covenant theology reached full development, bringing together as he did the positive elements in Voetian orthodoxy and Cocceian federalism, writes:

---

[1]Stephen Charnock, *The Existence and Attributes of God* (Reprint; Grand Rapids, Baker, 1996).

[2]John Calvin, *Institutes*, 1.13.2, emphasis supplied.

...it is necessary above all things, for the perfection of the human understanding, to be well acquainted with what it ought to know and believe concerning its God. And it may justly be doubted, whether he does not worship a god entirely unknown, nay, whether he at all worships the true God, who does not know and worship him, as subsisting in three persons. Whoever represents God to himself in any other light, represents not God, but an empty phantom, and an idol of his own brain.[3]

Interestingly, because he believed that God 'speaks sparingly of his essence' in Scripture (*Institutes* 1.13.1), Calvin hardly treats in any systematic fashion at all the attributes of God in his *Institutes* as I have attempted to do in this series, the nearest thing to a treatment of them by him occurring in *Institutes*, 1.10.2 where even there, basing his comment on Jeremiah 9:24, he speaks of God's mercy, judgment, and justice as the 'three things [that] are especially necessary for us to know' about God although he immediately declares that

neither [God's] truth, nor power, nor holiness, nor goodness is thus overlooked. For how could we have the requisite knowledge of his justice, mercy, and judgment unless that knowledge rested upon his unbending truth? And without understanding his power, how could we believe that he rules the earth in judgment and justice? But whence comes his mercy save from his goodness. If, finally, 'all his paths are mercy,' judgment, justice, in these also is his holiness visible.

This is pretty much the sum and substance of Calvin's systematic exposition in his *Institutes* of God's attributes as such, if you can even call it that.[4] But when he

---

[3]Herman Witsius, *The Economy of the Covenants Between God and Man*, translated by William Crookshank (Reprint; den Dulk Foundation, 1990; distributed by Presbyterian and Reformed), I:52.

[4]I do not intend to suggest that Calvin did not mention other

treats the doctrine of the Trinity he spends all of Book 1, Chapter 13 doing so – forty pages in 'The Library of Christian Classics' edition. From this one gets a sense of the significance that Calvin attached to the Trinity as the 'special mark' that distinguishes God from idols. This is the primary reason he argues that since the one living and true God is, in point of fact, a Trinity, if we think and/or talk about God and his attributes as if he were simply an undifferentiated divine Monad with no thought of his triunity we are, as a matter of fact, thinking of a God that has no existence. We are – how does Calvin put it? – thinking of 'the bare and empty name of God' that is *not the true God* at all! And how does Witsius put it? We are thinking of 'an empty phantom and an idol'. In sum, if we do not give due regard to God's triunity as we reflect upon his nature we have created for ourselves and are talking about an idol. Because I am convinced that Calvin is right, this is my rationale for concluding this series on the attributes of God with an address devoted entirely to God's triune nature. With this as background, let us now pray for divine guidance.

---

attributes of God; I am only saying that he did not treat them together in a systematic fashion. We are indebted to Benjamin B. Warfield who in his article, 'Calvin's Doctrine of God,' in *The Works of Benjamin B. Warfield* (Reprint; Grand Rapids: Baker, 1991), 168-9, lists the following attributes Calvin often mentions in his *Institutes*, together with their book and chapter locations: 'There is one only true God who is a self-existent, simple, invisible, incomprehensible Spirit; he is infinite, immense, eternal, and perfect in his Being, power, knowledge, wisdom, righteousness, justice, holiness, goodness, and truth'; he is severe, clement, merciful, pitying, gracious, beneficent, and benign; he is our Lord, Creator, Sustainer, Governor, Judge, and as our defender and protector he is our Father. When one recalls that God's essence is the sum total of his attributes this list of attributes hardly supports Calvin's contention that God speaks 'sparingly' in Scripture of his essence.

Prayer

Most holy and most merciful Father who together with your all-glorious Son and your blessed eternal Spirit are the triune God and who, as the only true and living God, are alone worthy of our adoration and praise: I praise and thank you for your kind and gracious providence that arranged for us to reflect upon your character the way we have this semester in these chapel services, and for the physical and mental powers you have given to each of us that have sustained us throughout our semester of studies and this series of addresses on your infinite, eternal, and unchangeable attributes.

We give all glory to you for what we have learned, as little as that learning might be, and we pray now, having learned more about you than we deserve, that you will quicken in us both a desire to know you even better and a more sincere love for you. If our learning about you has not increased our love for you and made us more fit to represent you, we ask you for your pardon for our sin; if it has, we know it is only because of your grace and we ask that you will carry on to completion your good work in us until the day of Jesus Christ when we will respond to your sinless love for us with a sinless love of our own. What rapture that day will be for us!

Be with us now and bless your Word as I declare it, I pray, for Jesus' cause and for our souls' benefit. Amen.

* * *

The Trinity's textual warrant

I begin this morning with this question: Why does the Christian church believe in God's triunity? The answer? Because the Bible teaches it. And as part of the biblical warrant for believing in it we have the following twenty biblical texts in which the three Persons of the Godhead are expressly mentioned together in one way or other:

Isaiah 48:16: '...at the time it happens I [a divine speaker] am there. And now the sovereign LORD has sent me, with his Spirit.'

Isaiah 61:1: 'The Spirit of the LORD is on me [a divine speaker], because the LORD has anointed me' (see Luke 4:16-21).

Isaiah 63:9-10: '...the Angel of [God's] presence saved them. In his love and mercy he redeemed them; he lifted them up and carried them all the days of old. Yet they rebelled and grieved his Holy Spirit.'

Zechariah 2:1-10: ' "I am coming, and I will dwell among you," declares the Lord. "Many nations ... will become my people. I will live among you and you will know that the LORD Almighty has sent me." '

Matthew 28:19: '...in the name of the Father and of the Son and of the Holy Spirit.'

Mark 1:10-11 (and the synoptic parallels): '...the Spirit descended on Jesus like a dove. And a voice came from heaven: "You are my Son, whom I love; with you I am well pleased."'

John 14:16-26: 'I will ask the Father, and he will give you another Counselor to be with you forever – the Spirit of truth...if anyone loves me, ... my Father will love him, and *we will come ... and we will make* our home with him ... the Counselor, the Holy Spirit, whom the Father will send in my name, will teach you all things....'

John 15:26: 'When the Counselor comes, whom I will send to you from the Father, the Spirit of truth who *comes forth from* [*ekporeuetai*] the Father, he will testify of me.'

John 16:7-15: 'Unless I go away, the Counselor will not come to you; but if I go, I will send him to you ... when he, the Spirit of truth, comes, he will guide you into all truth.... All that belongs to the Father is mine. That is why I said the Spirit will take from what is mine and make it known to you.'

Romans 8:1-11: 'You ... are controlled not by the sinful nature but by the Spirit, if the Spirit of God lives in you. And in anyone does not have the Spirit of Christ, he does not belong to Christ.... And if the Spirit of him who raised Jesus from the dead is living in you, he who raised Christ from the dead will also give life to your mortal bodies through the Spirit, who lives in you.'

1 Corinthians 12:3-6: 'There are different kinds of gifts, but the same Spirit. There are different kinds of service, but the same Lord. There are different kinds of working, but the same God works all of them in all men.'

2 Corinthians 13:14: 'May the grace of the Lord Jesus Christ, and the love of God, and the fellowship of the Holy Spirit be with you all.'

Galatians 4:4-6: '...when the time had fully come, God sent his Son ... to redeem those under the law that we might receive the full rights of sons. Because you are sons, God sent the Spirit of the Son into our hearts, the Spirit who calls out, "Abba, Father." '

Ephesians 1:3, 14: 'Praise be to the God and Father of our Lord Jesus Christ, who has blessed us ... having believed, you were marked in [the Lord] with a seal, the promised Holy Spirit.'

Ephesians 2:18: '...through [Christ] we ... have access to the Father by one Spirit.'

Ephesians 4:4-6: '...there is ... one Spirit ... one Lord ... one God and Father of all....'

2 Thessalonians 2:13-14: '...from the beginning God chose you to be saved through the sanctifying work of the Spirit and belief of the truth. He called you ...

that you might share in the glory of our Lord Jesus Christ.'

Titus 3:4-6: 'But when the kindness and love of God our Savior appeared, he saved us ... because of his mercy. He saved us through the washing of rebirth and renewal by the Holy Spirit, whom he poured out on us generously through Jesus Christ our Savior.'

1 Peter 1:2: '[You] have been chosen according to the foreknowledge of God the Father, through the sanctifying work of the Spirit, for obedience to Jesus Christ and sprinkling by his blood.' And

Jude 20-21: '...dear friends, ... pray in the Holy Spirit. Keep yourselves in God's love as you wait for the mercy of our Lord Jesus Christ to bring you to eternal life.'[5]

However, we are not restricted for our evidence for the Trinity just to the biblical affirmations in which all three persons are mentioned in a specific context. Since the deity and personal subsistence of the Father may be viewed as a given, the evidence for the Trinity is also discoverable in the totality of biblical data that teaches the deity of Jesus Christ and the distinct personhood of God the Holy Spirit. Said another way, whatever biblical evidence of whatever kind wherever expressed in Scripture that can be adduced in support of the deity of Christ and the distinct personhood of the Holy Spirit is also evidence for the doctrine of the Trinity. And the biblical evidence supporting these two doctrines is manifest and massive. The evidence for Christ's

---

[5]But not the Hebrew title *ĕlōhîm*, or 1 John 5:7-8 of the Received Text! See respectively my *A New Systematic Theology of the Christian Faith* (Second edition; Nashville, Tenn.: Thomas Nelson, 1998), 154, and Bruce M. Metzger, *A Textual Commentary on the Greek New Testament* (Third edition; New York: United Bible Societies, 1971), 716-18, for the reasons for excluding these as evidence for the Trinity.

deity includes the Old Testament's adumbrations and predictions of a divine Messiah, Jesus' own self-testimony in word and deed, his bodily resurrection from the dead, and the New Testament writers' united witness to his deity, specifically their employment of *theos* ('God') as a Christological title in Acts 20:28, Romans 9:5, Titus 2:13, Hebrews 1:8, 2 Peter 2:1, John 1:1, 1:18, 20:28, and 1 John 5:20. And the evidence for the Spirit's distinct personhood includes the *personal* pronouns that the Scriptures use of him in John 15:26, John 16:13-14, Acts 10:19-20, and Acts 13:2, the *personal* attributes such as wisdom (Isa. 11:2, 1 Cor. 2:10-11), will (John 3:8, 1 Cor. 12:11), and power (Isa. 11:2, Mic. 3:8, Acts 10:38, Rom. 15:13, and Eph. 3:16) that the Scripture ascribe to him, and the many *personal* activities (Mark 13:11b, Acts 13:2, 21:11, Luke 12:12, Rom. 15:30) that the Scriptures attribute to him.

Beyond controversy, if the biblical witness is given its just due the God depicted therein is, while one God, also three distinct Persons at the same time. I wish we had time to consider the biblical data in greater detail[6] but we must now move to a consideration of the church's doctrine of the Trinity.

The Church's doctrine of the Trinity
Christians of the first five centuries – as monotheistic in their outlook as the ancient Israelites and who in fact believed that they were worshiping Yahweh, the God of Israel, when they worshiped God the Father, God the Son, and God the Holy Spirit – began to formulate their doctrine of God in Trinitarian terms. That is to say, the early church's creedalized Trinitarianism was a deduction from its conviction that Jesus Christ and the Holy Spirit were both distinct divine persons. The formulating process itself, precipitated in the first three

---

[6]See my *A New Systematic Theology of the Christian Faith* (Second edition; Nashville, TN: Thomas Nelson, 2002), chapter 8, for these details.

centuries particularly by the emergence of 2nd century Gnosticism and the Logos Christologies, by 3rd century Origenism and Monarchianism, and by early 4th century Arianism, brought the church to a basic but real crystallization of the doctrine of the Trinity in the Nicene Creed of 325, a crystallization that it continued to refine, especially with regard to the person of God the Son, in the Nicaeno-Constantinopolitan Creed of 381, the 5th century anti-Nestorian statement of the Council of Ephesus in 431, and the *Definition of Chalcedon* in 451.

The efforts of these ancient Fathers who formulated these creedal statements are to be respected and revered. Their creedal statements make it clear that three doctrines are absolutely essential to the biblical God's triunity:

♦ First, there is but one living and true God who is eternally and immutabably *indivisible* in his essence; this is the Bible's doctrine of monotheism, and to deny this doctrine is to fall into the error of tritheism.

♦ Second, the Father, the Son, and the Holy Spirit are each *distinct* Persons – please note: *distinct* but not separate since comprising as they do in their unity the one *indivisible* God they mutually indwell each other[7]); this is the Bible's doctrine

---

[7]This aspect of orthodox Trinitarianism – the doctrine of the *perichōrēsis* that is largely the teaching of the Cappadocian theologians and John of Damascus in his *Exposition of the Orthodox Faith*, Book IV, Chapter XVIII – is vital to the divine unity. I believe it is necessarily true given the two facts that the triune God is one indivisible divine Being and that each person has the entire fullness, that is, the entire undivided Being, of God in himself (see Col. 2:9), but I do not think it is true for the reason that is usually given for it, namely, Jesus' statement in John 10:38 (see also 14:10, 11; 17:21, 22): 'The Father is in me, and I [am] in the Father.' How could Jesus' contemporaries, simply by observing his works, have deduced the doctrine of the ontological coinherence or interpenetration of the

of the three Persons' distinct personal properties, namely, the Father's ingeneration, the Father's eternal generation of the Son (the meaning of which it is quite impossible to explicate safely beyond the idea of internal order within the Godhead) and the Spirit's eternal procession from the Father and the Son (about the meaning of which again it is safe to say that we know virtually nothing beyond the idea of internal order within the Godhead[8]), and to deny this doctrine and these distinguishing properties is to embrace some form of modalism.

♦ Third, the Father, the Son, and the Holy Spirit are each *fully and equally* God; this is the Bible's

---

Persons of the Godhead? They could, however, have deduced from an observation of Jesus' miraculous works that his ministry was in accord with God's will and enjoyed God's blessing and that God was in some sense *in union with* him and that he was in some sense *in union with* God. An analogy here would be Reformed theology's interpretation of the preposition *en* in Paul's *en Christô* phrase and his *Christos en humin* phrase (Col. 1:27), the same preposition found in John 10:38. Does any Reformed theologian contend that Paul's phrases speak of a mutual ontological coinherence or interpenetration of persons? Is it not consistently asserted that these phrases speak of the Christian's vital spiritual union with Jesus Christ? When Jesus prayed that all of his people 'may be one, Father, *just as* [*kathôs*] you are in me and I am in you. May they also be *in us*' (John 17:21), has any Reformed theologian ever contended that he was praying that Christians would experience a mutual ontological coinherence or interpenetration of persons with each other and with the Godhead? When Jesus stated that the glory the Father had given him he had in turn given to his people 'that they may be one *just as* [*kathôs*] we are one' (John 17:22), has any Reformed theologian ever contended that he was teaching that Christians would experience a mutual ontological coinherence or interpenetration of persons? Has not Reformed theology consistently taught that Jesus was praying for the church's observable spiritual oneness in purpose, in love, in action in this world?

[8]Morton H. Smith, *Systematic Theology* (Greenville, S.C.: Seminary Press, 1994), I, 152, affirms that the exact nature of the Son's eternal generation and the Spirit's eternal procession 'is a mystery to us'. So also a host of other writers.

doctrine of the three Persons' *homoousian* 'identity in divine essence', and to deny this doctrine is to embrace some form of essential subordinationism within the Godhead.

The many attempts to discover parallels and analogies to the nature of the Trinity in the Scriptures, heathen religious thought, physical nature, the spheres of logic and grammar, the processes of the mind, and philosophical reconstructions,[9] in my opinion, are not helpful, first, because in none of them does one find tripersonality in unity of substance, and second, because we do not even know for certain what it is exactly for which we are attempting to find an analogy since there is not yet total unanimity of opinion even to this day among Christian theologians about the meaning and nature of the Father's generation of the Son and the meaning and nature of the Spirit's procession from the Father and the Son. Nathan R. Wood in his *The Secret of the Universe*[10] suggested that the universe's three-dimensional space (length, breadth, width) and three aspects of time (past, present, future) reflect the triune nature of the Creator. But again, the concept of personality is wanting in both analogies and neither has anything that resembles the 'generation' and 'procession' of the scriptural Godhead, whatever these terms may mean; therefore they break down as legitimate parallels. Therefore, I agree with Herman Bavinck that none of the proffered parallels and analogies 'can prove the divine trinity; for that doctrine we are dependent wholly on Scripture.'[11]

---

[9]See Herman Bavinck, *The Doctrine of God* (Reprint: Grand Rapids: Baker, 1977), 321-30.

[10]Nathan R. Wood, *The Secret of the Universe* (New York: Revell, 1932).

[11]Bavinck, *The Doctrine of God*, 322. Benjamin B. Warfield expresses the same opinion in 'The Biblical Doctrine of the Trinity' in *Biblical and Theological Studies*, edited by Samuel G. Craig (Philadelphia: Presbyterian and Reformed, 1952), 22-7: '...the doctrine of the Trinity is purely a revealed doctrine ... There are

The last-mentioned conciliar statement above – the *Definition of Chalcedon* – remains unsurpassed as an apologetical, ecumenical, and clarifying statement regarding God the Son incarnate. No other human creed has ever been written that captures as well as it does the exact balance of Scripture and permits all that the Scriptures say about God the Son incarnate to be given their just due. With its 'four great negative adverbs' it has become the touchstone of Christological orthodoxy throughout Christendom for the last fifteen hundred and fifty plus years, surviving the division of the church into Eastern and Western churches in 1054 and in Western Christendom the division of that church into Roman Catholicism and Magisterial Protestantism in the 16th century. It has continued to claim the allegiance of the church universal to this very day as it marks the terminal point, and legitimately so, of all speculation that would discard either its 'one Person' teaching or its 'two natures' teaching so as to eliminate the super-naturalness of the Incarnation and the incarnate Christ and thus the doctrine of the Trinity. And history is replete with examples that justify the oft-made observation that 'when one moves in his Christology beyond the boundaries of Chalcedon he has decided to choose a heresy'.

John Calvin and the Reformation emphasis

There is, however, one aspect of Nicaeno-Constantinopolitan Trinitarianism that many 16th and 17th century Reformation leaders called into question. By their creedal phrases, 'begotten out of the Father,' 'that is, out of the being of the Father' (which Nicene

---

no analogies to it in Nature, not even in the spiritual nature of man, who is made in the image of God.' In this article Warfield also discusses B. Keckermann's argument for the Trinity from God's self-consciousness, Richard of St. Victor's argument for it from the nature of love, and Jonathan Edwards' ontological argument for it, and demonstrates the flaws and inconclusive nature of each argument.

phrase was replaced in the Niceano-Constantinopolitan Creed of AD 381 by the phrase 'before all ages'), and 'God out of God, Light out of Light, very God out of very God,' the Nicene Fathers intended to teach, first, that only God the Father is 'God in his own right',[12] second, that he is the source of the Son, and third, that the Son derives his essential being as God from the Father through an eternal 'always continuing, never completed' act of begetting on the Father's part. They believed and taught that the Father, by his act of eternally generating the Son, is the 'beginning' (*archē*), the 'fountain' (*pēgē*), and the 'cause' (*aitia*) of the Son's essential deity (*theotēs*). That is to say, in the approving words of Roger Beckwith, 'central to the teaching of the Creeds' is the notion of 'an eternal impartation of the divine being and nature by the Father to the Son, whereby the Father is Father and the Son is Son'.[13] They also intended to teach that the Father (the later phrase 'and the Son' was added to the Creed here probably by the Third Council of Toledo in Spain in 589), by his act of eternally 'processing' the Spirit, is the 'beginning' (*archē*), the 'fountain' (*pēgē*), and the 'cause' (*aitia*) of the Spirit's essential deity (*theotēs*). They show no apparent awareness that such teaching by implication *denies to the Son and the Spirit the attribute of self-existence* that is necessarily theirs as divine Persons of both the tri-personal Yahweh of the Old Testament and the triune God of the New Testament, and without which they could not be *theotic* at all inasmuch as self-existence is an absolutely essential attribute of the three persons.

The Nicene Fathers were satisfied that they had carefully guarded the full deity of the Son (and by extension of the Spirit) by their affirmation of the *homoousia* and by their statement that the Son was

---

[12]Donald Macleod, *Behold Your God* (Revised and expanded edition; Ross-shire, Scotland: Christian Focus, 1995), 200.

[13]Roger Beckwith, 'The Calvinist Doctrine of the Trinity,' *Churchman* 115/4 (2001), 308-15.

'begotten not created.' But their language, if not their theology, in spite of their commendable intention by it to distance the church from Sabellianism, suggests both the Son's subordination to the Father not only in modes of operation but also in a kind of *essential* subordination in that he is not God *a se* but God *out of* (*ek*) the Father by the latter's ever-continuing act of generation that in effect denies to the Son his *autotheotic* self-existence as God, and the Spirit's essential subordination to the Father (and the Son) in that he is not God *a se* but God by an ever-continuing procession from the Father (the *filioque* was added later) that in effect denies to the Spirit his *autotheotic* self-existence as God. The Nicene language also raises the basic *epistemological* problem of how an unbegotten, a begotten, and a processing essence can be *simultaneously* the *same* essence and the *theological* problem of how the one divine essence can be *simultaneously* unbegotten, begotten, and processing, depending upon the Person of the Godhead being considered, without implying tritheism. In any event this became by and large the doctrine of the church and it went virtually unchallenged for well over a thousand years. Indeed, as Donald Macleod, Principal and professor of systematic theology at the Free Church of Scotland College in Edinburgh, observes: '... [this] subordinationist strain [implying tritheism] has continued right down to the present day, even in orthodox Christology.'[14]

John Calvin in the 16th century contended against all subordination of the Son to the Father with respect to his divine essence (as well as all subordination of the Spirit to the Father and the Son with respect to his divine essence). While his Trinitarian thought was not quite the total innovation that it is sometimes said to be since there were antecedents for it over a millennium before him in the Trinitarian constructions of some of the ancient fathers such as Gregory Nazianzus, Cyril of

---

[14]Macleod, *Behold Your God*, 201.

Alexandria and Augustine of Hippo, Calvin did 'conceive more clearly and apply more purely than had ever previously been done the principle of equalization in his thought of the relation of the Persons to one another, and thereby ... marks an epoch in the history of the doctrine of the Trinity.'[15] By doing so, in the words of Gerald Bray, Anglican Professor of Divinity at Beeson Divinity School, Birmingham, Alabama, Calvin 'found the key to a more deeply orthodox trinitarianism' that avoided 'any hint of causality in the terms "generation" and "procession".'[16] While he was willing to hold that the Father is the 'beginning of deity' within the Godhead (*Institutes*, 1.13.23, 25), Calvin explains that he means by the word 'beginning', not the Father's bestowing of essence to the Son (*Institutes*, 1.13.26), but rather 'in respect to order ... the beginning of divinity is in the Father' (*Institutes*, 1.13.24, 26). That is to say, he endorsed the doctrine of the Father's eternal generation of the Son, not with respect to his essence as deity, but with respect to his Sonship that he derives from the eternally 'generated' relationship in which he stands to the Father. In sum, Calvin employed the doctrine to distinguish between the Father and the Son with respect *to their order* within the Godhead, but he did not endorse the doctrine as being true, as we just said, with respect to the Son's divine essence. With respect to the Son's divine essence, Calvin argued, the Son is – and this is the key to which Bray refers – *autotheotic*. And he repeatedly argues that the Son is God *of himself* because Scripture names him Yahweh (*Institutes*, 1.13.20, 23), an argument that Charles Hodge of Old Princeton Seminary found to be 'conclusive'.[17] Indeed,

---

[15]Benjamin B. Warfield, 'Calvin's Doctrine of the Trinity,' *The Works of Benjamin B. Warfield* (Reprint; Grand Rapids: Baker, 1991), V:230.

[16]Gerald Bray, *The Doctrine of God* (Downers Grove, Illinois: InterVarsity, 1993), 201, 204.

[17]Charles Hodge, *Systematic Theology* (Grand Rapids: Eerdmans, n. d.), I:467.

if the Son is not *autotheotic*, Calvin argued, he is not *theotic* at all. He concluded his exposition of the Trinity by declaring that the ancient speculation that the Father's eternal generation of the Son's essence as an *always* continuing process was 'of little profit', unnecessarily 'burdensome', 'useless trouble', and 'foolish' 'since it is clear,' he states, 'that three persons have subsisted in God from eternity' (*Institutes*, 1.13.29).

By his exposition of Scripture Calvin 'not only attacked all forms of Origenism [see *Institutes*, 1.13.23-29], but also the Sabellianism latent in the Western tradition.'[18] And his successors at Geneva, as well as a mass of representative Reformed teachers of the period, followed Calvin's insights, all teaching that the Father, the Son, and the Spirit are properly to be regarded as *autotheotic*, the three Persons being 'united with each other ... by their mutual fellowship and coinherence – the Cappadocian doctrine of *perichōrēsis* in God, applied at the level of person, not essence,'[19] which is to say as well that, even though the three Persons are 'of themselves' essentially, they do not possess the quality of aseity independently of each other which would suggest tritheism. Rather, they share the quality of aseity that inheres in the one undivided divine essence that each fully possesses. And while some Protestant churchmen such as George Bull and William Pearson wrote defenses of the statements of the Nicene Creed a good many Reformed theologians and pastors in more recent times have deemed it appropriate and necessary to follow Calvin's exposition. For example, **Charles Hodge**, professor of systematic theology at Old Princeton Seminary, taking exception,

---

[18]Bray, *The Doctrine of God*, 201. This latent Sabellianism is due to the influence to varying degrees of Neoplatonism in the tradition reflected in its reading back into the *ontological* Trinity the inter-Trinitarian relations known to us from the economical Trinity's activities in the economy of redemption. On this influence of Neoplatonism on Nicene thought, see Bray's helpful comments in his *The Doctrine of God*, 28-35, 40-1, 158, 168-9.

[19]Bray, *The Doctrine of God*, 202.

not to the facts themselves of the subordination of the Son and the Spirit to the Father and the Son's eternal generation, but to the Nicene fathers' explanations of them,[20] declared that

> the fathers who framed [the Nicene] Creed, and those by whom it was defended, did go beyond [the] facts [of Scripture] concerning the Son's subordination to the Father as to the mode of subsistence ... instead of leaving the matter where the Scriptures leave it, [they] undertake to explain what is meant by sonship, and teach that it means derivation of essence. The First Person of the Trinity is Father, because he communicates the essence of the Godhead to the Second Person; and the Second Person is Son, because he derives that essence from the First Person. This is what they mean by Eternal Generation. Concerning which it was taught [that] ... the person of the Son is generated (*i.e.* He becomes a person) by the communication to Him of the divine essence.[21]

With respect to the Reformers' attitude toward these Nicene affirmations, Hodge continues:

---

[20]Hodge, *Systematic Theology*, I:468. Strangely, both Hodge (*Systematic Theology*, I:462) and Warfield ('Calvin's Doctrine of the Trinity, *Works*, V:250) draw a distinction between the Nicene Creed as such and the theology of the Nicene fathers who produced it. By drawing this distinction they give their endorsement to the Creed as written while at the same time calling into question some of the doctrinal thinking of the ancient fathers that lay behind some of the Creed's particular formulations. I find this confusing, to say the least. A creed will normally *contain* the doctrine and *reflect* the theology of those who compose it. This means in the present case, in my opinion, that if they would be critical of the Nicene fathers' doctrine in certain areas, as Hodge and Warfield are, they ought also to be equally critical of the formulations that are the products of that doctrine should they appear in the Nicene Creed. Neither is willing to be consistent and thus do this.

[21]Hodge, *Systematic Theology*, I:465, 468.

The Reformers themselves were little inclined to enter into these speculations. They were especially repugnant to such minds as Luther's. He insisted on taking the Scriptural facts as they were, without any attempt at explanation.... Calvin also was opposed to going beyond the simple statement of the Scriptures.[22]

Benjamin B. Warfield, professor of polemic and didactic theology at Old Princeton Seminary, states in his elaborate article, 'Calvin's Doctrine of the Trinity':

[Calvin] seems to have drawn back from the doctrine of 'eternal generation' *as it was expounded by the Nicene Fathers.* They were accustomed to explain 'eternal generation' (in accordance with its very nature as 'eternal'), not as something which has occurred once for all at some point of time in the past – however far back in the past – but as something which is always occurring, *a perpetual movement of the divine essence from the first Person to the second,* always complete, never completed. Calvin seems to have found this conception difficult, if not meaningless.[23]

As proof of his assertion, Warfield cites, as I did earlier, Calvin's closing words in *Institutes,* 1.13.29.

Then in concert with the Nicene fathers' opposition to the Arian heresy, Calvin found the notion that the Son's generation occurred punctiliarly or once for all at some point of time in the distant past also equally abhorent, for this would mean that before that point of time in the past he did not exist and that he had been created. The only alternative left is the one that he himself espoused, namely, the simple affirmation that '...three persons have subsisted in God from eternity' (*Institutes,* 1.13.29). By this his meaning appears to be, writes Warfield, that the Son's generation

---

[22]Hodge, *Systematic Theology,* I:466.

[23]Warfield, 'Calvin's Doctrine of the Trinity,' *The Works of Benjamin B. Warfield,* V:247 (emphasis supplied).

must have been completed from all eternity, since its product has existed complete from all eternity, and therefore it is meaningless to speak of it as continually proceeding. If this is the meaning of his remark, it is a definite rejection of the Nicene speculation of 'eternal generation.'[24]

Warfield continues:

The principle of [Calvin's] doctrine of the Trinity was ... the force of his conviction of the absolute equality of the Persons. The point of view which adjusted everything to the conception of 'generation' and 'procession' as worked out by the Nicene Fathers was entirely alien to him. The conception itself he found difficult, if not unthinkable; and although he admitted the facts of 'generation' and 'procession,' he treated them as bare facts, and *refused to make them constitutive of the doctrine of the Trinity.* He rather adjusted everything to the absolute divinity of each Person, their community in the one only true Deity; and to this we cannot doubt that *he was ready not only to subordinate, but even to sacrifice, if need be, the entire body of Nicene speculation.* Moreover, it would seem at least doubtful if Calvin ... thought of [the] begetting and procession as involving *any communication* of essence.[25]

Warfield notes further:

...the direct Scriptural proof which had been customarily relied upon for [the] establishment [of the Nicene Fathers' doctrine of 'eternal generation'], [Calvin] destroyed, refusing to rest a doctrinal determination on 'distorted texts.' He left, therefore, little Biblical evidence for the doctrine..., except what might be inferred from the mere

---

[24]Warfield, 'Calvin's Doctrine of the Trinity,' *Works*, V:248.

[25]Warfield, 'Calvin's Doctrine of the Trinity,' *Works*, V:257-58 (emphasis supplied).

terms 'Father,' 'Son,' and 'Spirit,'[26] and the general consideration that our own adoption into the relation of sons of God in Christ implies for him a Sonship of a higher and more immanent character, which is his by nature.[27]

Warfield is certainly correct to conclude that Calvin, while he rejected its speculative elaborations, held to the substantial core of the Nicene tradition.[28] I think it is in this sense (the substantial core without the speculative husk) that Calvin felt he could honestly write in *Institutes* 4.9.8: '...we willingly embrace and reverence as holy the early councils, such as those of Nicaea, Constantinople, Ephesus I, [and] Chalcedon, ... in so far as they relate to the teachings of faith,' in precisely the same way that Warfield could write (again, the substantial core without the speculative husk): '...the great body of the Reformed teachers remained good Nicenists.' For he immediately goes on to say:

> But they were none the less, as they were fully entitled to be, good 'Autotheanites' ['God of himself-ites'] also. They saw clearly that a relation within the Godhead between Persons to each of whom the entire Godhead belongs, cannot deprive any of these Persons of any essential quality of the Godhead common to them all. And they were determined to assert the full and complete Godhead of them all.[29]

Too, while it was never Calvin's intent to create a party – he simply wanted to reform the church by restoring a scriptural theology in it – Warfield observes that Calvin's treatment of the Trinity, nevertheless, marking as it did an epoch in church history,

---

[26]For these inferences see *Works*, V:168-70.
[27]Warfield, 'Calvin's Doctrine of the Trinity,' *Works*, V:278. See also V.248, fn. 86.
[28]Warfield, 'Calvin's Doctrine of the Trinity,' *Works*, V:279.
[29]Warfield, 'Calvin's Doctrine of the Trinity,' *Works*, V:275.

did not seem a matter of course when he first enunciated it. It roused opposition and created a party. But it did create a party: *and that party was shortly the Reformed Churches, of which it became characteristic that they held and taught the self-existence of Christ as God* and defended the application to Him of the term αὐϛτόθεοϛ[*autotheos*]; that is to say, in the doctrine of the Trinity they laid the stress upon the equality of the Persons sharing the same essence, and thus set themselves with more or less absoluteness against all subordinationism in the explanation of the relations of the Persons to one another.[30]

Warfield had elaborated upon this 'aroused opposition' earlier in this same essay in these words:

...strange as it may seem, theologians at large had been accustomed to apply the principle of consubstantiality to the Persons of the Trinity up to Calvin's vigorous assertion of it, with some at least apparent reserves. And when he applied it without reserve it struck many as a startling novelty if not a heretical pravity. The reason why the consubstantiality of the Persons of the Trinity, despite its establishment in the Arian controversy and its incorporation in the Nicene formulary as the very hinge of orthodoxy, was so long in coming fully to its rights in the general apprehension was no doubt that *Nicene orthodoxy preserved in its modes of stating the doctrine of the Trinity some remnants of the conceptions and phraseology proper to the older prolationism of the Logos Christology,* and these, although rendered innocuous by the explanations of the Nicene Fathers and practically antiquated since Augustine, still held their place formally and more or less conditioned the mind of men – especially those who held the doctrine of the Trinity in a more or less traditional manner. The consequence was that when Calvin taught the doctrine

---

[30]Warfield, 'Calvin's Doctrine of the Trinity,' *Works*, V:251 (emphasis supplied).

in its purity and free from the leaven of subordinationism which still found a lurking place in current thought and speech, he seemed violently revolutionary to men trained in the old forms of speech and imbued with the old modes of conception, and called out reprobation in the most unexpected quarters.[31]

One can now understand why Warfield strikingly acknowledges what for him are the following three causes for astonishment:

We are *astonished* at the persistence of so large an infusion of the Nicene phraseology in the expositions of Augustine, after that phraseology had really been antiquated by his fundamental principle of equalization in his construction of the Trinitarian relations; we are *more astonished* at the effort which Calvin made to adduce Nicene support for his own conceptions; and we are *more astonished still* at the tenacity with which [Calvin's] followers cling to all the old speculations.[32]

In his article to which I previously referred, 'The Biblical Doctrine of the Trinity,' Warfield summarized the history of the development of the Christian doctrine of the Trinity as follows (I will place in bold the four significant names from this history as Warfield rehearsed it):

In the conflict between [the Logos-Christology and Monarchianism] the church gradually found its way ... to a better and more well-balanced conception, until a real doctrine of the Trinity at length came to expression, particularly in the West, through the brilliant dialectic

---

[31]Warfield, 'Calvin's Doctrine of the Trinity,' *Works*, V:233 (emphasis supplied). Opposition during the Reformation Age came from both Romanists (primarily) and Lutherans and later from some Arminians.

[32]Warfield, 'Calvin's Doctrine of the Trinity,' *Works*, V:279 (emphasis supplied).

of **Tertullian**. It was thus ready at hand, when ... the
Logos-Christology ... ran to seed in what is known as
Arianism...; and the church was thus prepared to assert
its settled faith in a Triune God, one in being, but in whose
unity there subsisted three consubstantial Persons.
Under the leadership of **Athanasius** this doctrine was
proclaimed as the faith of the church at the Council of
Nice in 325 AD, and by his strenuous labors and those
of 'the three great Cappadocians,' the two Gregories and
Basil, it gradually won its way to the actual acceptance
of the entire church. It was at the hands of **Augustine**,
however, a century later, that the doctrine thus received
its most complete elaboration and most carefully
grounded statement. In the form in which he gave it,
and which is embodied in ... the so-called Athanasian
Creed, it has retained its place as the fit expression of
the faith of the church as to the nature of its God until
today. The language in which it is couched, even in this
final declaration, still retained elements of speech which
owe their origin to the modes of thought characteristic
of the Logos-Christology of the second century, *fixed
in the nomenclature of the church by the Nicene Creed
of 325 AD, though carefully guarded there against the
subordinationism inherent in the Logos-Christology,
and made the vehicle rather of the Nicene doctrines of
the eternal generation of the Son and procession of the
Spirit, with the consequent subordination of the Son and
Spirit to the Father in modes of subsistence as well as
of operation.* In the Athanasian Creed, however, the
principle of equalization of the three Persons, which was
already the dominant motive of the Nicene Creed – the
homoousia – is so strongly emphasized as practically
to push out of sight, if not quite out of existence, these
remanent suggestions of derivation and subordination.
It has been found necessary, nevertheless, from time to
time, vigorously to reassert the principle of equalization,
over against a tendency unduly to emphasize the
elements of subordinationism which still hold place
thus in the traditional language in which the church
states its doctrine of the Trinity. In particular, it fell

to **Calvin**, in the interest of the true Deity of Christ – the constant motive of the whole body of Trinitarian thought – to reassert and make good the attribute of self-existence (*autotheotos*) for the Son. Thus Calvin takes his place alongside of Tertullian, Athanasius, and Augustine, as one of the chief contributors to the exact and vital statement of the Christian doctrine of the Triune God.[33]

A careful reading of this summary will show that Warfield believed, first, that the Nicene Creed, by its doctrines of the eternal generation of the Son and the procession of the Spirit, implies 'the consequent subordination of the Son and Spirit to the Father in modes of subsistence as well as of operation' as well as 'suggestions of derivation and subordination'; second, that Calvin, over against this subordination of the Son and Spirit in subsistence to the Father, finally made good the attribute of the Son's (and the Spirit's) self-existence, thereby taking his place as the fourth major contributor to the exact statement of the doctrine of the Trinity; and third, that by so doing Calvin made a critical adjustment to the theological implications in the language of the Nicene Creed at the point of Nicea's implied subordinationism of the Son by derivation from the Father.[34]

---

[33]Warfield, 'The Biblical Doctrine of the Trinity' in *Biblical and Theological Studies*, 58-59 (bold supplied).

[34]Written as this article was in 1915 for *The International Standard Bible Encyclopedia* whereas Warfield's earlier article, 'Calvin's Doctrine of the Trinity,' was written in 1909 for the *Princeton Theological Review*, VII, 553-652, I think we should assume that the later article also represents Warfield's mature thinking on the doctrine of the Trinity, only considered from the biblical perspective. I also think we should assume that Warfield's understanding of both Nicea's doctrine of the Trinity and Calvin's understanding of Nicea as he represents both in these two articles is essentially the same in both articles. I underscore this because Robert Letham who has criticized my exposition of Calvin's Trinitarianism told me that he appreciated Warfield's exposition of Calvin's doctrine of the Trinity in the 1909 article but wished Warfield had never written what he

John Murray, professor of systematic theology at Westminster Seminary, states regarding Calvin's view of the 'catholic' doctrine of the early fathers' eternal generation of the Son:

> Students of historical theology are acquainted with the furore which Calvin's insistence upon the self-existence of the Son as to his deity aroused at the time of the Reformation. Calvin was too much of a student of Scripture to be content to follow the lines of what had been regarded as Nicene orthodoxy on this particular issue. He was too jealous for the implications of the *homoousion* clause of the Nicene Creed to be willing to accede to the interpretation which the Nicene Fathers, including Athanasius, placed upon another expression in the same creed, namely, 'very God of very God' (*theon alēthinon ek theou alēthinou*). No doubt this expression is repeated by orthodox people without any thought of suggesting what the evidence derived from the writings of the Nicene Fathers would indicate the intent to have been. This evidence shows that the meaning intended is that the Son derived his deity from the Father and that the Son was not therefore *autotheos*.[35] It was precisely this position that Calvin controverted with vigour. He maintained that as respects personal distinction the Son was of the Father but as respects deity he was self-existent (*ex se ipso*). *This position ran counter to the Nicene tradition.* Hence the indictments levelled against him. It is, however, to the credit of Calvin that he did not allow his own more sober thinking to be suppressed out of deference to an established pattern of thought

---

did about Calvin's understanding of it in the 1915 article. By saying this Letham is implying that Warfield's understanding of Calvin's doctrine, or at least his expression of it, degenerated rather than matured with the passing of years. I would urge, however, that the 1915 article helps us better understand Warfield's intended exposition of Calvin's Trinitarianism in the 1909 article.

[35]See, for example, Athanasius' *Expositio Fidei* where he clearly states that the Son derives his deity (*theotēs*) from the Father. See also his *De Decretis Nicaenae Synodi* §§ 3 and 19.

when the latter did not commend itself by conformity to Scripture and was inimical to Christ's divine identity.[36]

Morton H. Smith, professor of systematic theology at Greenville Presbyterian Theological Seminary, South Carolina states that the Nicene theologians taught that 'the Father is the beginning, the fountain, the cause, the principle of the being of the Son' and that 'the Son derives his essence from the Father by eternal and indefinable generation of divine essence from the Father to the Son.' He then notes:

> Calvin was the first one to challenge these ... two speculations. He taught that the Son was *a se ipso* with regard to his deity. He did not derive his essence from the Father. There is no warrant in the Scripture for the subordination of the Son in his essence to the Father. The same may be said of the Holy Spirit. He is *a se ipso* as regards his essence.[37]

Finally, **Donald Macleod** laments the fact, as did Warfield, that 'the valuable work done by John Calvin in this area has been largely ignored,'[38] observing:

> Subordinationism survived the introduction of the *filioque* as it had that of the *homoousion*, largely because the successors of the Nicene theologians were content to reproduce their language and sentiments uncritically.... This stubborn residue of subordinationism provided the background to John Calvin's formulation of the doctrine of the Trinity.... His whole concern is to maximize the

---

[36]John Murray, 'Systematic Theology,' *Collected Writings of John Murray* (Edinburgh: Banner of Truth, 1982), 4:8 (emphasis supplied).

[37]Morton H. Smith, *Systematic Theology*, 1:152.

[38]Macleod, *Behold Your God*, 201. Macleod adds here the qualification: '...apart from the prevalence of a certain suspicion that [Calvin] was unsound on the doctrine of the eternal sonship' (see fn. 39).

equality between the Father and the Son, and he is ill at ease with any suggestion of subordination. While he retains some of the language of causality he denies that the Father is in any sense the *deificator* ('god-maker') of the Son. The Father gave the Son neither his being nor his divinity.... [Because the Son and the Holy Spirit are both Yahweh] the essence of the Son and the Holy Spirit cannot be subordinate in any sense to the essence of the Father because it is one and the same essence, equally self-existent in each person. Consequently, such terms as 'begotten' and 'proceeding' apply only to the persons of the Son and the Spirit, not to their essence.[39]

I would urge, therefore, with Calvin and these cited theologians, that Christians should believe that God the Father is 'the beginning of activity, and the fountain and wellspring of all things' (*Institutes*, 1.13.18). But they should not believe that the Father, through an eternal act of begetting in the depth of the divine being that is *always* continuing, is begetting the Son's essential being as God out of his being, which act thereby 'puts this second person in possession of the whole divine essence.'[40] They should believe, rather, that the Son with respect to his essential being is wholly God of himself from all eternity, to whom as God the Son the Scriptures attribute 'wisdom, counsel, and the ordered disposition of all things' (*Institutes*, 1.13.18). Of course, they should also believe that the Son as the second Person of the Godhead derives his incommunicable *hypostatic* identity from the 'generated' relation that he sustains 'before all ages' to God the Father, the first Person of the Godhead (what this 'generation' means beyond 'reasoned order'[41] and the distinction just noted I cannot

---

[39]Donald Macleod, *The Person of Christ* (Downers Grove, Ill.: InterVarsity, 1998), 149-51.

[40]Berkhof, *Systematic Theology* (New combined edition; Grand Rapids: Eerdmans, 1996), 94.

[41]The main reason I express hesitancy in saying more about the meaning of the Son's 'eternal generation' than to say it teaches

say and will not attempt to say), and that the Father by
his incommunicable property as Father precedes the
Son within the Godhead by reason of order.

As for the Nicaeno-Constantinopolitan doctrine of the
Father's 'eternal processing' of the Spirit out of himself,

'reasoned order' within the Godhead is that the arguments commonly
offered for saying more are in my opinion suspect. To wit: (1) It is
often said that the very titles 'Father' and 'Son' imply that the Father
generates the Son out of himself; but this is to freight the titles with the
occidental ideas of 'source of being' and 'essential superiority' on the
one hand and of 'dependence of being' and 'essential subordination'
on the other, when according to John 10:30-36 the title 'Son'
denotes, first, *sameness of nature* and *equality* with the Father, and
second, infinite reciprocal affection between Father and Son. (2) The
Johannine term *monogenēs* (John 1:14, 18; 3:16; 1 John 4:9),
traditionally translated 'only begotten,' is said to teach that the Son
is generated by and out of the Father; but there is a wide consensus
today that the term does not mean 'only begotten,' alluding to some
form of generation of the Son on the Father's part or to the virginal
conception of Jesus, but means rather 'one and only,' 'only one of
his kind,' or 'unique.' Warfield, for example, writes in 'The Person
of Christ,' in *Works* (Reprint; Grand Rapids: Baker, 1991) II:194:
'The adjective 'only begotten' conveys the idea, not of derivation and
subordination, but of uniqueness and consubstantiality: Jesus is
all that God is, and he alone is this.' See also, for example, BAGD,
monogenēs, *A Greek-English Lexicon of the New Testament*, 529; Dale
Moody, 'God's Only Son: The Translation of John 3:16 in the Revised
Standard Version,' in *Journal of Biblical Literature* LXXII (1953), 213;
Richard N. Longenecker, 'The One and Only Son,' in *The Making
of the NIV* (Grand Rapids: Baker, 1991), 117-24; Karl-Heinz Bartel,
[*monogenēs*],' in *The New International Dictionary of New Testament
Theology*, edited by Colin Brown (English edition; Grand Rapids:
Zondervan, 1976), 2:725; and D. R. Bauer, 'Son of God,' in *Dictionary
of Jesus and the Gospels*,' edited by Joel B. Green, Scott McKnight,
and I. Howard Marshall (Grand Rapids: InterVarsity, 1992), 775a.
(3) The Father's statement, 'You are my Son; today I have begotten
you' (Ps 2:7), does not refer, as is commonly opined, to an activity
going on in the depths of the divine being but according to Acts 13:33
refers to the Father's raising of our Lord from the dead on the first
day of the week. (4) Jesus' statement that the Father 'gave to the Son
also to have life in himself' (John 5:26) is said to teach that the Father
communicates the divine essence to the Son, but a consensus has
by no means been reached that these words refer to an ontological
endowment. It is entirely possible and, in light of the context (see
5:22-23, 27), more likely that this statement refer to an aspect of

the biblical evidence for such ranges from slight to zero, based as it is in the main upon the single statement 'who comes forth from the Father' found in John 15:26. A host of recognized scholars, such as B. F. Westcott, Alfred Plummer, J. H. Bernard, J. Oliver Buswell, Jr., Raymond E. Brown, Loraine Boettner, F. F. Bruce, Leon Morris, James I. Packer, Donald A. Carson, Gerald Bray, and Paul Helm,[42] contends that the 'coming forth' here, in accordance with John 14:26, much more probably refers not to an intra-Trinitarian relationship between the Father and the Spirit but to the Father's dispatching the Holy Spirit into the world on his salvific mission of mercy.

Therefore, I would also urge that Christians should not believe that the Holy Spirit, through an eternal act

---

the incarnate Son's *messianic* investiture. The only conclusion that one can fairly draw from such data, among other data that could be cited (see Warfield, 'Calvin's Doctrine of the Trinity,' *Works*, V:277, fn 135), is that the Scriptures upon which the Nicene Fathers based their teaching of the Father's communication of his essence to the Son fail to provide clear warrant for the teaching.

[42]John 14:26 and 15:26, Palm Helm maintains, 'refer to the role of the Holy Spirit in the economy of salvation; they say nothing about the eternal relationship of the Father and the Son to the Spirit as it is in itself' ('Of God, and of the Holy Trinity: A Response to Dr. Beckwith,' *Churchman* 115/4 [2001], 352). However, I should note that, unlike the other scholars I have named here, Helm affirms this as part of his larger argument that *all* the biblical and especially the New Testament data advancing the concepts of divine Sonship and Spirithood are intended to reveal God in the economy of salvation and *not* as he is in himself, that is to say, that the Son's 'begetting' is a metaphor for his Incarnation (and the Spirit's 'proceeding' is a metaphor for his manifestation at Pentecost): 'I believe that [the verses regarding the relationship between Father and Son to which Roger Beckwith alludes such as John 1:3; 6:38; 10:36; 16:28; 17:5, 24; Colossians 1:16; Hebrews 1:2; Revelation 3:14] may all be understood, without exception, in the references they make to 'Father' and 'Son', as reading back into the eternal relationships of the godhead what became true at the Incarnation' (357).

With Helm's larger argument I cannot agree. The persons of the Godhead have eternally existed within the ontological Trinity of proceeding in the depth of the divine being that is *always* continuing, is continually proceeding out of the Father and the Son as to his essential being as God, which acts 'puts the third person in possession of the whole divine essence.'[43] They should believe, rather, that the Holy Spirit with respect to his essential being is wholly God of himself from all eternity, to whom as the Spirit of God and of Christ (Rom. 8:9) the Scriptures assign 'the power and efficacy of [the divine] activity' (*Institutes*, 1.13.18). Of course, they should also believe that the Holy Spirit as the third Person of the Godhead derives his incommunicable *hypostatic* identity from his 'procession' before all ages from both God the Father, the first Person of the Godhead, and God the Son, the second Person of the Godhead (what this 'procession'

---

as the Father, the Son, and the Holy Spirit. A couple of examples showing this, beyond those Beckwith advanced, will have to suffice. First, a careful exposition of the word 'son' in the parable of the wicked farmers (Matt. 21:37; Mark 6; Luke 20:13) will show that Jesus represented himself as the Son *before* his mission and as God's beloved Son *whether he be sent or not*. As Geerhardus Vos writes in his *The Self-Disclosure of Jesus* (Reprint; Phillipsburg, N.J.: Presbyterian and Reformed, 1978), 161-3: 'His being sent describes ... his Messiahship, but this Messiahship was brought about precisely by the necessity for sending one who was the highest and dearest that the lord of the vineyard could delegate.... The sonship, therefore, existed *antecedently* to the Messianic mission.' This is also the case in Paul's use of the word 'Son' in Romans 1:3, 8:3, 32 and Galatians 4:4. These verses clearly suggest that the Son enjoyed an existence with God the Father prior to his being sent into the world on his mission of mercy and that in this preexistent state he stood in a relation to the Father as the Father's unique Son (see also Col. 1:16-17 where the Son is said to be 'before all things'). Second, the Word that John 1:1 coordinates in the beginning with *God* before the creation of all things with its *pros ton theon*, is in its counterpart in 1 John 1:2 coordinated in the beginning with the *Father* with its *pros ton patera*, showing that John was thinking of the Word who was in the beginning with God in John 1:1 in *personal* terms as the Son of the Father. And of course the Spirit of God was engaged in the beginning with creation (Gen. 1:1).

[43]Berkhof, *Systematic Theology*, 97.

means beyond 'order' and the distinction just noted and how it differs in nature from the Son's 'generation' I cannot say and will not attempt to say except to assert that it issues from the Father and the Son while the latter is from the Father alone), and that the Father and the Son precede the Holy Spirit within the Godhead by reason of order.

We may sum up all we have said so far this way: There is no *essential* subordination of the Son to the Father and no *essential* subordination of the Holy Spirit to the Father and the Son within the one undivided Godhead that each fully possesses, but there is 'a reasoned order' (*Institutes*, 1.13.20) that brooks no essential subordination within the one undivided Godhead, with the Father being the first Person of the Godhead, the Son as the Son of the Father therefore being the second Person of the Godhead, and the Holy Spirit as the Spirit of the Father and the Son therefore being the third Person of the Godhead. I would, therefore, caution against both an uncritical employment by the church of the language of the Niceno/Constantinopolitan Creed because of the subordinationist and tritheistic implications therein and the uncritical presumption that the Trinitarian statement of the *Westminster Confession* intends to incorporate without any modification the flawed language of the earlier Creed.

Westminster Trinitarianism: Nicene or Reformed or Both?

A knowledgeable person will ask here, 'But does not *Westminster Confession of Faith*, II.ɪɪɪ, itself state:

> In the unity of the Godhead there be three persons, of one substance, power, and eternity: God the Father, God the Son, and God the Holy Ghost: the Father is of none, neither begotten, nor proceeding; the Son is eternally begotten of the Father; the Holy Ghost eternally proceeding from the Father and the Son?

And is this not the language of Nicea?' To both questions we respond, yes, most assuredly. But the questions now become: What did the framers of the *Confession* intend by their confessional statement? Did they intend their statement in the unqualifiedly 'Nicene' sense or in the 'Calvinistic' or Reformed sense?

Robert Letham of Westminster Theological Seminary, Philadelphia, has criticized my questioning whether the Trinitarianism of the *Westminster Confession of Faith*, II.iii is 'Nicene' or 'Reformed'[44] – by 'Reformed' here I simply mean the *non-speculative* view of 'eternal generation' and 'eternal procession' espoused by John Calvin and his followers – a question that I do not regard as out of bounds to raise. I suggested in the first edition of my *A New Systematic Theology of the Christian Faith* that the view of the *Confession* is the latter but not in any totally new or radical way, of course; indeed, I acknowledged that the language of the *Westminster Confession* is that of the earlier Nicene and Niceno/Constantinopolitan Creeds. But Letham argues in rebuttal that by so doing I have severed the Magisterial Reformation away from the ancient church – a breech that Calvin himself had employed every fiber of his being to avoid.

Letham contends that I arrived at my conclusion by 'building an unprovable hypothesis on an insupportable theory.' But have I? When we learn that Calvin's Trinitarianism 'created a party,' even the Reformed churches (so Warfield), whose view of God was a 'change of perception' that was 'fundamentally different' from the past in the belief that 'the persons of the Trinity are equal to one another in every respect' (so Gerald Bray[45]),

---

[44]Robert Letham, 'Review' of my *A New Systematic Theology of the Christian Faith* in *Westminster Theological Journal* 62 (2000):319, and from a subsequent telephone conversation that I initiated with him.

[45]Bray, *The Doctrine of God*, 197, 200. Bray's phrase, 'fundamentally different' (*The Doctrine of God*, 197), is probably a bit strong; 'different in some respects' would, I believe, be truer as a description. But I do agree with Bray when he writes in *The Doctrine*

why should we not consider whether the *Westminster Confession of Faith*, the high-water mark of Reformed confessional writing, just might have intended by its very sparse statement on the Trinity in II.ɪɪɪ to side with Calvin's non-speculative understanding of the Trinity over against the Nicene Fathers' more expansive and sometimes speculative understanding of the doctrine? Particularly pressing does this question become if we recall that

> when during the first weeks of its sessions,[46] the Westminster Assembly was engaged on the revision of the Thirty-nine Articles, and Article viii on the Three Creeds came up for discussion,[47] objection was made to the ἐκ θεοῦ [*ek theou*] clauses. It does not appear that there was any pleading for the subordinationist position: the advocates for retaining the Creeds rather expended their strength in *voiding the credal statement of any subordinationist implications*.[48]

---

of God, 198: 'Many people [wrongly] assume that Calvin's defense of the Trinity ... was intended mainly as a refutation of heretics like Servetus, and offers little that could be termed new.' In my opinion, Paul Owen is among such people for he is surely wrong when he states in 'Calvin and Catholic Trinitarianism: An Examination of Robert Reymond's Understanding of the Trinity and His Appeal to John Calvin,' in *Calvin Theological Journal* 35:2 (2000), 270, 273, emphasis his, that '...however zealous Calvin was to preserve the authentic deity of each of the Persons of the Trinity, it needs to be recognized that he saw himself, not as *improving* upon earlier trinitarian dogma, but rather *defending it* in all its pristine purity from heretics such as Michael Servetus and Valentine Gentile.' Robert Letham as well, minimizing Calvin's rejection of the subordinationist language of Nicea, may be among such people.

[46]The Westminster Assembly began to meet on July 1, 1643. Its work on the Thirty-Nine Articles extended from July 8 to October 12, 1643.

[47]Article eight states: 'The Nicene Creed ... ought thoroughly to be received and believed.'

[48]Benjamin B. Warfield, 'Calvin's Doctrine of the Trinity,' *Works*, fn. 137 (emphasis supplied). Chad B. Van Dixhoorn in 'Reforming

Why should we not conclude, then, when these same men, their earlier debates on Article viii of the Thirty-Nine Articles having prepared the way for a more summary mode of procedure, turned because of Parliament's new instructions to them soon after the signing of the Solemn League and Covenant to the task of writing a new confession of faith – the confession that we now know as the *Westminster Confession of Faith* – that they would have had the same opposition to the subordinationist implications of Nicea in this new confessional expression of their Trinitarianism? In fact, as Alex F. Mitchell observes, 'the so-called Athanasian Creed is shrunk up into the single sentence' of II.iii,[49] concerning which reduction John Murray states:

> [Chapter II, Article iii's] brevity is striking and its simplicity is matched only by its brevity. Both surprise and gratification are evoked by the restraint in defining the distinguishing properties of the persons of the Godhead. *It had been Nicene tradition to embellish the doctrine, especially that of Christ's Sonship, with formulae beyond the warrant of Scripture. The Confession does not indulge in such attempts at definition.* Later generations lie under a great debt to Westminster for the studied

---

the Reformation: Theological Debate at the Westminster Assembly' (Ph.D. dissertation; University of Cambridge, 2004), I, 253, provides the following information about the later status of the Thirty-nine Articles before the Parliament: 'The uncertain status of the [three] Creeds and of the Thirty-nine Articles as a whole was underlined once more by the House of Commons on 13 October 1647 when it drafted propositions "touching Church Government, and of an Exemption for tender Consciences." The exemptions, it was made clear, did not extend to any toleration of popery or to the "Printing, Publishing, or Preaching" of the first fifteen of the Thirty-nine Articles "as they have been cleared and vindicated by the Assembly of Divines. Yet ... the Commons allowed one exception to the Thirty-nine Articles: the Eighth Article and its recommendation of the creeds".'

[49]Alex F. Mitchell, *Minutes of the Sessions of the Westminster Assembly Divines* (Edinburgh: William Blackwood and Sons, 1874), li.

reserve that saved the Confession from being burdened with such *speculative notions* as commended themselves to theologians for more than a thousand years, but to which Scripture did not lend support. Hence all we find on this subject is the brief statement: 'the Father is of none, neither begotten nor proceeding; the Son is eternally begotten of the Father; the Spirit eternal proceeding from the Father and the Son.'[50]

Does not this collocation of data suggest that a difference does exist between Nicene Trinitarianism and what I would characterize as the non-speculative Trinitarianism of the Westminster Assembly? I think so and would suggest that, while it is possible (but only barely) that the Westminster divines intended to stand uncritically by the earlier creeds and to affirm the early church's particular doctrines of the Father's *continuing* generation of the Son out of himself and the Spirit's *continuing* procession out of the Father and the Son with respect to their *essential* being as God, much more likely is it that they intended their brief Trinitarian statement – clearly shorn of virtually all of the Nicene verbiage and thus its unbiblical speculations and implications – to be understood, in keeping with Calvin's more scriptural insights, as an expression denoting the eternal 'order' in the Godhead, that is, the Father, being 'of none,' with respect to his hypostatic identity is the first Person of the Godhead; the Son, 'eternally begotten' with respect to his *hypostatic* identity, is the second Person of the Godhead, and the Holy Spirit, 'eternally proceeding' with respect to his *hypostatic* identity, is the third Person of the Godhead.[51] I find it difficult to believe, in

---

[50]John Murray, 'The Theology of the Westminster Confession of Faith,' *Collected Writings of John Murray* (Edinburgh: Banner of Truth, 1982), 4:248 (emphasis supplied).

[51]Chad Van Dixhoorn in email correspondence, dated June 2, 2005, agrees with me that 'the speculative side of the creedal statement is absent' in the *Westminster Confession of Faith*, but he

light of the clear fact of our *Confession*'s omission of much of the subordinationist language of Nicaea, that its framers simply leaped back over Calvin's treatment of the Trinity as if it were non-existent and returned uncritically to the flawed formula of Nicea with its speculative subordinationism in essential subsistence of the Son to the Father (and later of the Spirit to the Father and the Son). As did a host of Reformed writers in the 16th and 17th centuries,[52] American orthodox

---

is not prepared to say with confidence that *WCF*, II.ɪɪɪ teaches only Calvin's view. He asks: 'Certainly there is room for Calvin's position, but did the Assembly close the door on the Bezan position, or that of Simler or Featley?' In email correspondence dated June 6, 2005 Van Dixhoorn concluded, because the Westminster divines were cautious in their creedal statement precisely because of Calvin's Trinitarianism that we know they discussed, that their statement 'does not incline toward either side of the debate, but allows both.'What is my response to Van Dixhoorn's conclusions? To his question I would respond in the negative. While the confessional statement in my opinion is essentially non-speculative and thus 'Calvinistic' in its expression, I would say that the Assembly's unembellished Trinitarian statement could still countenance positions that were 'more Nicene' than was Calvin's, since, after all, as Warfield said, while 'the great body of the Reformed teachers [were] good Autotheanites,' they also 'remained good Nicenists' as well, as indeed was Calvin, who would not have intended to expel Nicenists who did not agree with them in every point from the Assembly. I say this even though I am confident that Calvin would have taken umbrage with Theodore Beza when he states: *filius est a patre per ineffabilem totius essentis communicationem ab patre* ('The Son is from the Father by an ineffable communication of the whole essence from eternity') and with Josiah Simler when he states: *negamus filium habere essentiam a Deo patre, sed essentiam genitam negamus* ('We do not deny that the Son has his essence from God the Father, but we deny a begotten essence'). As for Daniel Featley, while it is true that he attempts to undermine Calvin's insights overall, yet when he states in his *The Dippers Dipt* (London, 1647), 190-91: 'I am of Whitakers mind that it is ... most truly and religiously spoken: *nam si ex se Deus non est, omnino Deus non est* ['For if [the Son] is not God of himself, he is not God at all'],' he positions himself by that statement, considered apart from the other things he said, squarely *within* Calvin's thinking.

[52]Gisbertus Voetius (1589-1676), Dutch Reformed pastor and professor of theology at the University of Utrecht, lists not only Calvin's

Presbyterian theologians such as Charles Hodge, Benjamin B. Warfield, John Murray, J. Oliver Buswell, Jr.,[53] Loraine Boettner,[54] Morton H. Smith, and the Scottish theologian Donald Macleod have followed Calvin's insistence that the second and third Persons of the Godhead, like the Father, are both *autotheotic*, that is, God in and of themselves, possessed as they each are with the one undivided, self-existent divine essence.

Letham's criticism arises from his concern that Protestants should not sever the Reformation cause away from the ancient church at such a strategically vital nexus as the doctrine of the Trinity. He contends,

---

successors at Geneva, Theodore Beza and Josiah Simler, but also 'the whole mass of representative Reformed teachers: Danaeus, Perkins, Keckermann, Trelcatius, Tilenus, Polanus, Wollebius, Scalcobrigius, Altingius, Grynaeus, Schriverius, Zanchius, Chamierus, Zadeel, Lectius, Pareus, Mortonus, Whittaker, Junius, Vorstius, Amesius, Rivetus,' as teaching that Christ is properly to be regarded as *autotheos*. See Warfield, 'Calvin's Doctrine of the Trinity,' *Works*, V:274, fn. 127. Van Dixhoorn thinks Voetius's list is too inclusive. Perhaps Beza and Simler should be eliminated. Romanists of the period who opposed Calvin's view (which fact in itself suggests that Calvin's view differed in some respects from Nicea) were Peter Caroli, Anthony Possevinus, Alphonsus Salmeron, William Lindanus, Peter Canisius, and Dionysius Petavius, all of whom concluded that his view was heretical. The two greatest Romanist theologians of the period, Gregory of Valentia and Robert Bellarmine, however, were more judicious and concluded that Calvin's meaning, while in error in the manner in which he expressed it, was nonetheless 'catholic' and orthodox.While Calvin had his occasional defenders among the Lutherans such as Meisner and Tarnov, generally the Lutheran theologians such as Tilemann Heshusius and Aegidius Hunnius condemned his view in the interest of the traditional Nicene representation of the Trinity. Excluding Arminius himself, the first Arminians, such as Episcopius, Curcellaeus, and Limborch evidence a distinct tendency toward an Origenistic subordinationism within the Godhead. Later members of the school, such as Samuel Clarke, even show a Socinian influence.

[53]J. Oliver Buswell, Jr., *A Systematic Theology of the Christian Religion* (Grand Rapids: Zondervan, 1962), I:110-12, 115, 119-20.

[54]Loraine Boettner, *Studies in Theology* (Grand Rapids: Eerdmans, 1951), 121-4.

as we have seen, that Calvin himself, solicitous to maintain catholic unity with the ancient church as evidenced by his frequent favorable citations of the early fathers, particularly Augustine, would have opposed such a severing with every ounce of strength in his being. But while Letham's concern is appropriate enough since it is certainly true that we should not sever the Magisterial Reformation away from the teaching of the ancient church where it is not necessary to do so, I believe that this is one of several instances (the ancient church's sacerdotal soteriology surely being another) in which it is *necessary* to do so, and I think I have shown that Calvin thought so too. And by his treatment of the Trinity, writes Warfield, Calvin entered the 'narrow circle of elect spirits' that includes the names of Tertullian and Augustine to whom 'the Church looks back with gratitude' for the contribution he made to the right understanding of the doctrine of the Trinity by his 'clear, firm and unwavering assertion of the αὐτοθεοτης [*autotheotēs*] of the Son'.[55]

I believe that Letham's problem with my exposition is due to his having too high a view of the ancient church's stature as a church authority. His high view is evident when he concludes his review of my *Systematic Theology* by posing to his readers Colin Gunton's 'vital' question:

> ...if we can no longer ... appropriate for ourselves the language of the past – for example, the affirmations of the Nicene Creed – then on what grounds are we able to judge whether we share the faith of the Fathers who formulated the Creed?[56]

---

[55]Warfield, 'Calvin's Doctrine of the Trinity,' *Works*, V:284.

[56]Regrettably, there is a tendency among Reformed thinkers today, following Thomas Oden's lead, to regard the early ecumenical creeds as 'classical Christianity' and therefore as the standard of orthodoxy and heresy. I say 'regrettably,' first, because these early creeds are too narrow to serve by themselves as the standard of orthodoxy and heresy because they are not *evangelical* creeds, failing as they do to enter into salvific matters with any fullness. They were

But Gunton's (and indirectly, Letham's) 'vital' question begs the whole question at the heart of our difference here. Is our primary concern to be to assure ourselves that we 'share the faith of the Fathers who formulated the Creed'? I think not. Is our primary concern to be to 'appropriate for ourselves the language of the past'? I think not. Is not our primary concern to be to make every effort to assure ourselves that our faith *first of all* passes biblical muster, employing the faith and creeds of the ancient fathers as secondary aids and helps as we seek to learn and to enunciate the truth of the infallible Scriptures? I certainly think so, and I believe that Letham thinks so as well. And is not the faith of the ancient fathers, while we revere their creedal labors, to be considered by us as a secondary authority to the authoritative teaching of Scripture itself? I certainly think so, and again I believe that Letham thinks so as well. Therefore, I do not think that it is essential

---

framed in the narrow context of the Trinitarian and Christological debates of the 4th and 5th centuries and are underdeveloped and virtually silent on salvific matters. There is nothing in them that the Judaizers whom Paul confronted in his letter to the Galatians could not have endorsed. Nevertheless, Paul condemned the Judaizers in the strongest possible terms because of their 'other gospel.' Quite obviously, Paul did not believe there was saving value in holding even to a *right* view of God as Trinity if one was also holding to a *wrong* view of the saving work of the Trinity. Herman Bavinck in his *The Doctrine of God*, translated by William Hendriksen (Grand Rapids: Baker, 1951), 285, observed, I believe rightly, that 'the Reformation has brought to light that not the mere historical belief in the doctrine of the Trinity, no matter how pure, is sufficient unto salvation, but only the true heart-born confidence that rests in God himself, who in Christ has revealed himself as the triune God.' Hence, orthodoxy and heresy must be determined by a fuller standard than the early ecumenical creeds. I say 'regrettably', second, because, while Holy Scripture is, of course, the final standard of orthodoxy and heresy (*see Westminster Confession of Faith*, I.viii, x), the *Westminster Confession* and its 'creedal children', the *Savoy Declaration of 1658* and the *Baptist Confession of 1689*, because of their fuller conformity to the teaching of Holy Scripture, provide the richer and fuller *creedal* expressions of the teaching of that 'final standard'.

to the contemporary Reformed church's commitment to the 'faith of the fathers' as set forth in the early ecumenical councils that it must accept their creedal pronouncements uncritically with no qualifications or adjustments. And as I have shown, neither did John Calvin.

As I have asked before on many occasions, I ask again: Should not our primary concern be to assure ourselves that our faith *first of all* passes biblical muster, employing the faith and creeds of the ancient fathers, while we revere their creedal labors, as uninspired *secondary* aids and helps as we seek to learn and to enunciate the truth of the infallible Scriptures? I certainly think so. And I could wish that more Reformed theologians and pastors were less concerned to be '*creedally* correct,' faulting in the process their brothers who have *biblical* reasons for not being as 'creedally correct' as they, and more concerned to avoid speculative distractions and to be *biblically* governed in their Trinitarian beliefs and pronouncements.

Application

Permit me before I close to make two short but very important applications concerning the value of the Trinity. First, the doctrine of the Trinity is a vital tenet of the true faith because, as Calvin observed, the one living and true God who revealed himself in Holy Scripture

> so proclaims himself the *sole* God as to offer himself [at the same time] to be contemplated in three persons. *Unless we grasp these, only the bare and empty name of God flits about in our brain to the exclusion of the true God.*[57]

Only faith in the one living and true God as trinity in unity and unity in trinity keeps one from idolatry. The

---

[57] John Calvin, *Institutes*, 1.13.2, emphasis supplied.

unitarian theist who rejects the doctrine of the Trinity has only 'the bare and empty name of God flitting about in his mind' (Calvin), 'an empty phantom and an idol' (Witsius).

Second, only the doctrine of the Trinity brings clarity and harmony to the totality of the salvific teaching of Scripture. When the triune personhood of God is given its proper place the several aspects of biblical soteriology fit together 'hand in glove' and form a glorious and harmonious whole. The unitarian theist who rejects the doctrine of the Trinity leaves both Old and New Testament salvation in a total shambles and utter confusion.

We must now bring this address, and with it, this series of addresses on God's attributes to a close. I want to express again to the faculty my gratitude for their invitation to me to deliver these addresses, but before I conclude I would urge you all again never to think or to talk about God as if he were simply an undifferentiated divine Monad but always to remember that the biblical God's *special* mark of distinction is his triunity. Never forget that it is the one living and true *tri-personal* non-corporeal Being who is infinite, eternal, and unchangeable in his being, wisdom, power, holiness, justice, goodness, and truth. I would also urge you to espouse Calvin's non-speculative view of the Trinity, and I would admonish you students to find in Calvin your model for your own theologizing. Ever make it your design, as did he, to go as far as Scripture goes in your theologizing and to stop where Scripture stops. Such an approach will invoke the blessing of God upon your ministry and you will avoid serious theological error. And always remember that the doctrine of the Trinity is the bedrock of all true gospel proclamation.

I must now issue one final caution before I let you go, and it is this: Because the catechetical definition we have been considering is not *per se* an *evangelical* definition, that is to say, because it does not define the gospel and what a person has to do in order to be saved, a person can believe from the heart every word of this catechetical definition and *still be lost* if in order to be saved he is trusting to any degree in his own character, and/or if in addition to his trust in God and his Christ he believes he must bring to the judgment bar of God at least some good works of his own, and/or if he is trusting in Christ plus the works of anyone else such as Mary and the saints. So one must clearly understand that there is a danger in reciting even the revered, time-honored Apostles Creed or any of the other early Trinitarian creeds if one assumes that by simply believing their tenets one is necessarily saved. For it is possible to believe the Apostles Creed and even the answers to the fourth and sixth questions of the *Westminster Shorter Catechism* – that 'God is a Spirit, infinite, eternal, and unchangeable, in his being, wisdom, power, holiness, justice, goodness, and truth' and that 'there are three persons in the Godhead: the Father, the Son, and the Holy Ghost; and these three are one God, the same in substance, equal in power and glory' – but also to believe at the same time that if one would go to heaven when he dies he must still put an 'and' or a 'plus' of his own presumably meritorious obedience after the triune God's saving work. But to do so is soul-destroying, for he who would trust in the triune God's saving work plus any of his own works that presumably possess some merit before God, according to Paul, has trusted in a 'different gospel that is no gospel at all' (Gal. 1:6-7). He must then keep the whole law perfectly (Gal. 3:10), making thereby Christ's cross-work of no value to him (Gal. 5:2). In so doing, he has alienated himself from Christ (Gal. 5:4a), has fallen away from grace (Gal. 5:4b), and has abolished the offense of the cross (Gal. 5:11). Brothers and sisters, it is not enough to be orthodox in knowing *who* God and Christ are. One must also be orthodox in believing *what* the triune God has savingly done for those for whom Christ died and trust in that work alone! So make sure you are trusting in Christ alone for your salvation!

With this admonition I have completed my exposition of the *Shorter Catechism* definition of God. To God alone be the glory for all that he has enabled us to accomplish in these eleven chapel addresses! As I now close, I would admonish us all to rededicate our lives and minds to the task to which God has called us, to get to know him better than we know anyone or anything else, to 'declare to both Jews and Greeks that they must turn to God in repentance and have faith in our Lord Jesus,' and finally, to 'finish the race and complete the task the Lord Jesus has given [us] – the task of testifying to the gospel of God's grace' (Acts 20:21, 24) – and to do so in such a way that with Paul we too will be able to say someday: 'I have fought the good fight, I have finished the race, I have kept the faith' (2 Tim. 4:7).

Let us pray:
Almighty triune Creator and Preserver of us all: As we conclude this semester's work and this series of addresses on your attributes, we praise you for your incomprehensible, omnipresent, everlasting, and unchangeable Being, for the riches of your wisdom and knowledge that are unsearchable and past tracing out, for your omnipotence by which you do precisely what you deem it proper to do, for the beauty of your transcendent and condescendent holiness, for your retributive righteousness by which you deliver us from our enemies and for your distributive righteousness by which you redeem us from our sins and justify us, for your gracious longsuffering and your lovingkindness, your pity toward and your mercy upon us, your compassion and tenderness when dealing with us, and for your perfections of perfect rationality, ethical steadfastness, and covenant faithfulness.

As we contemplate your triune Being and character, we become invalid in our efforts at adoration and praise.

We recognize that no thoughts or words of ours can adequately capture the wonder of your Triunity or the majesty of your sovereignty.

We can only bless your name that you set your love upon us before the creation of the world and have been working ever since to give us to your beloved Son as his bride, to the praise of the glory of your grace.

We thank you, our heavenly Father, for your beloved Son who became man for us men and our salvation.

We thank you, holy Father and holy Son, for your blessed Holy Spirit who dwells within us as our Counselor, teaching us to cry 'Abba, Father' (Rom. 8:15) and to confess with our mouths, 'Jesus is Lord' (1 Cor. 12:3).

Be with us now as we go to our other work and never allow us to outlive our love for you. In the name of the Father and of the Son and of the Holy Spirit we pray. Amen.

Please stand for the doxology to our God:
'Now to the King eternal, immortal, invisible, the only God, be honor and glory forever and ever. Amen.'

APPENDIX TO THE ELEVENTH ADDRESS

HOW WE SHOULD MAKE THE CASE
FOR THE DOCTRINE OF THE TRINITY

Recently Robert Letham of Westminster Theological Seminary, Philadelphia used my exposition of the Trinity as a foil for his theologizing on the *filioque* clause in the church's creeds. Even though he acknowledges that 'much New Testament scholarship[1] argues that the procession [of the Spirit from the Father referred to in John 15:26] refers to economic activity only ... and not at all to eternal antecedent realities in God himself,' in a lecture delivered at Mid-America Reformed Seminary on November 10, 1999 entitled 'East is East and West is West? Another Look at the *Filioque*,' Letham, citing my *A New Systematic Theology of the Christian Faith*, stated: 'Robert L. Reymond thinks that referring this to immanent realities in God is to go beyond the bounds of Scripture.'[2] But this is patently *not* true. I believe, and I say so in my *A New Systematic Theology*, that such

---

[1]See my *A New Systematic Theology of the Christian Faith* (Second edition; Nashville, Tennessee: Thomas Nelson, 1998), 337-40, where I provide the evidence for Letham's acknowledgement here regarding the opinion of New Testament scholars and other orthodox theologians by referring my readers to B. F. Westcott, Alfred Plummer, J. H. Bernard, J. Oliver Buswell, Jr., Raymond E. Brown, Loraine Boettner, F. F. Bruce, Leon Morris, James I. Packer, and Donald A. Carson.

language indicates the reality of a reasoned *order* within the Godhead: The Holy Spirit is the *third* Person of the Godhead, *not* the first or the second. But because of his misunderstanding, Letham opposes my alleged position by citing as his rebuttal witness the Jesuit scholar, Bertrand de Margerie, who declares that this restriction of John 15:26 to the Spirit's temporal mission is

> a simplistic exegesis that lacks a theological background and is the work of exegetes who fail to reflect on the logical and metaphysical presuppositions of the scriptural texts.[3]

What de Margerie means here is that if I as well as 'much New Testament scholarship' would reflect on 'the logical and metaphysical presuppositions' behind the simple phrase in John 15:26 (a statement that occurs, by the way, only one time in the entire New Testament), *ho para tou patros ekporeuetai*, to be translated 'who from[4] the Father is coming forth,' as well as upon the teaching of John 14:16, 26; 16:7, 13-15; and 20:22, we would conclude that the statement teaches by implication that in the infinite depths of the divine Being a necessary, 'always continuing yet ever complete' act of the first and second persons in the Trinity is occurring whereby 'they ... become the ground of the personal subsistence of the Holy Spirit, and put the third person in possession of the whole divine essence, without any division, alienation or change' (L. Berkhof's definition of the Spirit's eternal procession).[5]

---

[2]Robert Letham, 'East is East and West is West? Another Look at the Filioque,' in *Mid-America Journal of Theology* (2002), Vol. 13:73.

[3]Bertrand de Margerie, *The Christian Trinity in History* (Petersham, Massachusetts: St. Bede's Publications, 1982), 169.

[4]Benjamin B. Warfield, 'The Biblical Doctrine of the Trinity' in *Biblical and Theological Studies*, 40, supplies the words 'fellowship with' after the word 'from.'

[5]Louis Berkhof, *Systematic Theology* (New combined edition; Grand Rapids: Eerdmans, 1996), 97. I should note that Letham

I think any fair-minded reader will conclude that such an involved deduction from John 15:26 is quite a stretch to say the least. One might even be pardoned for wondering if the Apostle John who wrote these words had even an inkling that his words were reflecting such an 'always continuing and yet ever complete' process[6] that makes the Father and the Son the ground of the personal subsistence of the Holy Spirit and that puts the Holy Spirit 'in possession of the whole divine essence, without any division, alienation or change' (Berkhof). In my opinion, to claim that such an interpretation was present to his mind and represents what he intended to convey by his statement would be to import into the Gospel the doctrinal conclusions from the controversies of the fourth and fifth centuries. I, for one, seriously doubt that John intended by his words such a teaching; but since this is only my opinion, no weight one way or the other should be placed upon this specific opinion of mine in the present context. But to assert as a generalization, as Bertrand de Margerie and Robert Letham do, because I and others refuse to 'logicize' and 'philosophize metaphysically' about John 15:26 and other biblical texts in order to arrive at *their* conclusions, that ours is 'simplistic exegesis that lacks a theological background' is pretty pompous, to say the least. One must find his consolation *vis à vis* such pomposity, I suppose, in the fact that this puts him in the company of men like John Calvin who, to cite Charles Hodge, was 'little inclined to enter into these speculations' and was 'opposed to going beyond the simple statement of the Scriptures' in these matters.[7]

---

in private correspondence dated 23 August 2003 does not accept Berkhof's definition, concurring with me that Berkhof's conception requires 'some kind of subordinate status for the Son and the Holy Spirit.'

[6] Berkhof, *Systematic Theology*, 93.

[7] Charles Hodge, *Systematic Theology* [Grand Rapids: Eerdmans, n.d.], I:466.

What concerns Letham primarily is this: In his opinion our (I am including in my 'our' here his acknowledged 'much New Testament scholarship') not reflecting on the 'logical and metaphysical presuppositions' of such a statement 'has the effect of undermining the reality and truthfulness of God's revelation by positing the idea that what God does economically does not necessarily indicate who he is.'[8] That is to say, according to Letham we may and must be willing to deduce what God is *in se* as the *ontological* Trinity from what the Bible represents the three Persons of the Godhead as doing *economically* in creation and redemptive history. Letham apparently holds this view even though he declares in a second lecture delivered on the same occasion as the first: 'We haven't got a clue what goes on in the ontological Trinity – it is completely beyond us ... we don't know the inner workings of the Trinity and can never know, and it may even border on sacrilege to talk about it.'[9] What? Haven't got a clue? May be blasphemous? Now Letham has confused me. I thought that he believes that the Trinity's economical activities are *just* that: clues to what 'goes on' in the ontological Trinity. Are not the Son's 'eternal generation' and the Spirit's 'eternal procession' 'inner workings' that Letham alleges 'go on' in the ontological Trinity and that he believes one who does not 'lack a theological background' (de Margerie) may and ought to infer from the Trinity's economical activities?

I have no problem, of course, with Letham's general sentiment as I indicated in Address Eleven when I noted that I believe such language reflects the reality of a reasoned order within the Trinity, as long as we do not overreach ourselves and arrive at additional conclusions that are based more on speculation than on clear biblical testimony and then declare these conclusions to be 'classic Christianity' and 'orthodoxy', which is

---

[8]Letham, 'East is East...,' *Mid-America Journal of Theology*, 73.
[9]Letham, 'The Holy Trinity and Christian Worship,' in *Mid-America Journal of Theology* (2002), Vol. 13:97.

what has too often occurred in the history of dogma.[10]
I think a similar concern is what led Calvin, after citing
Augustine's explanation of the relation between the
Father and the Son in his *Institutes of the Christian
Religion*, 1.13.19, first to declare: '...it is far safer to stop
with that relation which Augustine sets forth [in the fifth
book of *On the Trinity*] than by too subtly penetrating
into the sublime mystery to wander through evanescent
speculations,' and then to state later in the *Institutes*,
1.13.29:

> Certainly I have not shrewdly omitted anything [from
> my discussion of the relation between the Father and
> the Son] that I might think to be against me: but while
> I am zealous for the edification of the church, I felt
> that I would be better advised not to touch upon many
> things that would profit but little, and would burden my
> readers with useless trouble. For what is the point in
> disputing whether the Father always begets? Indeed, it
> is foolish to imagine a continuous act of begetting, since
> it is clear that three persons have subsisted in God from
> eternity.

But if the economical activities of the Persons of the
Godhead do not *necessarily* reflect the eternally
continuing activities going on in the infinite depths of
the ontological Trinity of the Father's eternal generation
of the Son's essence and the Father's and the Son's
eternal procession of the Spirit's essence, what may we
say with some degree of certainty (because Scripture is

---

[10]A case in point is the doctrine of the *filioque* itself. Given, for
the sake of argument, the Spirit's procession in the Nicean sense,
does the Spirit eternally proceed from the Father alone or from
the Father *and the Son* (*filioque*)? Eastern Christendom maintains
the former is correct; Western Christendom maintains the latter is
correct. Both think the other is unorthodox. And the *filioque* clause
has continued to this day to be a major cause of contention between
Western Christendom and the Eastern churches even though the
biblical evidence would indicate that both are in error.

not silent here) that they do reflect? In response to this question I have suggested elsewhere that their economical activities reflect not only *the reality of 'reasoned order'* within the Godhead but also *the division of redemptive labor* eternally and immutably determined upon in the pre-creation covenant of redemption. Benjamin B. Warfield expands upon this redemptive feature, writing:

> There is, of course, no question that in 'modes of operation,' as it is technically called – that is to say, in the functions ascribed to the several persons of the Trinity in the redemptive process, and, more broadly, in the entire dealing of God with the world – *the principle of subordination is clearly expressed.* The Father is first, the Son is second, and the Spirit is third, in the operations of God as revealed to us in general, and very especially in those operations by which redemption is accomplished. Whatever the Father does, He does through the Son ... by the Spirit. The Son is sent by the Father and does His Father's will...; the Spirit is sent by the Son and does not speak from Himself, but only takes of Christ's and shows it unto His people...; and we have Our Lord's own word for it that 'one that is sent is not greater than he that sent him' (Jn. xiii. 16). In crisp decisiveness, Our Lord even declares, indeed: 'My Father is greater than I' (Jn. xiv. 28); and Paul tells us that Christ is God's, even as we are Christ's (I Cor. iii. 23), and that as Christ is 'the head of every man,' so God [the Father] is 'the head of Christ' (I Cor. xi. 3). *But it is not so clear that the principle of subordination rules also in 'modes of subsistence,' as it is technically phrased; that is to say, in the necessary relation of the Persons of the Trinity to one another....* It may be natural to assume that a subordination in modes of operation rests on a subordination in modes of subsistence; that the reason why it is the Father that sends the Son and the Son that sends the Spirit is the Son is subordinate to the Father and the Spirit to the Son [in modes of subsistence]. But we are bound to bear in mind that *these relations of subordination in modes of operation may just as well be due to a convention,*

an agreement, between the Persons of the Trinity – a 'Covenant' as it is technically called, by virtue of which a distinct function in the work of redemption is voluntarily assumed by each. It is eminently desirable, therefore, at the least, that some definite evidence of subordination in modes of subsistence should be discoverable before it is assumed.... It must at least be said that in the presence of the great New Testament doctrines of the Covenant of Redemption on the one hand, and of the Humiliation of the Son of God for His work's sake and of the Two Natures in the constitution of His Person as incarnated, on the other, *the difficulty of interpreting subordinationist passages of eternal relations between the Father and the Son becomes extreme.* The question continually obtrudes itself, whether they do not rather find their full explanation in the facts embodied in the doctrines of the Covenant, the Humiliation of Christ, and the Two Natures of His incarnated Person.[11]

I noted in the first edition of my *A New Systematic Theology of the Christian Faith* that the subordination in modes of economic operation on the part of the Second and Third Persons of the Godhead, as Warfield suggested above, may well rest not on modes of essential subordination but on the relational order within the Godhead and on the eternal Covenant of Redemption that reflects that order, for which eternal plan there is a large amount of biblical support and thus requires no speculation at all[12] – within which Covenant, as I just suggested, the *order* of relational (*not* essential) subordination between the Father and the Son and between the Father and the Son on the one hand and the Spirit on the other doubtless determined the division of the three Persons' redemptive labors – and I would have asserted this in the second edition of my *A New Systematic Theology* had it not been

---

[11]Warfield, 'The Biblical Doctrine of the Trinity,' in *Biblical and Theological Studies*, 53-5, emphases supplied.

[12]See my *A New Systematic Theology of the Christian Faith* (First edition; Nashville, Tennessee: Thomas Nelson, 1998), 337-8.

for the fact that my publisher placed me under rather strict space limitations in the rewriting of any chapter for the second edition and therefore this suggestion had to be omitted due to lack of space. I also stated in the first edition that

> to look elsewhere for the warrant for these proposed on-tological relational subordinations within the Godhead, that is to say, to press back behind the eternal covenant of redemption and to attempt to think about the ontological Trinity 'behind' and 'apart from' all redemptive considerations, is to think about the Trinity bereft of all content save only for its barren triadic existence. But the covenant of redemption, properly construed, will not permit even Genesis 1 and the doctrine of God as Creator to be considered apart from redemptive considerations [because even his creative activity was initiated with redemptive considerations in mind according to Ephesians 3:9-10].[13] It is eminently desirable, therefore, that definite, virtually irrefutable exegetical evidence for [any] proposed eternal subordinationism within the Godhead in modes of subsistence should be offered before the church is asked to accept them.[14]

I am aware that I will be charged with espousing a theological method that reflects more the so-called Radical Reformation than the Magisterial Reformation (a witless charge that I roundly deny) when I say this, but for myself I think that the doctrine of the Trinity should be argued and explicated *biblically*, with a *minimum* of theological or philosophical speculation on the church's part. Calvin even states:

---

[13]See my *A New Systematic Theology of the Christian Faith*, chapter 13 on 'God's Eternal Plan of Salvation.'

[14]Reymond, *A New Systematic Theology of the Christian Faith* (First edition), 338.

I could wish [such terms as 'Trinity,' 'Person,' etc.] were buried, if only among all men this faith were agreed on: that Father and Son and Spirit are one God, yet the Son is not the Father, nor the Spirit the Son, but that they are differentiated by a peculiar property.[15]

Note that Calvin includes no reference here to 'God out of God', 'Light out of Light', 'very God out of very God', or 'out of the being of the Father', in what he regarded as essential to the depiction of orthodox Trinitarianism. Indeed, he writes in the Preface to his *Expositio impietatis Valen. Gentilis* (1561):

...the words of the Council of Nice run: *Deum esse de Deo.* A hard saying [*dura locutio*], I confess; but for removing its ambiguity no one can be a more suitable interpreter than Athanasius, who dictated it. And certainly the design of the fathers [he could likely have had Gregory Nazianzen and Augustine particularly in mind here] was none other than to maintain the origin which the Son draws from the Father in respect of Person, without in any way opposing the sameness of essence and deity in the two, so that as to essence the Word is God *absque principio* [without beginning], while in Person the Son has his *principium* [beginning (but with reference to order)] from the Father.

By his phrase 'A hard saying' Calvin seems to have meant that 'the form of the statement is inexact – the term *Deus* requiring to be taken in each case of its occurrence in a non-natural personal sense – and that, being inexact, it is liable to be misused in the interests of a created God,'[16] which is what the heretic Gentilis was teaching. He may also have intended to suggest that a less ambiguous way (he specifically states that

---

[15]Calvin, *Institutes*, 1.13.5.
[16]Warfield, 'Calvin's Doctrine of the Trinity,' *The Works of Benjamin B. Warfield* (Reprint; Grand Rapids: Baker, 1991), V:249.

there is 'ambiguity' about it) should have been chosen of saying that the Son draws his origin with respect to his Person from the Father than the harsh locution *Deus de Deo* which certainly is capable of being misunderstood as teaching that the Son owes his divine essence to the Father. But in either case, it is quite clear that Calvin, speaking elsewhere of the Creed's 'battology',[17] was willing to be critical of the linguistic formulas of the Nicene Creed and doubtless some of the understanding lying behind it, as do I!

So confessing as I do that there is only one living and true God who is eternally and immutably indivisible, I believe that the case for the doctrine of the Trinity is just the biblical evidence, of whatever kind, for the deity of Jesus Christ and the distinct personal subsistence of God the Holy Spirit. Said another way, whatever biblical evidence, wherever expressed in Holy Scripture, that can be adduced in support of the deity of Jesus Christ and the personal subsistence of the Holy Spirit is probative evidence for the Christian doctrine of the Trinity. The classic exegetical method known as 'grammatical/ historical exegesis' absent the Nicene speculation, I submit, is the only proper way to support and explicate this core doctrine of the Christian faith.

---

[17]In his dispute with Peter Caroli, a theologian of the Sorbonne, Calvin refers to the Nicene Creed's 'battology', not to controvert the Creed's words but simply to make it clear that he did not feel 'confined to the very words of the old formulas in his expression of the doctrine of the Trinity' (Warfield, 'Calvin's Doctrine of the Trinity,' *Works*, V:210-11).

SUBJECT INDEX

PERSONS INDEX

SCRIPTURE INDEX

2 Timothy
1:9 82, 164
2:13 99, 110, 158, 289
2:19 255
3:15-17 16
4:1 113
4:7 338
4:18 77

Titus
1:2 156, 284, 287
2:13 303
3:4-6 302
3:5 164, 228

Philemon
17-19 228

Hebrews
1:2 41, 324
1:2-4 262
1:3 56
1:8 303
1:10-12 74
1:14 47
4:12 113
4:13 113, 121
4:16 57
6:4-8 113
6:17-18 34, 99, 158
6:17-19 287
6:18 284
7:25 75, 90
7:27 89
9:12 89
9:25-26 89
9:28 89
10:10-14 89
10:23 289
10:25 65
10:26-31 113
11:4 191
11:10 30
11:27 34
12:14 182
12:28 65, 99

12:28-29 196
12:29 29
13:5 89
13:8 75, 93, 99

James
1:13 158
1:17 99, 238
2:13 113
2:19 27
3:8 189
3:17 122, 258
4:5 232
4:12 113

1 Peter
1:2 302
1:5 90, 167
1:12 135
1:15-16 182
2:7 113
2:8 113
2:23 113
2:25 57
3:12 113
3:18 89
4:17 113
4:18 113

2 Peter
1:2 200
1:3 21, 200
1:20-21 16
2:1 303
2:3-10 113
2:6-8 204
2:17 208
3:7 113
3:9 248
3:10 162, 167
3:12 162
3:13 168

1 John
1:2 277, 325
1:5 29, 181
1:9 211, 289

3:2 185
3:7 113
3:8 113
3:18 41
3:20 121
4:4 169
4:8 29, 238, 243
4:8-10 243, 254
4:9 323
4:9-10 239
4:10 29
5:6 268
5:7-8 302
5:12 43, 194
5:20 268, 303

Jude
4-6 113
6 204
7 204
13 113, 208
15 113
20-21 302

Revelation
2:27 165
3:14 324
4:6-8 177
4:8 176
4:10 77
4:11 27
9:17-18 207
11:15 77
14:3 189
14:7 113
14:9-11 113
14:10 56, 207
14:17-20 113
15:1 113
15:3-4 211
15:4 176
16 113
18:20 253
19:1-3 113, 253
19:6 152
19:11-21 113
19:20 207

Christian Focus Publications
publishes books for all ages

Our mission statement –

STAYING FAITHFUL
In dependence upon God we seek to help make His infallible Word, the Bible, relevant. Our aim is to ensure that the Lord Jesus Christ is presented as the only hope to obtain forgiveness of sin, live a useful life and look forward to heaven with Him.

REACHING OUT
Christ's last command requires us to reach out to our world with His gospel. We seek to help fulfill that by publishing books that point people towards Jesus and help them develop a Christ-like maturity. We aim to equip all levels of readers for life, work, ministry and mission.

Books in our adult range are published in three imprints.
Christian Focus contains popular works including biographies, commentaries, basic doctrine and Christian living. Our children's books are also published in this imprint.
Mentor focuses on books written at a level suitable for Bible College and seminary students, pastors, and other serious readers. The imprint includes commentaries, doctrinal studies, examination of current issues and church history.
Christian Heritage contains classic writings from the past.

Christian Focus Publications, Ltd
Geanies House, Fearn, Ross-shire,
IV20 1TW, Scotland, United Kingdom
info@christianfocus.com

For details of our titles visit us on our website
www.christianfocus.com